D1290200

Second Chance

By
Ryan Troutman

JOZEF SYNDICATE

Parts of this memoir are written as told by Lisa Leon. Special thanks to Kayla Huggins of Jacksonville , Florida for her editorial guidance and support that initiated this book.

ISBN 978-1-944155-21-6
EBook ISBN 978-1-944155-23-0
Library of Congress Catalogue Number 2016939786

Contact Ryan Troutman
contact@ryantroutman.com
(904) 595-6015

Printed in the United States of America

~~~~
RYAN TROUTMAN

Advance Praise for Ryan Troutman

I'm so glad to know you. As a first responder when we see scenes like this we can only hope for recovery stories like yours!

Cassandra Null, Tallahassee, Florida

Ryan, this is amazing. I'm so proud of you. I remember this so well and will never forget it. I can't wait to read your book! You are seriously such an inspiration.

Victoria Coker, Oxford, England

You're an amazing man Ryan I'm glad I had the chance to meet you and we will cross paths again soon.

Devante Watts, White Bear Lake, Minnesota

I love this! So proud of my best friend!

Kirsten David, Jacksonville, Florida

Proud of you, man. You're an inspiration to me and I'm sure a lot of people. The way you have lived your life after that accident is truly an example of living life to the fullest, and I couldn't be happier for you bro. I definitely want a signed copy of that beast when it comes out!

Johnny Sours, Jacksonville, Florida

Thanks for sharing, Ryan! This is proof that with the right attitude you can overcome any obstacle or difficulty life may bring!

Akbar Alam, Arlington, Virginia

This is awesome, Ryan! I remember after you told me the story that you were hoping one day to write a book of it. So wicked you accomplished it!

Anna Pennington, Vancouver Island, BC, Canada

Get behind this guy. One of the most inspirational and upbeat people I've ever met. We can learn so much from him and this experience. Every respect, Ryan.

Joshua Gallagher, Brisbane, Australia

"Your perseverance and incredible outlook on life is so inspiring! I can't wait to read your story!"

Britney Khauv, Jacksonville, Florida

RYAN TROUTMAN

We are all so glad you proved to have the incredible strength to defy the odds and pull through. Not only to just survive, but to make a full recovery and I think anyone can see you have been even more full of life since. We thought we lost you that night, and I bear witness to the fact that your life is important to a whole lot of people and you deserve to be here buddy.

Jesse Casey, Richmond, Virginia

I can't wait to read your book. It is such a huge accomplishment. I moved to Idaho in 2007, and I had no idea you had been in an accident. Watching your world travels has been such a joy. You are an inspiration to many and will go far in life because you have such a pure heart and spirit. You have always been great. I look forward to watching this next chapter unfold for you.

Meredith Nicole Atkins, Jacksonville, Florida

Ryan, life is a journey....You have taken your second chance and ran with it. That 9 years have past is still hard to believe. That is a night I will never forget and I thank god for you each night. I'm am so proud of you and so thankful to be a part of your life. I cannot wait to read your journey in your words, BUT I will have to have a very large box of tissues. I love you.

Rae Lamia, Jacksonville, Florida

Ryan,

You have faced many challenges along the way
and never gave up.
I could not be more proud of the man you've become.
One with strength, perseverance,
and the most beautiful passion for life!
Each day
you are making your mark on this world
and on everyone you meet.
I wish everyone could see the world through your eyes.
You are truly an inspiration.
I love you with all my heart!
You will always be my hero!

Mom,

You've seen me at my best
and helped me through my worst.
Your unconditional love
has supported me in everything
I've ever done.
You've loved me
like no one ever could
I am your boo-man
and you are my hero.
You saved my life.

RYAN TROUTMAN

TABLE OF CONTENTS

Fun For All, All For One ---8

Let's Get Moving ---20

The Missing Link ---23

Mother Knows Best---27

Family Reunion --35

Fighting to live --37

Stop, Drop, and Talk --40

Rebuild Me ---48

Mr. Sneaky Snake---55

Don't Stop Believing --57

Ding, Ding, Ding ---68

Morgan has Questions --77

Morgan's Day --80

Eye Never Saw It Coming --------------------------------------85

Recovery is Discovery---90

Houston, We Still Have a Problem ----------------------------100

I Always Did Like Rollercoasters ----------------------------104

Still in a Galaxy Far, Far Away -------------------------------108

I'm Walking on Sunshine ---------------------------------------113

Like-minded --122

The Miracle Mile --126

Me, Myself, and My Money--135

I'm Not Dreaming--143

Therapeutic Days and Talladega Nights -----------------------------149

This Wasn't an Episode of Glee -------------------------------------154

You Can Always Dig a Hole Deeper---------------------------------163

Paying 'Respects' --182

Even Photoshop Couldn't Fix This -----------------------------------187

Grade Me Now--192

That Vitamin C Song Everyone Knows ---------------------------200

Beer Basted BBQ --207

Man, I Love College. --217

Life in the Fast Lane--225

'Cause the Party Don't Start Till I Walk In ---------------------------239

Play hard, but work harder--246

The Day Center of Our Lives --259

Thoughts for You --268

The Show Must Go On--270

Fun For All, All For One

February 18, 2007, was the day I died.

I was sixteen years old, and like any other teenager, my life revolved around friends, girls, and video games. My best friend, Kyle, lived around the corner from me with his two brothers, Daniel and Ben. We lived in a small neighborhood that from an aerial view looked like the shape of a lollipop. Our neighborhood was our kingdom. Our one, looping road was always battered by skateboard wheels, poorly-made ramps, and a bunch of kids trying to avoid becoming what our parents called "young adults."

We were all waiting for that one form of identification that told the world we were free. A dim-lit, blurry, half-cracked smile on a little state-issued card proclaimed that we were ready to lead our own lives. Kyle's newly acquired, used Camaro was an added bonus.

"Let's start planning our first trip!" I blurted out. "No time better than the present. There's a ton of places I'm already thinking of going."

Kyle shot me a look of discontent. "I'd be fine with just driving up someplace and grabbing cheeseburgers," he said dryly.

Ben and I exchanged puzzled glances.

"Definitely not!" I argued. A fast-food restaurant of all places. What was unique or memorable about that?

"No. No," I said.

It hit me after a moment that I was being domineering; but, was wanting a fun night out on the town a crime?

"Okay. Then, tell me about your grand ideas?" Kyle snapped sarcastically.

"We should throw some short boards in the trunk and head to the ocean!" I exclaimed.

Kyle opened his mouth to argue, but I cut him off. "I'd much rather go surfing than just grab cheeseburgers. I'm not even hungry." Agitation spilled from my voice. "Let me guess, after cheeseburgers you want to sit safely in a movie theatre like a good boy?"

"Whoa! Take a chill pill, man," Ben stifled a chuckle. "Let's go downtown. There's a show playing tonight at The Empire. We can check out some bands. It goes pretty late into the night too which is cool."

We were silent for a moment pondering Ben's idea. He was much more into the music scene than we were, and a concert sounded fun.

"I wouldn't be against it," Kyle said finally.

"Me neither," I agreed.

"I don't think I'm going to go. Too many crazies down there," Daniel sighed, disinterested. I wasn't surprised. Daniel wasn't one for large crowds or loud noises. He was the poised one. I snickered to myself at the thought.

"Alright then, it's decided. We'll go downtown tonight and see the show," I declared.

Kyle and Ben nodded. A wave of eagerness washed over me. I didn't know much about The Empire other than the fact that it was a frequent hangout for scene, hardcore, and goth kids. Regardless, it was something new for us.

Something fresh.

I ran home knowing I would need my mom to agree to another night out. For some reason, she was reluctant and determined to stall my plans. She decided I would have to clean my room and make sure all my homework was finished before she would agree. Easy breezy! This was the one time I actually had cleaned my room and finished my homework earlier in the week. I could overhear her and Tony, my step dad, discussing my plans. It really wasn't that big of a deal—just Ben, Alex, and me hanging out like we normally do. For the second time, the look on my mom's face showed her hesitation, but she acquiesced.

"Okay, Ryan, you can go," she said.

"Yes!" I celebrated with a clap.

"Let me know when you make it," she said while I hugged her good-bye.

After digging through clothes' hampers to find the only band t-shirts we owned, Kyle, Ben, and I set forth on a night of excitement—one that was free from the shackles of adolescence. We were moving up in the world.

We said goodbye to my mom and hopped in the car. The Camaro reeked of a new car smell that floated from the blue tree-shaped air freshener dangling from the rearview mirror. Kyle plopped down behind the wheel and indicated that he saved the front seat for his very best friend. I looked to the back seat with a smirk. Ben sighed and shrugged his shoulders, wishing he had shotgun privileges. As the key turned, the car suddenly sputtered on, sounding the alarm that declared our independence.

Tonight was going to be a test and I planned on passing it with flying colors, I thought. The drive was invigorating. Despite being in the passenger seat, I felt in control. The Camaro's stereo wasn't the greatest, but it still weaseled out a few catchy tunes. In unison, we shouted the lyrics from the tops of our lungs, preparing ourselves for what lie ahead.

As we drove across the main bridge, Kyle rolled down the windows. I reveled in the crisp air kissing my face. Scintillating headlights and street lights in the distance blurred together as we zoomed towards downtown.

The sun was beginning to descend, and etched shades of orange, red, and lavender began to stain the sky above us.

RYAN TROUTMAN

A smile danced across my lips as we passed high-rise buildings and various night clubs. We were nearly there. Jacksonville's city square came into view and Kyle glanced over at me.

"It's a little past here."

I nodded excitedly.

"Whoo!" Ben cheered. "Finally!"

We rounded a corner and saw a worn, red graphite one-story building that had a line of young punks standing outside waiting to pay their dues to the bouncer.

Adjacent to the unkept building laid a worn parking lot with faded white lines that singled out several cars. Kyle pulled into the lot, parked, and switched the car off. He clasped both hand tightly around the steering wheel and declared, "The time has come!" Ben and I laughed at his melodramatic comment before shuffling out of the car.

The streetlights shined a flickering glow down on us as we stepped out of the car. A nervous energy surged through our bodies. We willed our feet forward.

As we approached the line, the sound of hoots and boisterous banter filled the air.

"Please! Anything will help!" cried a dirty homeless man hovering near the crowd asking for money.

The kids felt no remorse. They scoffed and teased him by flashing dollar bills and hiding them when he stepped forward. A boy wearing blood-constricting jeans and a dark gray shirt with "I Am The Sphinx" scribbled across the front spit a wad of slimy mucus toward the man.

"There! See what you can buy with that!" he cackled. His friends screamed in laughter and applauded his goading. They inched closer towards the entrance. In their wake, clouds of smoke and ash bellowed out of the front door.

"We might leave this place with lung cancer," Ben whispered.We took two steps closer to the slim door that was cut into the left front of the building. After twenty minutes, we finally ended up in front of a burly man with a lumberjack's beard. He rose from his stool surveying us. His tattered black t-shirt was soaked in the stench of cigarette smoke.

"NEXT!" The bouncer shouted, summoning us closer. He clearly detested his job or lamented the mounting line of overly excited teenagers.

Before Kyle or I could react, we were all startled by the screech of a microphone being mounted to its stand. We lit up with excitement.

"Ten bucks," the bouncer mumbled.

The three of us plunged into our pockets to fish out dollar bills.

"Here you go, sir," I said, handing over a wad of crinkled bills. No matter how invincible we felt, we were still just a bunch of teenagers. We extended our balled fists to allow him time to mark a black X across each hand as a not-so-subtle indication that we were underage. The branding didn't bother us, in fact it would be our most noticeable proof of entrance into The Empire.

I beheld my marked hands with admiration and a slight dose of pride. I would use these Xs to boast my unofficial acceptance into a drug- and alcohol-free lifestyle everyone called "Straight Edge." Even though my commitment would still be limited to my circle of underage friends and classmates. My cult-like commitment would soon fade with the marks.

Each of us shuffled into the smokey darkness.

"This place is awesome!" Ben hooted while mock head banging.

"Someone got started early," Kyle laughed.

I chuckled and glanced around. The Empire was larger than it appeared from the outside. There were chairs and tables scattered about the front, and a neon-lit bar straggled in the dead center. A small, elevated stage stood on the far left side of the room. Sam Adams placards and old stickers from performing bands plastered the walls sparsely.

Multi-colored lights danced above our heads and painted the area in candescent hues of green, red, blue, and yellow. A smirk danced across my face. This was the life.

Ben was the first to move. Kyle and I followed eagerly. We moved past the bar and headed toward the stage.

We awkwardly meandered near a group of more qualified fans. From their looks, this wasn't their first show. One of the veterans appeared to be in his mid-twenties. He was covered in tattoos and had gauges in his ears that made him look like he had just left an indigenous Maasai tribe. His girlfriend glanced over at us with a look of discontent. It was a well-practiced expression, I surmised. Just below her eye sat an ink-smear that at one point might have been a cute heart or a pony tattoo. Now, it was just a faded reminder of how many times she'd cried herself to sleep.

"I'm ready for this shit to start already!" I yelled.

Curse words typically weren't apart of my vocabulary, but tonight made me feel like a new man. Kyle and Ben noticed the adrenaline filling my eyes.

"Yeah! Let's get this show goin—"

Kyle's celebration was cut off as the sound of a snare drum began pounding through the speakers. Repeatedly, the musician tamed his drumhead with a stick. BOOM.. BOOM.. BOOM.. the sound continued as silhouettes danced in tune to their beats.

"Hey guys! We're I Am The Sphinx, and this song is called 'I Want to be Mauled by a Panther'!" A shadowed man shouted into the microphone.

The three of us expected the band to erupt in whining guitar solos, fast double bass pounding, and raspy screams. Surprisingly, he grabbed his sticker-tagged guitar and began softly strumming individual chords in a soothing, melodic kind of way. We glanced at each other. Dumbfounded.

"Is this the right show?" Kyle asked.

I shrugged my shoulders and pawned the answer off on Ben. His thin shoulders tensed in a similar fashion leaving the question unanswered. The crowd was too relaxed for our comfort. Each fan swayed back and forth, mesmerized by the guitar's chime.

"If this keeps up much longer, we're going home," Kyle commanded. His authoritative voice was supported by the shiny key in his pocket. I didn't want to leave regardless of how soft the music was. I just wanted a fun night with my friends.

Just as I opened my mouth to rebut Kyle's directive, my gut was pummeled with a fist. The crowd broke out into a pit of slinging arms, high-kicking legs, and twirling beer bottles. I Am The Sphinx suddenly picked up into an ear-ringing, disorganized sound. The vocalist's high-pitched voice rattled the microphone with unrecognizable words.

Chaos ensued in the pit as the strained sounds blasted from the speakers.

"Ryan!" Kyle screamed from a distance.

The audience swung their arms and fists, dancing in a mixed two-step shuffle and hypnotic windmill motion. It was like we were lost in a forest of chaotic delinquents and couldn't find our way through to safety. I dodged swinging limbs and spiked bracelets, praying for a reprieve. From the corner of my eye, I could see Kyle extending his arm from the edge of the pit.

I quickly grabbed his sweaty, trembling hand and lunged for safety. This was not what we expected. I'd been to some rock concerts in the past, but this was just violent.

"Are you ok?" Kyle asked with an uneasy grin.

"I've never been better," I replied sarcastically. Ben watched as the two of us distanced ourselves from the thrashing.

Near the stage groups of kids continued to throw their bodies around maniacally. They called this "dancing." Over at the bar sat the older crowd. They seemed so out of place against the mayhem. The fluorescent lights painted our faces. We were a part of an aberrant masterpiece.

RYAN TROUTMAN

"Dude, you got nailed!" Ben chuckled as he rose from the depths of dancing bodies. I saw the elation in his eyes. This is what he wanted. This is why we came.

As the lights dimmed, the instruments went quiet. The crowd erupted in applause, aggressive fist-pumping, and shrill whistling. The three of us just watched. After a moment, we joined in on the praise.

"We've got to get closer for the next song!" Ben rallied.

Kyle and I reluctantly inched closer to the pit of people.

"Alright everyone! Again, we're I Am The Sphinx! We've got some great bands playing tonight! So, listen up and don't forget to tip your bartenders! Let's all make some noise!" The lead vocalist boomed, inspiring another roaring cheer. "This next song is called 'Bob's Voyage Through the Windshield'!"

The crowd readied themselves for another brawl. A large, muscular man moved in front of me, blocking my view of the stage. Salvation came in the strangest form. I wanted to be a part of the fun, but I didn't want another blow to the stomach. I silently thanked my protector.

As the song began, the crowd became a hurricane of bodies once more. The electric guitar whined through chords as the drummer pummeled his cymbals. Loud crashing sounds crept across the ceiling and even grabbed the attention of the bar crowd. The man in front of me, who I had rightfully dubbed my bodyguard, began to shake in a rhythmic manner. The uncoordinated music was somehow gracefully flowing through his tapping feet and nodding head.

Without a moment's notice, the large man's fists came soaring into my forehead. He repeatedly swung his arms backwards in swift, circular motions. In all the years of my childhood, I'd never gotten into a fight. At least now I could say I kind of knew what it was like. My opponent seemed to be oblivious to his flurry of blows. Before he could flail another punch, I managed to duck out of sight. My assailant's eyes drifted over to me; he was more aware than he seemed, maybe even pleased.

RYAN TROUTMAN

This was my first hint.

I was in the wrong place.

Snickers from onlookers ensued, but I ignored them and shifted my gaze back to the stage which had quieted. I contemplated ways to twist this into a more masculine story. I liked the idea of going back to school and telling all of the ladies I was at The Empire throwing punches with the guys.

The next gig was about start up. Once they introduced themselves, the crowd spurred them on and the atmosphere swelled back to life.

The level of energy in the room bewildered me. The song's tempo sped up and the people in the pit began running around frantically. A flurry of flailing limbs and brutalizing thrusts penetrated the air once more. It was oddly mesmerizing.

A frenzied mosh erupted within the circle pit. A scrawny kid with shaky eyes spun towards me. I saw myself in this kid. Just another over-zealous teenager trying to fit in among an opposing crowd. Now, he was caught in a tornado of twirling limbs and had no exit strategy.

After a moment, a courageous glint rippled across the boy's face. His jet black, neatly ironed hair whisked in the air as he made a run through the circle. One attempt at slipping through the crowd caused him to collide with the mass of oncoming moshers. His twig body crumpled across the floor as stomping feet paraded over his mascara-marked face.

Kyle and I locked eyes in horror. This was monstrous. No one was helping him; to them, this was normal.

One final strum of the guitar ended the song and set. "Thanks everyone! We had fun tonight!" The vocalist exclaimed. His thankful words were cushioned by countless curse words and derogatory remarks. My face fell. This was a far cry from the hair-raising round of applause I was waiting for.

My gaze ran back to the helpless boy. He was upright now limping his way towards the bar. I sighed in relief. He was okay —for the most part.

RYAN TROUTMAN

The mood equalized once more. As another band started setting up on the stage, metal tunes began to screech down from the speakers that dangled from the roof. We noticed small, folding tables stationed near the entrance. They were setup and filled with t-shirts, keychains, hats, and various band gear.

"Sweet!" Kyle exclaimed. "Come on, guys!" He made his way to the merchandise tables. Ben and I followed suit. A souvenir to mark the moment was mandatory.

Tonight, I became a man. Not a boy sitting at home playing video games. This moment would be defined by my needs and wants—or so, I told myself.

The three of us stopped at a table filled with character and catch phrase t-shirts. Out of all of the tables this one seemed to be the most promising. I looked from t-shirt to t-shirt taking in the sayings and remarking on the funny ones. One caught my eye. It was a black shirt with red, streaked writing that read "My friends stand beside me" and revealed an image of bloodied brass knuckles wrapped in barbed wire. I looked up at the disinterested vendor manning the table.

He was a tall guy with pale skin and shaggy black hair. I cleared my throat roughly, and he locked eyes with me. He was unmoved by my questioning eyes and took a sip of his beer.

"How much are these?" I finally asked.

"Thirty bucks," he grumbled.

"I..I'll take i—" I stopped short. Thirty bucks was a lot of money. From the corner of my eye, I spotted an array of belts spread across the table beside the vendor. One of them stood out. It was a generic black belt with AK-47s scattered on a pleather surface and the phrase "Your ghost is a gift" embossed down the length of the belt.

"Do you want the shirt or not?" The man asked with a temper.

"How much is the belt?" I asked, unfazed by his attitude.

"Twenty bucks," he replied, rolling his eyes.

"Pass me that one!" I directed, motioning toward the belt.

The grin on my face shot upwards into a toothy smile at the idea of saving ten bucks and rocking my new memento.

The man sighed and grabbed the belt off of the table. I dug a crumpled twenty dollar bill out of my pocket and handed it to him. He shoved the belt at me and began tinkering on his cellphone.

I slid the belt through the empty loops of my jeans, unaware of the truth in the ambiguous phrase.

"Are you ready?!" Kyle shouted from a distance, pulling me out of my reverie. He and Ben were already at the door waiting, empty-handed. I hurried towards them eager to show off my souvenir.

"Check it out!" I exclaimed and started to lift my shirt.

"Whoa! Nobody needs to see that!" Ben joked.

I rolled my eyes, but smiled in spite of myself. As we walked out of the building, I felt the cold air whip across my cheeks. The moon casted an eerie glow across the towering buildings as my beautiful city slept the night away.

We retraced our steps along the tattered sidewalk, maneuvering around the broken glass and dried vomit. The homeless man had disappeared. As we turned the corner, the Camaro's faded black hood glistened under the moonlight. Smiles crept across our faces.

We did it.

"Shotgun!" Ben announced as we neared the Camaro.

This made my blood boil. I looked for a way to counter his proclamation.

"Let's play rock-paper-scissors! Best two out of three. The winner gets front seat," I refuted.

Kyle stared at us. "How old are you guys again?" He teased.

"Shush, the adults are talking," Ben shot back.

Kyle laughed to himself. Ben's daring eyes urged me on. We readied our hands.

"Rock...paper...scissors...shoot!" We chanted as our fists smacked down on our palms.

RYAN TROUTMAN

"Boom!" Ben yelled, as his paper covered my rock.

My face went pale. I never lost at this game. My eyes cut inwards and my shoulders tensed.

"Alright, alright. Let's do this," I muttered roughly.

"Rock...paper...scissors...SHOOT!" We shouted again.

My body sank in sorrow as Ben's scissors cut right through my paper. Kyle's jaw dropped. "No way!"

My feet gripped the ground. I took one deep breath and dove towards the front door. Thankfully, Kyle had unlocked it. I swung the door open and climbed in, letting the seat cushion catch me as I jerked the door closed and pressed down on the lock.

Ben's eyes were dreary in defeat.

"Let's go! Get in already!" I screamed through the window.

Ben slumped towards the other side of the car and climbed into the lonely backseat.

"Dude, don't worry about it. We're having an awesome night, and we'll be home soon anyway," Kyle said reassuringly, before climbing into the driver's seat.

LET'S GET MOVING

The ignition coughed and chugged when Kyle turned the key. We were off.

"That was so awesome! You got leveled by that tall dude!" Ben beamed from the backseat. All was forgiven. I smiled to myself. It never took Ben long to mellow out.

The Camaro crept down dimly-lit roads, humming in the night. I looked outside of the window blankly. I had no idea where we were.

"How do we get home?" I asked, glancing over at Kyle.

"I got this," he replied with a confident grin. "Don't worry."

I was convinced and tinkered with the dial on the stereo. Familiar jams began to stream out of the old system. My feet tapped in tune to the edgy guitar riffs and ringing baselines. I could faintly hear Ben singing along to the chorus. The return trip consisted of a lot of narrow roads and one-way streets, until we merged onto the interstate. The expressway was oddly bare for ten o'clock traffic. I glanced around at the passing signs looking for anything that looked familiar.

"Relax, Ryan," Kyle said nudging me. "We'll make it back home."

I smiled to myself. Kyle had always been relatively synergetic with what I was thinking. I suppose that's why we ended up being best friends. We made things easy for one another.

RYAN TROUTMAN

A green sign illuminated in the glare of the Camaro's headlights. The words upon it eased my nerves. We were nearly home. This was a great ending to a kickass night. I cranked the stereo's volume to the max as Ben and I popped around in our seats, fist-pumping like the kids at the show. Kyle grinned at us and decided to elevate the mood even further.

He grasped the steering wheel with two hands and drove his foot down onto the gas petal. The car huffed as it accelerated. We went wild. Adrenaline was coursing through our veins. I embraced it, allowing a smile to dance across my lips. The speedometer's needle surpassed 100 miles per hour. Streetlights, concrete walls, and silhouettes of buildings blurred past me as I stared out the window. The faint smell of gasoline crept through the car, snapping me back to Earth.

Up ahead was a small bridge. I expected to see a direct path home on the bridge's other side, but I didn't. We sped across the peak of the bridge and panic gripped me. I knew where we were now; one of the sharpest turns in the city lie up ahead.

At this speed we wouldn't be able to make it. The thrill ceased as realization kicked in. This was it.

Our eyes widened in horror as we quickly neared the turn's concrete wall. Our lyrical karaoke suddenly turned into horrifying shrieks. Kyle turned the wheel roughly, but we couldn't avoid it.

The car slammed into the concrete wall with a deadly impact. It dug into the passenger side door, shredding what little paint was left. My body jerked around as the car spun out of control. The faint scent of gasoline abruptly changed into the scent of heated metal and smoke. Darkness took over. Screeching metal howled in the night amidst our screams. I could hear my side door give way. The night's cold wind bombarded the inside of the car.

My eyes snapped open.

RYAN TROUTMAN

Kyle was the only person wearing a seatbelt, and Ben was guarded by our front seats. I was vulnerable, exposed to the tempest. In an instant, we crashed into something solid.

My body was thrown out of the gaping hole that was once the passenger side door. I flew through the cold air, writhing uncontrollably.

Dying.

I hit the asphalt hard. My forehead collided with the street and blood began to pour from my face. My skin was shredded by the road's unrelenting gravel as my body slid down the pavement.

The world finally grew still. I was mangled, broken, and worn. My legacy was about to end with me bleeding to death in the middle of the street.

The air evanesced from my lungs as my synapses slowed. My jaw was ripped open and dipped over the right side of my face. Blood continued to leave my body, taking the small measure of strength I had left with it.

Death was cradling me now.

I would never get to see my loved ones again nor be able to express how much I cared for them. My parents would never be able to see me graduate or get married and have a family. My brother and sister would be devoid of their big brother. All of my dreams would truly be no more than just dreams.

RYAN TROUTMAN

THE MISSING LINK

The Camaro lie in ruins against the side of the street. Kyle and Ben remained in the car. They were both unconscious as the car wheezed smoke and metal clanked.

My dismantled body marinated in a pool of warm, sticky blood. The night returned to its ghostly silence. We were all in our resting places now.

Miraculously, there was a woman who had witnessed the crash. She stood in the distance stupefied into stillness. After a moment, she rushed over to the car.

"Hello?! Hello?! Are you ok?!" She cried.

The sight and stench terrified her.

She surveyed Kyle and Ben intently, searching for any form of movement. Her wide eyes darted back and forth as her hands were held high above her head. Fear rattled through this woman's body.

"Thank God!" The woman rejoiced as Kyle began to slightly open his eyes. He ached but still moved his head to check on me and Ben.

"Where is Ryan?" He murmured weakly.

"He's in the backseat," the woman replied, extending a shaking finger towards Ben. Kyle painfully twisted to see his brother. His eyes grew wide at the realization that I was no longer in the vehicle.

"No! Where is Ryan!" Kyle yelled.

RYAN TROUTMAN

The women's eyes widened in horror. "What do you mean? Was there someone else with y—"

"Yes! Ryan! My friend!" Kyle broke in.

The woman surveyed the front and back seats of the car frantically. "I don't see him!" She cried.

She felt the weight of responsibility. She pulled out her cellphone and forcefully mashed 9-1-1 into the keypad. The phone rang only once before she shouted through the speaker. "Hello!? I'm at a car accident scene. There are teenagers who are hurt! Hurry! Send someone!" She bellowed.

"Alright, ma'am, I need you to calm down and tell me where you are located," the operator said mechanically.

"We're on the bridge leaving downtown to head back to Southside. The car is near the turn that goes under the I-95 overpass," the woman replied with a little more composure.

"Alright, hang tight. Police and paramedics will be there shortly," the 911 operator assured her.

"There is no time! There's a boy that's not even in the car! I don't know where he is!" The woman shouted into her smartphone.

"I will let them know," the operator said calmly.

The phone call ended and the woman's eyes glanced back over to Kyle and Ben.

"You two stay seated. Help is on the way," she explained. The woman turned away from the mangled car and stared off into the darkness. She felt helpless. There was another boy somewhere out there, she reminded herself.

The night's cold, crisp air floated through the darkness. Minutes felt like hours. The dismal silence was soon interrupted by sirens and flashing lights.

Police, paramedics, and firefighters arrived at the scene. They began to pile out of their vehicles. An officer approached the trembling woman.

"Ma'am, we'll need a statement," the police officer directed at her. "Can you explain what happened here?"

"The car smashed into the wall. It bounced around and ended up on the side of the road," she explained. There was a sense of caution apparent in the woman's voice. Her hands were clasped at her waist. Stress caused her jittery fingers to crawl across her hips like spiders. She didn't know what to do with herself. The officer wrote on his notepad and nodded his head.

"There was a third boy! We don't know where he is," she continued.

The officer glanced over at Kyle in the driver's seat.

"That boy the driver?" He asked more like a statement than a question. The woman shrugged her shoulders wearily.

"Alright, thank you. Stay here and I'll touch base with you in a moment," the officer instructed before turning away.

His colleagues had begun detouring oncoming traffic, while paramedics scoured the street searching for me. After a few minutes, a female paramedic shouted, "I found him! He is over here! Hurry!"

They rushed over.

"How is he doing?!" Asked a male paramedic beside her.

"Hand me a bag. He isn't breathing!" The woman directed as she swung her open hand backward awaiting the equipment. They quickly passed the woman a long tube connect to a bag resembling an empty liter bottle. She lunged the tube down my throat and leaned in to push it down farther. Instinctively, my mouth bit down on the cylindrical catheter.

"Dammit! He bit down!"

This wasn't a first in her line out of work, but they were running out of time.

"Put him in the back, we don't have anymore time! We need to get him to the hospital!" A third paramedic ordered.

They hoisted my body on to the rigid stretcher and rolled me back to the ambulance.

"I'm pumping!" The paramedic cried as she squeezed the bag repeatedly—hoping the bit tube would allow oxygen to flow.

RYAN TROUTMAN

They came to a halt in front of the double doors of the ambulance.

"Get him in the back!" She commanded. Her team obeyed and wheeled me into the back of the vehicle.

"We need to hurry!" Another paramedic shouted.

The siren roared as the ambulance raced toward the trauma center. Regardless of how much oxygen was pumped into me, my body wanted—needed—more.

Ben was rushed to the hospital in a second ambulance. Despite his body being responsive, he was in bad condition. Kyle was held at the scene for questioning. If I died, they were ready to charge him with vehicular manslaughter.

MOTHER KNOWS BEST

All of the houses in my small neighborhood began to quiet down. My mom and stepdad were getting ready to go to sleep.

"Something isn't right," my mom said, standing next to the bed fiddling with the sheets. "I have tried calling him numerous times, but it keeps going to voicemail." She felt this eerie feeling come over her. Anxiety set in as chills began to creep down her spine. Without taking a second to think, she quickly changed clothes and began making her way out of the bedroom.

Tony raised his head. He sat up in bed and threw his feet to the floor. "What are you doing? Where are you going?" He said quickly. "If he needed us, he would call. He might still be there or they might have stopped to grab food."

Those words did nothing to soothe my mom. By now, her instincts were on high alert. "I know, I know, but I won't be able to sleep tonight not knowing where he is." Just as she responded, there was a knock at the door.

Their eyes widened in fear.

They quietly stared each other down. Nothing was said, but yet they understood what that knock meant. Something was wrong. My parents bolted toward the front door. Tony whipped it open and stared into Daniel's moonlit eyes.

"They got into a car accident. Ryan's a little bit hurt," Daniel reported.

"What do you mean a little bit hurt?"

RYAN TROUTMAN

"I don't know," he said. His hands were stuffed in his pocket.

"Where's Kyle and Ben? Were they wearing seat belts?" My mom's questions were hitting Daniel faster than he could answer.

"Where is Ryan?"

"Trauma."

My mom immediately felt the air knocked out of her. As her heart began to pound, she felt a cold sting deep in her bones. Tears filled her eyes.

She watched as every ounce of color faded from Daniel's face. He gave her one last look and turned to head to the hospital where his brothers were.

Being a nurse all of her adult life, my mom knew no one went to the trauma center for being "just a little hurt."

Instinctively, Tony grabbed his keys and prepared to leave. My mother called her best friend, Janet, unable to stop the tears from rolling down her face. Her breathing was unsteady as the line began to ring. She pressed the phone to her ear, anxiously awaiting Janet's voice.

"Hello," a familiar voice replied.

"Ry-Ryan's been in a car accident. He's been taken to trauma," my mother said hurriedly.

"I'll be right over!" Janet replied, realizing the urgency. My mom hung up the phone, thankful that Janet lived right around the corner. My parents stood trembling in shock. It wasn't long before Janet came hurrying through the door. She embraced my mother and then Tony. Time was precious. My mom just wanted to get to me.

"I'll look after Morgan and Logan. Go to Ryan," she motioned toward the door.

"I can't thank you enough," Tony whispered to Janet. "Let's go," he directed at my mom. They both shuffled out of the door. In seconds, they were backing out of the driveway and headed down the road. Tony sped his way past the quiet residences, glancing occasionally at my mom. She was shaking, lost in her own fears.

"God, I hope he is ok," Tony whispered in a prayer.

My mom's eyes darted around in the car manically. She was hoping for the best, but preparing for the worst. This was her life. Life and death's vicious cycle was something she understood all too well. For more than twenty years, my mom nursed patients through some of their worst illnesses. Her entire career had been taking care of children in a pediatric hospital. A nightmare came true on this night when one of her children became a patient. She went into mom mode but maintained the eye and wisdom of a seasoned nurse.

After a moment, she pulled out her cellphone and began punching in numbers on the keypad. Everyone needed to know. She called my grandparents and aunt, filling them in on what little she knew.

My mom began to cry more and said to Tony, "This is bad!"

"You don't know that, maybe it's just some broken bones."

"It's trauma! It's trauma," my mom was crying, quietly; occasionally she let out, "He has to be okay." It was almost like my mom was fighting a battle within herself. Looking through the eyes of denial, my mom tried forcing her will on the outcome. "He's okay. He's okay. Ryan will be okay." But the nurse inside of her kept saying, "It's trauma..."

On the interstate, they passed the scene of the accident. From their angle, the Camaro didn't appear to be damaged.

Silence lingered between my mom and Tony. The thought of this all being an exaggeration played through their minds. But, they didn't see the other side of the car. They couldn't see the side that was crushed inward and was missing its door. My side.

My mom was shaking and shivering and crying. When they arrived at the trauma hospital, her chest tightened. As soon as she walked through the doors, denial couldn't comfort her anymore. She had to face reality.

Tony's car squealed up to the front door of the emergency room. My mom's attention moved to a blinking message on her phone. My grandparents were on their way. Tony stopped and let my mom out of the car, then sped off to find parking.

My mom raced through the hospital corridors in search of her sixteen-year-old boy.

"Where is he?!" She asked several of the nurses, who responded with blank stares. She caught a paramedic passing by.

"Where is my son! I need to see my son!" She screamed at him.

"Calm down, ma'am," the man said dryly. He paused and looked into my mom's pleading blue eyes. "Are you here for the accident that just occurred?"

"Yes! Yes! Where is he?!" My mom implored.

"Are you the mother of the passenger or the driver?"

"The passenger," she said quickly. The paramedic could tell by my mom's fearful tone which passenger she was referring to. She was getting more impatient now. She needed to find her boy. She needed to know what was going on.

A nurse interjected and began talking to the paramedic, stealing his attention. My mom glanced around looking for a reprieve, but there was none. The waiting room was full of anxious families and a surly dread that surrounded the cold air.

My mom locked heated eyes with the paramedic and moved in front of him. She wouldn't be ignored. He broke away from the nurse and turned towards my mom.

"Ma'am I'm going to need you to follow me," he instructed grimly.

His brief words were not enough. My mother continued to probe for information on my condition as he led her past the waiting room.

"Is he alive?" She asked.

The paramedic stopped and turned to face my mom. His comforting hands lightly grasped my mom's shoulders. His frigid demeanor melted away.

"He is now," he softly replied.

My mom's face became outraged.

"What do you mean by 'he is now'?!" What happened? I demand some answers!" She declared.

The paramedic evaded the question and continued walking. My mom huffed as she trailed behind him. This was her child's life. She wasn't going to blindly sit on the sidelines.

As she followed the paramedic down the hallway, she felt a light squeeze on her arm and turned to find Tony beside her.

"Have you heard anything?" Tony asked.

My mom shook her head in a worried frustration.

"They haven't given me any information. I don't even know where he is."

Tony's face fell, but straightened after a moment. He couldn't fall apart right now; it wouldn't help anyone.

"Maybe they're taking us to him now," he tried, attempting to comfort her. My mom said nothing. Her face was stone cold. She just wanted to find her son. Nothing else mattered.

They continued pacing through the halls closely tailing behind the paramedic. The sounds of crying patients and light moans filled their ears as they continued down the corridor. My mom dropped her head in misery; she'd never been on the patient end before.

Then, the paramedic stopped in front of a private room and turned to them. It was an open rectangular shaped room with chairs lined down the sides and a small couch at the end with a table that had a phone and a lamp.

My mom's anxiety and fear increased. She started crying more and said, "No, no, I'm not going in there." Being a nurse, my mom knew when the chaplain is called in and waiting for you, it's not going to be good.

"Where is my son? Is he alive?"

"Ma'am why don't you just wait, someone will be out to talk to you," he responded.

My mom asked louder, "Is he alive?!"

RYAN TROUTMAN

The paramedic looked at her desperation and said quickly, "He is right now."

"Is he intubated?"

He knew then she had medical knowledge. My mom was hysterical and not going to let him leave without telling her something. He said, "He is intubated now. We were unable to intubate him at the scene; he clamped down on the tube. He was a GCS of three and was posturing at the scene."

My mom fell to her knees crying hysterically. The paramedic reached to lift her and said, "Please. You need to speak to the chaplain while you wait for an update on your son."

Tony opened the door to find an older man in a black robe sitting in the middle of the room. Chairs lined the walls of the small chapel. The man glanced up at my parents expectantly as they entered the room and took a seat. They didn't want to hear the Word of God right now. The only word that held merit was that of the doctors.

"Is my son alive?" My mom asked roughly.

The chaplain nodded. She sought more answers, but her queries were met with vague nods or three word denials. My mother found no help or consolation in this poor man. He still hadn't moved on to providing the Divine Word. His purpose had been reduced to curtailing my mom's questions.

"I don't know, I don't know," he echoed continuously. Until, my mom finally recoiled in her chair, defeated. My mom was hysterical, crying saying, "He's on a ventilator! He's a three GCS! My God. He can't die! He can't die!" Tony began to cry and held my mom tight. The chaplain sat quietly, attempting to comfort them with tissue for their noses.

"The paramedics offered their support and said they are working on your son. As soon as they can they will be out to talk to you. You know he's critical, and they are doing everything they can right now," the chaplain said. Tony and my mom sat on the couch at the end of the room.

My mom was in shock and full of disbelief. She felt helpless. "I'm supposed to protect my children, and now, there is nothing I can do," my mom cried. "Ryan is fighting for his life, and all I can do is wait and pray that he will live!"

"You should call Tom. This is bad," Tony said softly.

"I can't talk to him right now," she rolled her eyes and shook her head.

"I will call him," he picked up the phone on the table and called my biological father, Tom. My mom was sitting next to Tony crying with her head on his shoulder.

The phone rang a few times, before my father's sleepy voice came onto the line.

"Hello," he yawned.

"Tom, Ryan has been in an accident, and they don't expect him to make it."

Tom did not respond.

"We're at the emergency room now, waiting to hear from the surgeons," Tony's voice cracked as he spoke.

"How'd it happen?" Tom asked slowly.

"We don't know. One of his friends came over to tell us about it, and we rushed up here," Tony replied.

"Well, I hope that he's okay and that the doctors give you some good news. Keep me updated…" Tom trailed off.

"W-we will," Tony hung up.

My mom said, "that's it, he knows. It's up to him to do with the information as he pleases. I don't have the energy to deal with him."

My father didn't make any heartfelt proclamations. He didn't offer to break our long distance barrier and drive down to look after his boy. He just wanted to be kept updated. That principle defined our tumultuous relationship, a series of phone calls, and brief tidbits into the happenings of my life.

My mom exhaled, picked up her phone, and dialed Janet's cell. Before Janet could say anything my mom began to sob into the receiver. "He can't die! He can't die! He can't die!" She cried.

Janet's voice had barely managed a retort before my mom hung up in despair. This cycle of calls to Janet continued until Tony wrenched the cell phone away from my mom and enveloped her in a hug. She cried against his shoulder.

Family Reunion

The operating room was frantically buzzing with doctors and nurses trying to keep down the swelling in my head. They dosed me with hypertonic saline and Mannitol to sustain my body.

On the other side of the building, my parents had been waiting for hours. The cries outside of the room ceased only to be replaced by new ones. My parents were growing restless, so they moved out to the hallway seeking anyone who could tell them something.

My grandparents, Pepa and Ms. Rae, and my Uncle Frankie wandered the hall in search of my mom. From a distance, Ms. Rae saw my mom and Tony sitting solemnly against a busy walkway near the chaplain's room. She hurried towards them. My mom stood to hug her dad. Pepa wrapped his arms around her and restored a little strength in them both. Tony hugged Ms. Rae whose body was shaking.

The medical staff began to move me back to the trauma center's patient hub. They hurried through the halls with shuffling feet and poised faces.

"Have you found him yet?" Ms. Rae asked.

"No, we—," Tony stopped mid-sentence. His eyes fastened on the bloody body laying on a stretcher that was being hurried down the hallway by a group of nurses.

"Oh, my God," my mom yelled.

"That's Ryan!" Tony shouted and grabbed my mom's arm.

RYAN TROUTMAN

My mom and Ms. Rae shrieked. They were startled. A stretcher with a dozen nurses and doctors crowded around it quickly passed them heading toward doors that led to the intensive ward. A nurse was bagging me with an ambu bag. My mom got a glimpse of the person lying lifeless on the stretcher as they quickly rushed past. The vision of seeing my lifeless body surrounded by medical staff aggressively working to breath for me seemed so surreal.

My family ran to follow the stretcher through the doors. They were quickly stopped by nurses who asked them to return to the waiting room.

They did as they were told and were met by more family. My mom did not speak to anyone. All she could do was sit and cry. Soon after, Daniel and his mother arrived.

After seeing them, my mom had to leave the waiting room and collect herself. Her heart hurt with worry and fear. She found the nearest restroom and let out the sorrow welding inside of her. After some time, she calmed herself and returned to the waiting room.

"I have a different idea," she told Tony, "let's go see Ben."

My mom quickly told one of the neighboring nurses that she and Tony wanted to check on Ben. The nurse reluctantly agreed. My mom's eyes shot to the direction that the nurses had rolled me, but I had already departed. It didn't matter. She was determined to find her boy.

FIGHTING TO LIVE

My mom buzzed at the door for the triage nurse to allow them entrance.

"Yes?" The nurse asked.

"May we see Ben Glovine?"

"He's in number six," the nurse said. The door clicked loudly when it unlocked. Tony pulled it open for the two of them.

They went directly to the small bed behind the sixth set of curtain walls that separated the critical patients. Ben was awake and alert, just groggy with a headache. He had a concussion and my mom could see the pain in his eyes. They stayed in Ben's room a few minutes before my mom started to slide back curtains to find me. Tony followed. She opened every curtain wall she could until she found me. When she did, she could hardly recognize me. Tubes and wires were connected to me everywhere. The ventilator was breathing for me. Everywhere she expected to see skin, she saw blood—even my eyes were swollen and bloody. A C-collar was clamped around my neck. The entire right side of my face had been peeled away by the road. Seeing me like this was horrific. My mom cried hysterically. Her body shook at the sight of me.

"Ry—ryan..."

Tony stared at me; his Cuban melanin faded, leaving a pale white face. He crouched down, fearfully, and ran his eyes down my body. The sight was too much for him. He turned and stepped out of the room, hiding the tears pooling in his eyes.

Nurses at a nearby station looked with wide eyes at Tony. They knew exactly what he just saw. One nurse slowly raised a pointing finger and directed Tony to the waiting room.

"Sir, your family is waiting back in the holding room. You can't be in there right now," the nurse said gently. Her eyes darted over to the doorway of my room where my mother now stood.

"He's a fighter. We finished his scans, but we need him to stabilize a bit more before you can see him. Can I ask you two to please wait in the private room?"

My mom joined Tony, and they nodded at the nurse. They blankly retreated to the waiting room where my cousins, aunts, uncles, and several other family members now gathered. The small room was filled with love and support.

Tony forced a straight face and addressed everyone. "He is still alive. They took the scans they needed, and now he is back in PICU," he announced.

"Oh thank God!" Ms. Rae shouted.

My aunts and uncles ran to hug my mom and Tony. Prayers and soft words of comfort swirled around in my mom's ears, but no sentiment quenched her worry.

"I can not lose my son!" My mom cried.

She slumped through the waiting room with a zombie-like crawl. She remembered seeing a Florida Highway patrolman in the hall and didn't think much about. This was a trauma center and she knew they dealt with trouble all of the time. From car accidents to gun shot wounds and everything in between. So it really didn't seem significant at the time.

Moments later my mom saw that same Highway Patrolman now standing in the hall outside of the waiting room. She began to wonder what his purpose was. So she slowly walked towards the man and said, "why are you here?"

He replied, "I am waiting to see if your son dies. If he does, I have to charge the driver."

My mom was angry. She hated him in that moment and felt as though he was the Grim Reaper. Lurking, just circling for death. Nothing else was said. She stormed off into the waiting room. Fortunately, it was full with family. Everyone returned to sitting in silence including Ben's uncles and brothers. My mom was still in shock, wishing that I'd wake up and this would all be nothing but a nightmare. The clock above their heads continued to tick as the moments of my short-lived life began to fade.

STOP, DROP, AND TALK

Kyle was still being held by police at the accident scene. Abrasive questioning and worry over the fate of his brother and best friend left him feeling vulnerable. A familiar voice echoed from a distance and grabbed his attention.

He looked up to see his uncle flashing his badge to one of the officers. He faintly heard his uncle explain that he was a private investigator. After a moment, Kyle's uncle started in his direction with the stout commanding officer in tow.

His uncle's voice was clear now.

"Let him go. His parents are not here with him, therefore you cannot keep him here. I am his uncle and can take it from here."

The officer huffed, but consented. "That'll be fine." He tilted his head up motioning for Kyle to stand. When he obeyed, he locked eyes with his uncle in silent pleading.

"Thank you for your time and assistance. Are there any other questions you need to ask before we leave?" Kyle's uncle asked, feigning civility.

"N..no sir, we've got everything we need," the officer grumbled.

Kyle's uncle tipped his hat at the officer and led Kyle away from the forlorn scene. He stopped in front of his car and regarded his nephew.

RYAN TROUTMAN

"Why were you driving that fast?" His uncle asked sternly. Kyle's eyes were empty. He stared downwards in a shameful posture. His uncle exhaled.

"I'll take you," he whispered, "to the trauma hospital."

As Kyle's uncle's blue Ford F-150 rolled away from the scene, Kyle gazed out at the idle remnants of his once new Camaro. Billows of grey smoke fogged his view of the shattered windows and crushed seats. His uncle watched Kyle through the rear view mirror. There was an unspoken question in Kyle's dejected eyes. With a deep breath, he offered, "It will be okay. We all make mistakes."

Kyle released a subtle sigh as the words stripped him of any sense of comfort.

———

It was five o'clock in the morning when the sliding glass doors of the trauma center parted and Kyle half-stepped his way inside. He wandered the halls aimlessly. He spotted a nurse and lightly tapped her on the shoulder.

She turned to him briskly. "Yes?" She asked irritably.

"Hello. Have you seen Ry-Ryan?" Kyle asked with hesitance.

"You're going to have to tell me more than just a first name. There's bound to be more than one Ryan at this hospital," she replied coldly.

"Troutman! I'm looking for Ryan Troutman!" He blurted out. Sweat covered his face that was scarred and bruised.

"Well, I don't know who that i—"

Kyle turned and barreled away from the nurse before she could continue. He needed to talk to someone who knew where his friend was. He was getting anxious. No matter how many people he approached or trailed after, they were too busy to answer his questions. His patience was slipping.

RYAN TROUTMAN

"Hey!" He screamed at a passing nurse. Her face rose from her patient information chart and she regarded him with confused eyes. His face and demeanor softened.

"Sorry. Excuse me, ma'am. Do you know where Ryan Troutman is?" Kyle asked again.

He was on the verge of tears. The nurse nodded sympathetically. She placed a comforting hand on his shoulder.

"Follow me," she directed.

Kyle tipped his head in obedience and let the nurse lead the way. She stopped in front of a glass door and turned to Kyle.

"They're in there," she said lightly.

"Thank you," Kyle breathed.

The nurse nodded and gave Kyle's shoulder a light squeeze before walking away.

Kyle peered through the fingerprints on the uncleaned door that opened into the private waiting room. He slowly turned the knob and forced himself to enter. As soon as he locked eyes with my family, he broke down in tears.

"I'm sorry! I'm sorry! I should've made sure he had his seatbelt on! I shouldn't have driven that fast! I'm sorry!" Kyle bellowed, as tears poured down his cheeks.

The horrid reception that Kyle expected never came to pass. He had been my best friend for almost all of my childhood. He spent the night at my house, ate dinner with my family, and was always there for me. He was my brother and like a son to my parents.

A shadowed man sat in the corner watching as Kyle cried his apologies to my family.

"Hey, Tom," a passing uncle muttered in the direction of the man. My dad peered up and gave an affirming nod. He distanced himself from my mom's side of the family. His unexpected appearance was met with ambivalence, but regardless this was the best way for him to stay updated.

My mother sat quietly in the corner, almost oblivious to Tom's and Kyle's presence. She was numb. No apology or sentiment of comfort could console her.

Kyle couldn't stop tears from rippling down his face as he vehemently apologized. My mom was still in shock with no energy to speak. Tony rose from his seat beside my mother and walked over to Kyle. He placed a consoling hand on Kyle's back.

His eyes strayed over to my mom and then back to Kyle.

"Let's step outside for a moment."

Kyle nodded and wiped his eyes. They departed the room and silently walked outside of the trauma hospital. Tony motioned for Kyle to take a seat on a bench against the wall just outside the entrance doors. Kyle exploded into tears once more.

"I'm so sorry," he sobbed.

Tony joined him on the bench and wrapped an arm around his shoulders.

"It's going to be okay." Tony whispered gently.

Kyle looked up at Tony in disbelief. The anger he was expecting was nonexistent. He let out a long sigh.

"But..what if it's not okay? What if he—"

Tony held his hand to silence Kyle. "You can't think like that. Nobody is mad at you. It will all be okay."

Tony sat quietly and allowed Kyle time to cry and collect himself.

"Let's go back in the room now," Tony said and Kyle nodded. The two of them made their way back into the grim waiting room and sat down on the blue, cushioned chairs. The silence in the room was unsettling. Worry and dismay sifted across everyone's tired faces.

The knob to the private room turned and a nurse entered the room. Everyone stared up at her expectantly.

"Could Ryan's mother and father please follow me?" She asked quietly.

My mom and Tom rose from their seats abruptly. Tony wanted to lunge out of his chair and provide all of the support possible. He wanted to be there for me and my mother but knew staying in the room with other family members would be best.

"I am going to take you both upstairs to the pediatric intensive care unit," the nurse said, turning back to open the door.

"Tha-thank you," my mom breathed out.

They followed the nurse out of the room and into the hallway. The beeping monitors and mild hysteria in the surrounding rooms were dizzying. My mom took relief in the elevator at the end of the hall.

My parents said nothing to each other as they ascended.

"Once we get to the ICU, I'll go over the procedures with you. I'll also tell you when you'll be permitted to see your son and where you can sleep and shower should you decide to stay in the hospital." The nurse explained softly.

The elevator stopped and they exited onto the ICU hallway facing the nurses triage. Glass doors opened revealing whirring machines and chattering nurses.

"It's just through here and on the left," she assured my parents.

They nodded and followed. She led them past the triage station and finally stopped in front of a large brown door.

"Now, you're going to have a sleeping area over there." The woman explained, pointing behind their shoulders at what appeared to be another lobby. Her finger shifted over to an area across from them. "Those two doors over there lead to women's and men's bathrooms. There, you can shower."

My parents nodded in understanding. As they approached the room and nurses desk, they were introduced to a neurosurgeon. This woman began to explain the procedure she just did and the purpose behind an ICP monitor. She informed them that I have a severe traumatic brain injury and a diffuse axonal bleed, which meant my brain was bleeding all over. She added that I was critical, had high levels of pressure in my brain, and a basilar skull fracture. She paused and let that information sit with my parents for a moment. Then she explained that the specialists and surgeons on duty were treating the bleeding and swelling with medications right now, but I still may not live. "The surgeon has told the nursing staff that the next several days were critical. Ryan's body can't take any excess stimulation so only you, mom, and you, dad, can see him right now," she explained gently.

"Now, when I let you in, you can't make a bunch of noise. You can't shout loudly," she concluded.

"I understand," my mom said in a near whisper.

"No questions, then?" She asked skeptically.

My parents shook their head slowly.

The nurse turned back to the door and let them inside the room. An intracranial pressure monitor had been put into my head and fluids from an I.V. sustained my body as I lay motionless upon the hospital bed. My mom rushed to my side and pulled up a chair. She exhaled and lowered herself down onto the seat. Her eyes surveyed my battered body. Tears pooled in her eyes, but didn't fall.

It was a small room. To the left was a window overlooking a parking lot. Beside the window was a recliner, machines, monitors, a ventilator, and six to seven I.V pumps all connected to my body. My mom watched her son lying there, fighting for his life. The sight of me made her feel like she couldn't breathe. Her soft whimpers were tamed by the doctor's orders to limit stimulation. Her feelings weren't important to her. All she wanted to do was stay strong for her child.

I had a tube down my throat. My body was connected to a machine that was breathing for me; and a central line jutted out of the left side of my chest. I.V. fluids continued to pump medication into me to try to decrease swelling in my brain and keep my blood pressure sustainable. The ICP monitor was a wire coming out of a small white styrofoam cup that was taped to the top of my head. My face was swollen and unrecognizable. It was as if the first several layers of my skin had been removed. My eyes had moisture gel with tape to keep them closed and from drying out.

The sight was horrific and forced my mom to face the reality of losing her first child. Her boy, who was always so full of life and energy, now laid there lifeless. They let my mom stay in the room with me. She continued sitting in a chair right beside the bed. Praying to God to not take her son away. She laid her head down on the sheets and held my hand. She sat in silence, watching the monitors and making sure the numbers didn't drop. The doctor said the ICP number shouldn't go above twenty. She watched the number shoot up and down across the screen far past that number.

Tom hung back unable to lift the heaviness in his chest. He started toward me, but paused mid-step. After a moment, he left the room. My mom scoffed and shook her head. It was just like him to leave. She rested her head beside me and closed her eyes.

At least now she could be with her son. It gave her a small measure of contentment. Within minutes she began to doze off.

My mom's heavy eyes later opened to Tom's face. He'd been softly shaking her awake. He bore a tired leer.

"You can sleep in one of the rooms with me if you like," he offered. She shook off his arm and stared at him intensely.

"Let me tell you something," her voice grew a sharp lilt whisper. "Do not touch me. Do not look at me. Do not talk to me. The only reason for you to be here is for Ryan."

Tom's face was constricted. He opened his mouth to argue, but the sight of me stilled the beast in his chest. He turned and left the room muttering to himself. My mom deflated and recoiled by my side once more. She nuzzled her head against the cushioned edge of my bed. The lullaby of beeping monitors and whirring machines slowly lulled her to sleep.

After a couple hours, my ICP numbers were still high, and the nurse was in and out tending to monitors and medicine. My mom asked if her being in the room right now was causing any of the monitors to jump. The nurse whispered "no, but it might be a good idea to go in the waiting room for just a bit and let us try to get him settled down."

While my mom did not want to leave my side, she wanted to do whatever was best for my chance at living. When she returned to the family waiting room, she noticed thirty kids from my school outside the doors. She couldn't believe the number of friends and classmates who had already heard what happened and decided to come to check on me.

Rebuild Me

The hospital bustled with people as the afternoon descended. Nurses checked their charts, and cleaning crews mopped the hospital floors with vigor. Sunlight poured through the windows highlighting my bandaged frame.

The steadfast shuffling of nurses woke my mom out of her uncomfortable, contorted sleeping position. She wiped the tiresome crust from her eyelids and peered at my monitors. My blood pressure was unusually high.

"Good morning. How did you sleep?" a nurse asked as she grabbed charts from my door's basket.

"Not that great."

"You can go into one of the side rooms and rest if you need to."

"No, I'm fine."

My mom rose to her feet wearily. The hospital room was tidy and untouched. Medical tubes and devices were all properly stationed in their holsters and my paperwork was stacked neatly beside the bed for the doctor's inspection.

My mom slunk into the bathroom to brush her teeth and wash off. She splashed water on face and stared back at herself in the mirror. Her eyes were slightly sunk in.

She wanted to cry, but bit back the tears. She straightened her hair and headed back to the room solemnly. She sat back down in the chair and exhaled.

RYAN TROUTMAN

She felt her phone buzz and pulled it out of her pocket. It was Tony. He was with my siblings, Morgan and Logan. He said he'd be back later with a change of clothes. She quietly thanked him. She couldn't be anywhere else right now.

"Knock, knock," a nurse quietly whispered through a cracked door. "You have some visitors."

"Thank you. Please send them in," my mom responded softly. Her eyes bulged at the sight of her boss from the dialysis center and her boss' son, Father O'Neill. Word—or tragedy—traveled fast. They sat with my mom offering thoughtful sentiments and the well wishes of other coworkers.

"It's going to be alright. I promise," my mom's boss whispered as she rested her comforting arm over my mom's shoulders.

"The Lord is with you," her son added. Father O'Neill knelt down beside my bed and bowed his head. His eyes closed and his lips began to softly mumble a prayer. My mother and her boss closed their eyes and joined him.

My mom needed all the support and prayers she could get, but sitting there listening to Father O'Neill perform the anointing of the sick—essentially my last rites—was difficult to hear. As she stood at my bedside, with the priest across from me, she cried. Her body was numb and her mind kept asking, *How did we get here? Why my son?*

"Please don't take him away from me," she whispered during the priest's prayer.

Later, the chaplain checked in on me, providing fervent invocation. He hugged my parents and extended an invitation to his church once I stabilized a bit. We weren't devout churchgoers, but my family found comfort in the invitation .

Waves of family members and friends followed as the day wore on, offering their condolences and silent cheers for a speedy recovery. The nurses and doctors came back and forth intermittently, checking my vitals and scribbling on their clipboards. My mom anxiously supervised the numerous exchanges.

Time felt as though it stood still; the goal and hopes were that the medications would control the bleeding in my brain and reduce the swelling, but all they could do is wait.

The medical staff allowed my mother to have a nursing role in my healing process and remain in the room. She changed my bandages as they filled my I.V. with antiseptic.

"We'll take it from here, Lisa," one of the nurses gently instructed. My mom nodded and took a step back as they tended to me. Tony arrived later that night. He stood outside of my room preparing himself. It was hard for him to see me like that and to feel my mom's sorrow.

Tony felt his phone vibrate and dug into his pocket. He pulled it out and flipped it open, bringing the phone to his ear.

"Our plane just landed."

He recognized his mother's voice. It stilled his nerves.

"A rental car is waiting outside for us, and we should be there in two hours," she informed him.

"Okay, we'll see you soon," Tony replied. Both of them took a deep sigh. The flight from Seattle was most unnerving. He hung up the phone and watched the procession of relatives and family friends cycle in and out of my room.

"You're very loved," Tony smiled to himself.

Janet joined the succession of visitors. Her presence served as my mom's anchor. She sat with her and dispelled some of the anxiety in the air.

"Hey, Lisa. How are you feeling?" Janet asked.

My mom glimpsed up at Janet's curious expression and shrugged her shoulders in response. She didn't know how to answer that question. She felt helpless. Numb. Janet squeezed my mom's hand empathically. "You've got a wonderful array of people on your side. We're here for you."

My mom faintly smiled. Janet moved next to me and began gently rubbing my feet. She reminisced with my mom about all of the childhood shenanigans that I'd gotten into, in hopes that it would spark a conversation. My mom stayed relatively silent chuckling and nodding at points, but offered nothing more than one word responses.

Through my unconscious stupor, My toes twitched against Janet's fingers much to their delight. Pain darted through my body.

"See, he's still here," Janet smiled and turned to my mom.

My mother's lip cricked up, but she remained silent. As a nurse, my mom knew the twitch was an unconscious response from a misdirected nerve signal and not a sign of me awakening. There were still too many unknowns to try to explain to Janet; she really didn't want to sadden her best friend with an explanation on the difference between conscious and unconscious movements. Janet stayed a little longer before hugging my mom goodbye.

Kirsten was the first schoolmates to visit me. Mom and Tony monitored me like bodyguards as she sat beside my bed. Eventually, her sincerity won them over. Even though we didn't spend much time together outside of school, Kirsten was like a sister to me. When my facade crumpled, she was okay with what lie underneath. Among the ambiguous years of trying to belong, she remained true.

More classmates cycled in and out the small room. The news of my accident spread like wildfire at my high school. As grateful as my parents were for the concern, they eventually tired and cleared the room out.

I was fragile. All the voices and people's presence in the small room were taxing on me and on my parents.

My dad popped in periodically to "stay updated." Over time, he coaxed a social worker to put him up in a room downtown and supply him with daily meal vouchers to minimize the strain of commuting and buying food. The transition was tumultuous, but my mother feigned civility.

That first night in PICU was nerve-racking. Tony stayed along with Pepa and Ms. Rae. People were sleeping in every chair of the waiting room. My mom was in the room with me. All through the night, family would come to see how I was doing. The ventilator kept making alarming sounds. I was on full assistance, meaning the machines were doing all the work of breathing. I made absolutely no contribution. The pressures on the ICP were still high, my heart rate was all over the place. The Foley catheter collecting my urine was putting out minimal dark urine which meant my kidneys were failing. The medical staff kept giving me medicine to keep my blood pressure up because it had sunk so low. Everything was failing, and all they could do was wait and watch. In the middle of the night, two nurses came in and spent more than two hours applying the Silvadine cream to my right side from head to toe. This is typically what they do to burn victims. Nurses would rub the cream on my bloodied raw flesh and wait for it to dry. Later, they would come and rip it off of my body to prevent scabbing.

The next morning, Dr. Tepend made rounds and Dr. Vetarve came in to assess my brain and the ICP monitor. My brain was still swelling, Dr. Vertarve said, and we would just have to wait and hope the swelling decreases and the bleeding stops with help of the medications.

"What if doesn't?" my mom asked.

"Let's cross that bridge when—if—we come to it."

"Is he going to live?"

"We can't answer that question, Lisa, we just have to wait," Dr. Tepend responded. "Ryan's kidneys are becoming affected. We are having a hard time keeping his blood pressure up and we have to watch him closely."

The sum of this conversation was to stop trying to know the ending of the story and just read it line by line. Waiting and watching seemed to be all my mom was told to do for several days.

Family and friends stayed at the hospital throughout the day and night for the first week. On the fourth night, another highway patrolman showed up and asked my mom how I was.

"No change," she said, hoping he'd just go away.

"Off the record, ma'am, I suggest you get a lawyer."

"A lawyer?" my mom asked, "I'm not suing anyone."

"You have no idea the amount of financial issues you are about to mount," he offered as politely as he could. My mom walked away. The financial issues were still not a priority. She walked into the waiting room in time to hear Pepa, Ms. Rae, Tony, other family discussing who would stay the night with her. She told them she thought she could handle the night alone and they could go sleep at their homes. After reassuring them and saying goodbye, my mom returned to my room. She would stay all night while everyone else went back home and tried to sleep off the thought of losing me.

Now alone for the first time, her fear took over. She couldn't stop thinking about the possibility of something going wrong in the night. In the corner was a recliner that would only half-way recline. She climbed into the seat and began to rest. Her face was dimly lit by the glow of many screens. The chirping and beeping sounds of machines working hard into the night was her only lullaby. Just as she began to fall into a light slumber, the monitors started beeping loudly. Nurses rushed in and began checking the screens. Moments later a resident arrived and began grabbing charts that were clipped to the door.

"Whats wrong?! What is going on?!" my mom cried. A resident ordered the nurse to increase certain medications and hang new ones. My mother's face twisted in fear and anger.

"What is wrong!" she shouted.

"Look, it's getting better," the resident pointed to a gleaming monitor, but the alarming beeps continued shrieking.

"If this doesn't stop soon, you better get the attending doctor on the phone now and figure out how to get him stabilized!" My mom commanded. She was so scared; she picked up her phone and called Janet. She answered the call only to hear my mom crying and mumbling an inaudible explanation of what was happening.

"I'm on my way." Janet once again jumped at the opportunity to offer support. After several hours, the medications were able to sustain a low blood pressure. The staff had to give me additional fluids which could pose another problem and strain my failing kidneys. When they fixed one problem, it seemed as if that caused an issue with something else. Being comatose, I offered no help and no resistance.

MR. SNEAKY SNAKE

One night when the hospital began to quiet down my dad popped by my room, seeking my mom.

"Knock, knock," he whispered, tapping lightly on my door.

"What?" my mom sat rigidly in the chair by my bedside.

He let himself in and forced a crooked smile. "Every time I come by you're in that chair. Your back is gonna get shot to hell like Th.—"

"What do you want?" my mom snapped.

His smile faded, and he fought to keep his voice even.

"I wanted to see if Morgan could stay with me tonight. I have a place not too far from—"

"Absolutely not," she interrupted. My mom knew Morgan didn't want to stay the night at the Ronald McDonald House with him.

"Whatever, I don't even know why I bother," he dully whispered.

He stormed out of the room abruptly. My dad's visits continued to be sporadic and often resulted in a verbal altercation of sorts. He developed a colorful reputation. His arrivals and departures consisted of lewd gestures and suggestive remarks towards the female medical staff. My mom watched in distaste as he eyed up the attending nurses' backsides. Eventually, he became known as "Mr. Sneaky Snake."

RYAN TROUTMAN

"You act like you don't trust me to be alone with him for five minutes," my dad sneered.

"I don't trust you and don't play me. You treat this place like your own personal hunting ground," my mom shot back.

My father glared at my mom.

"Tom, just stop. This is supposed to be about, Ryan."

"It is about—"

"It's not. It's about what you can take."

Tony appeared in the doorway with his hands crossed. He cleared his throat silencing them. "Do we have a problem here?" he asked with a stout tone.

My dad was still fuming.

"Okay, Mr. High and Mighty," my dad grumbled. He shook his head and left the room.

Don't Stop Believing

The days became a continuous cycle. The mornings and afternoons were comprised of intensive operations, scans, and tests on my weak and limp body. Most evenings were designated times for my room to be as quiet as possible. All of this was beginning to take a toll on my parents.

The cold hospital room became my home. Among the blind darkness, my parents sought to add a bit of light and a sense of home. Jack Johnson played on Tony's portable stereo and mom kept surfing movies on an endless loop.

The doctors encouraged them to do things that I'd be able to recall. They obliged. My mom and Tony alternated between telling me stories and playing my favorite songs.

They kept a calm face, but they were slowly being unnerved. Everyday I laid in bed, eyes closed, unmoved, and broken. Everyday they were forced to helplessly wait and hope.

One day Dr. Eyliat, a nephrologist my mom worked with in pediatric dialysis came to visit. Fortunately, he had privileges at the trauma hospital to view my reports. My mom told him the staff is concerned with my kidney function because I was only putting out minimal amounts of urine and now my body was retaining all of my fluid.

"Can you take a look at the monitors and tell me what you think?" she asked, believing he would.

He gently examined me, look through my charts, and pressed a few buttons on the beeping machines. Suddenly a depressing look crept across his face. "Lisa, we just need to pray," he softly replied.

Soon after his visit, the nurses started a continuous Veno-Venous Hemofiltration dialysis to remove some fluids from my body. I was becoming less and less recognizable. My body was swollen from head to toe with fluid. The staff constantly checked on the monitors in hopes my body would improve enough for surgery. My lower jaw was still hanging loosely from my face and needed immediate attention.

That night Janet and my mom were in the room alone. They conversed about many stressful topics that unfortunately needed to be discussed.

"Do you mind waiting a moment? I am going to run to the restroom. I'll be right back." my mom kindly whispered before tip-toeing out into the hallway.

She returned moments later and saw an uneasy look on Janet's face. Her finger shook, pointing towards my idle body to bring attention to another problem. When my mom turned to face me she was frightened to see that blood was oozing from my nose and ears. Her trembling hand reached for the nearest phone.

"Hello?! Can you get here right now? Ryan has blood coming out of him!" she yelled into in phone.

"Someone'll be right there."

The doctor came to check my blood for cerebrospinal fluid. Because of the magnitude of my brain injury, the doctor quickly ordered more medication to try to stop the bleeding, but the flow of blood from my brain was severe. They worked through the night to stop the bleeding and were finally able to stabilize me once again.

The next day, a seventeen-year-old boy was life-flighted in and put in the room across the hallway from mine. His family was in the waiting room talking with my family as they waited for their son to come from surgery. He was riding a four wheeler with a friend in the woods and they hit a tree. The boy hit his head and was laying nearly dead in the dirt. Out of fear, his friend went home and didn't tell anyone about the accident for a few hours. Now, the boy had a brain injury and was taken immediately to surgery to try to relieve pressure in the brain. He had a external ventricular drain in his brain collecting all of the cerebrospinal fluid. My family comforted them as best as their own fears for my life would allow them.

Two nights later, my mom heard the familiar alarming from motors and sprang up thinking they were mine until she heard people rushing in and out of the boy's room. His mother was crying hysterically outside my door. They were coding him for what felt like several hours. My mom held on to me for dear life with silent tears rolling down her cheeks, knowing there was still a possibility she could be facing the same horrific scenario.

The next morning, she walked out to go to the restroom and noticed a crowd of people standing near the boy's room. His mother walked over to mine, hugged her, and said "I hope your son does well, we just had to let ours go." My mom didn't know what to say or do. All she could say back was how sorry she was. The boy's mother turned away, sobbing, almost being carried out. In that moment my mom knew they had to stay vigilant, push harder, and believe more for me to wake up.

Family and friends continued to visit staying overnight to support my mother and Tony. They faced a plethora of issues that impacted my recovery: I wasn't urinating, my kidneys were failing, my blood pressure was steadily dropping, and the duress in my head intensified. Day after day, my fever remained and my sodium levels bounced from high to low. A large collar brace held my jaw together. Bandages covered my battered limbs.

The nurses routinely filled my I.V, hoping to sustain me. My body was thirsting for fluids despite how balanced my insulin was. In just a few days, I went from not being able to pass urine at all to not being able to regulate the release of it.

Fourteen days had gone by and I was still in a coma. Then, a respiratory therapist and two nurses came into the room one night with a startling announcement. My mom was alone.

"We are going to try to wean Ryan down off the ventilator."

"Absolutely not!" my mom yelled. "You will not do this tonight without a full staff!"

It was a stalemate, and mom wasn't bulging.

The therapist and nurse rescinded and agreed to return the next day. When they returned, they were unsuccessful in weaning me off. I still could not breathe on my own at all. My jaw was broken and I was in the second week of my coma. Finally, Dr. Tepend came into the room.

"Ma'am, we've done all that we can," He began. "We cannot keep Ryan on the ventilator with the endotracheal tube. We need to perform a surgery to continue giving him air and to repair his jaw. We will switch the air source to a trach, and see if he begins breathing on his own."

"No," my mom complained, "I don't want him to have a trach."

"This is not the same trach you are thinking of. This is a trauma trach. Hopefully it is short term and can be reversed. It has to be done if we want Ryan to breath and breath on his own. During this surgery we will also operate on his jaw."

"My son can barely maintain his other vitals; he hasn't opened his eyes, and you want to remove his breathing apparatus?" My mom asked incredulously.

"His body will not push itself if we keep enabling him. He needs this surgery. Surely you understand this better than most," he said pointedly.

My mom relented even though she felt I was not stable enough. Dr. Tepend walked to the nurses' triage to schedule the surgery immediately. She was frightened, worrying that I wouldn't survive. For a moment, she couldn't slow down the pounding in her head. She needed an escape.

"Bad time?"

My mom and Tony spun around to see Tom standing in the doorway.

"Everything alright here?" He locked eyes with my mom.

She nodded curtly and moved out of Tony's hold.

"What do you need?"

Tom glanced over at Tony and then back at my mom. His hesitance made my my mom's face fall.

"What is it, Tom?" She asked knowingly.

"Uh-um, could we all talk outside the room?" Tom faltered.

My mom nodded and shot a sideways glance at Tony. She was already dreading the conversation. Several of my family members were dispersed around the waiting room. Disapproving eyes shot to my father as he emerged from my room.

"I'll probably have to head out soon," Tom said quietly.

My mom's expression hardened. A few more gazes turned in my dad's direction. Before my mom could outburst he continued.

"I have a place and meals here and there, but I can't afford the necessary things without a job. I'm not leaving the area. I will be around; I just have several interviews lined up."

My mom tried to keep her voice even. "Ryan's probably going to have surgery within the next day or so, Tom."

"Surgery for what? I wasn't told anything about a surg—."

"They would like add some consistency to his air flow and wean him off of his ventilator. His jaw is still broken."

"That's just stupid! His damn machine beeps and alarms half of the time I'm in the room."

"He has to start being conditioned to breathe on his own."

"Uh-huh," he mumbled, "Well, keep me upd—"

"Updated. Sure." My mom closed her eyes and reopened them, fighting back the agitation coursing through her body. "Do what you have to do, Tom." She muttered finally. "You should probably spend some time with him before you head out. It's been a while."

Tom nodded and slipped back into my room.

My mom stepped out of the room and decided to ride the elevator instead of going near the crowd of family and friends. She needed a little escape—a little peace.

Family and friends came to support me on the morning of my surgery. Everyone brought coffee and breakfast, neither of which my mom could enjoy.

"Good morning," Tony sleepily said to my mom while setting down a box of bagels.

"Thank you," she stared down at the caffeinated elixir steaming up from the table beside her.

"When are they taking him?" Tony asked. The squinched look on his face made it apparent that the sip of coffee he just had was scalding hot.

"Should be any min—"

"Good morning. We're here to take Ryan up." A nurse walked in and hinted that the bagels and coffee be moved away. Behind her was a line of medics ready to roll me away.

The respiratory therapist and nurses disconnected me from the ventilator and added a manual bag in its place. They hoisted me onto a stretcher and began rolling me down the hallway, headed for the operating rooms.

They stopped in front of glass double doors. The surgeon and anesthesiologist met my mother and the nurses in the hall for my mom to sign a consent form. My comatose body began to buck on the tube. A nurse quickly pulled a syringe from her pocket and stabbed my right hip leaving behind strong medicine that immediately sedated me. My mother kissed me and began to walk toward the waiting room.

After a rolling journey of little air, a nurse ran through the operating room's double doors saying, "Take him back!"

"What's the problem?" the therapist asked.

RYAN TROUTMAN

The nurse shook his head and waved his arms.

"We can't go in there right now," he seethed.

The nurses exchanged glances.

"Why?" the second nurse piped up. Her jet black hair was pulled tightly into a bun and her figure proved she had experience lifting weights.

"Apparently, some gang member got shot, and until they are done using the rooms, they won't let anyone else in. There was some incident in the waiting room from the connected parties. He needs to come back later. He's critical..." The nurse's voice trailed off.

The respiratory therapist nodded reluctantly and angled my stretcher around. They rolled me back to my room. My mother froze as she watched the nurses hurriedly move me back into place and reconnect the ventilator. Her eyes narrowed, and her cheeks became flushed.

"What in the hell are you doing?" my mom yelled. She moved in front of the nurses.

"We're holding Ryan here for a little while. There was a shooting near the hospital, and a—" one of the nurses responded.

"You couldn't have checked on that before you took away my son's oxygen?" My mom asked angrily.

The second nurse stepped forward and lightly placed a comforting hand on my mom's shoulder. My mom faintly recognized her, but still pulled away indignantly.

"It'll be alright, Lisa. Ryan will be taken to surgery as soon as the wing becomes available. I apologize that we were not notified prior to rolling him down there,"

My mom threw her hands in the air and stormed away. She took a minute to compose herself before she slowly descended into madness. Nothing was improving regardless of how many times she heard "it'll be alright." Things weren't alright but she was still expected to keep a controlled face.

She walked into the now crowded waiting room where the shooting victim's family gathered. The family was loud and police were questioning them and completing reports. My family had to have police protection in the room because they were afraid there was going to be gang retaliation.

My mom stomped through the crowd angry and yelling, "if my son dies because of some low life drug dealer bumping his surgery, I'm going to raise hell in this place!" She stormed out the room and headed back to my room. Tony was there. One step into the room, she fell into his arms, unable to hold back the tears. His supportive hold was warm and comforting. The two of them sat down on a nearby couch. It was only minutes before my mom began to doze off.

Many minutes had passed until she awoke to Tony's soft smile. She smiled back and wiped her eyes.

"Sorry, I didn't mean to fall as-"

"Don't be sorry," he kneeled and kissed her, "You needed sleep."

"How long was I out?"

"Not long," he gave out a slight chuckle. "You got fidgety when I tried to move you, so I let you stay here."

"And Ryan-"

"Is perfectly fine. Dr. Tepend would like to talk to you, though."

"Is it bad?"

"No, from what I gathered, I think Ryan can get the surgery done now."

My mom nodded and rose from her chair, stretching her arms and back. She was greeted by Dr. Tepend as she entered my room. "We would like to proceed with the surgery." He started. His eyes turned apologetic. "Sorry about the miscommunication earlier. It's been a little crazy around here."

"It's okay. I know that things happen," my mom replied.

"Now, the surgery will take several hours. We'll probably hold him for an hour afterwards, just to make sure that everything is okay. Then we'll place him back here. We'll have a nurse send word once the procedure is complete just to keep you adequately informed." Dr. Tepend explained.

My mom opened her mouth but Dr. Tepend held up his hand and continued speaking.

"Lisa, we can't have you present during the surgery."

"But…"

"In his state, everything is intricate and sensitive. You have to trust us."

My mom nodded, glancing over at me. She watched as the nurses repeated the steps of taking me off of the ventilator and putting a bag in it's place. The nurses undid the break on my bed and rolled me towards the door.

"We'll take good care of him." Dr. Tepend assured her.

"O-okay." My mom nearly whispered.

She watched as Dr. Tepend and the nurses filed out of the room with my bed in tow. She stared at the empty doorway for a while, lost in thought.

"Lisa…" Tony's voice pulled my mom out of her trance. She glanced over at him blankly.

"S-sorry," she mumbled. "What is it?"

"While you were sleeping earlier, I asked Janet to look after the kids. But I should probably head back." Tony paused and motioned to a white paper bag sitting on the small stand beside where my bed used to be. "I made a quick food run and brought you soup and sandwiches for whenever you get hungry. I'll probably send your brother by later with a change of clothes for you."

My mom stared at Tony thankfully. She could see the fatigue in his eyes and yet he was unquestioningly thoughtful. She didn't know what she'd do without him.

"Thank you," she said.

"You're welcome. I love you, and we'll get through this."

"I love you, too," my mom kissed Tony goodbye. For the first time, she opted to relax in one of the resting areas. It was more inviting than she expected. It was a small room, but the bed was relatively comfortable. She curled up against the blankets and nuzzled the pillow. Despite her desire to stay awake, she slowly drifted off into a deep slumber.

A gentle buzz in my mom's pocket made her stir. Her eyes opened, and she lazily sat upright. Her phone continued to vibrate. She yawned and weakly fished it out of her pocket. My dad's name danced across the front screen. She rolled her eyes, but reluctantly brought the phone close to her ear.

"Hello," she said wearily.

"So, when were you planning on telling me that our son was taken to surgery?" Tom questioned roughly.

"He wasn't taken in that long ago, Tom. I was waiting until they were finished."

"I called Ryan's room looking for you and when you didn't pick up I was routed to the front desk," my dad fumed. "I had to find out from one of the nurses! You said you'd keep me up—"

"Keep yourself updated!" My mom exclaimed. "You're his father. I'm not your mother or your wife! If you want to know what's going on, then be here. That's why you came here initially, right? To be updated?"

"Don't start!" Tom screeched into the phone.

My mom struggled to keep her voice even.

"Look, you're the one who left to go job hunting."

My dad was silent for a moment. Venom spilled through his voice. "Lisa, I can't keep driving up to that hospital and buying cafeteria food if I don't have any money. Those damn vouchers only last for so long. I'm done living like that. Everything was fine when I left yesterday. They weren't busting through the doors shouting 'he's dead' now were they?"

My mom didn't respond.

His tone softened slightly. "I can't stop every part of my life and neither can you, you've got two other kids at home just in case you forgot."

Fire brimmed in my mom's eyes. She was livid.

RYAN TROUTMAN

"I'm done with you, Tom. All these years you've been some translucent shadow of a person. You're not a father and haven't been. You show up here and expect the seas to part for you. It doesn't work that way. Don't forget to tell your prospective employers what kind of man you are!" My mom roared back. She could faintly hear my dad shouting obscenities.

"Mrs. Leon," a tiny voice called.

My mom quickly turned her head. A short nurse with short back hair and a plump frame stood in the doorway. "Sorry, I didn't mean to interrupt," she apologized in a whisper.

My mom shook her head vehemently. She quickly hung up the phone and stood to her feet.

"Is Ryan okay?"

The nurse nodded and smiled at my mom who was slightly embarrassed about a staff member witnessing her outburst.

"The surgery went really well," she answered happily. "He'll be able to breathe on his own again, but it will take time." She led my mom back to my room.

"My poor baby," she said seeing the tube in my neck, connected—still—to a ventilator. "Thank God, he's still alive," she whispered to herself although the nurse heard her and nodded her head in silent agreement.

DING, DING, DING

My mom and Tony reveled in my latest success. I was far from being completely healed, but this was a great start. Ms. Rae and my grandfather, Pepa, sat by my bedside as I lie in a bedridden stupor. "Keep fighting," Pepa would softly whisper in my ear, smoothing my forehead.

Visitors cycled through my room paying their respects and rejoicing at my successful surgery. Without any real glimpse of hope, the days and nights were long and filled with everyone waiting for that one spec of hope or one tiny improvement. My mom closely watched the monitors. She followed my urine output. In one day, I went from minimal urine output to more than 3,000 milliliters in a matter of hours. My mom gleamed with excitement. *His kidneys are working!* she immediately thought. But sadly that was not the case. Now something else had gone awry. The increased urine output indicated diabetes insipidus, meaning the pituitary gland had been damaged in my brain. The urine was not really urine, it was just large amounts of "free" water. My sodium levels were dangerously low and could have posed another critical issue to correct. The medical staff soon gave me Desmopressin because the pituitary gland was no longer doing its job.

My dad began to show up less and less as time wore on. It angered my family, but my mom began to accept the reality. Then suddenly after weeks of absence, he reappeared.

RYAN TROUTMAN

It was raining that evening and the hospital was unusually quiet. Tony had already left to rejoin Morgan and Logan. My mom stood still against the wall, peering out of the window pensively.

"Hi, Lisa." There was bitterness in the greeting. My mom turned to see Tom and the pale, worn face of a dirty blonde whose mascara hung thick around her dark eyes. She wore a scanty tank top with faded blue jeans.

"Who's this?" my mom asked examining the woman.

"His girlfriend," the woman answered.

"Charmed," my mother said sarcastically.

"Oh, she's fancy," the woman said, cutting her eyes at Tom. Irritation flickered across my mom's face. She couldn't be around Tom anymore and his plus one was a new type of idiocy.

"I'm going to give you some time with him," my mom's eyes shot to my dad's girlfriend. "Please try not make too much noise. He's still really sensitive right now."

My mom moved past them swiftly and froze once she hit the lobby. She had the sudden urge to cry. She pulled her cellphone from her pocket and dialed Janet but hung up before the phone began to ring. Her mind ran to Tony, but he was probably tending to the kids.

She shook her head angry with herself. She couldn't keep burdening everyone else around her. My mom crept to the single-stalled restroom in the corner of the short corridor. She gently closed and locked the door behind her.

She collapsed to the floor and broke down in tears. In that moment, she felt like the world had stopped in order to highlight how bad things were looking for her child. Her crying continued until the sound of running feet silenced her whimpers. She rose and opened the door.

She could see nurses spilling into my room. She bolted down the hallway. The closer she got the louder my monitors beeped. When she ran into the room, she and Dr. Tepend locked eyes.

"Ryan isn't resting well. His pressure shot up."

RYAN TROUTMAN

"When was his last dosage of medication?"

"A few hours ago."

My dad stood frozen in the corner watching the nurses readjust my I.V.s. His girlfriend inched closer to Dr. Tepend determined to participate in the conversation.

"Yeah, can't they just make a hole in his head and let all the pressure out?"

Both my mom and Dr. Tepend turned to look at her in disbelief. My mother's blood began to boil. She rose a shaking finger and pointed towards the door.

"You need to leave," she paused, "NOW!"

"Come on. Let's get out of here," my dad mumbled. He grabbed his girlfriend's arm and dragged her away. As the night wore on the nurses equalized my pressure again. The days that followed were even more disorderly.

At times my vitals were normal and at other times they bounced up and down violently unleashing the horrid squawks from each machine. As news of my condition traveled, my dad's family paid me a visit. They were genuinely concerned with my health and wanted to offer their loving support. One night, my aunt and uncle entered my room without warning.

"Hey," my uncle greeted.

My mother snapped her head up from my bedside and rose. She was silent for a moment. She couldn't remember the last time she'd seen them. They had hardly spoken when my parents were married, but the current situation only made things more awkward. My uncle was the first to take a step forward.

"Hello," my mom finally replied. "You can come up to the bed if you'd like. Please do not make any loud noises or mess with anything."

"Alright. Thank you. We won't be long," my aunt said.

My mom moved to the far corner of the room to give them the space closest to me. They slowly walked over to my bedside. My aunt let out a gasp as they stood motionless beside my still body.

RYAN TROUTMAN

"Is he still in a coma?" my aunt asked.

"Yes," my mom said quietly as she walked toward the doorway. Tony's voice floated through the noisy hall and into her ears from a distance.

"I'll be right back," my mom muttered, leaving the room. My uncle carefully eased his cellphone from his pocket. He angled the phone over my battered body and snapped a picture. He nodded at my aunt and slipped the phone back into his pocket. #nofilter.

My mom and Tony returned. My uncle greeted Tony with a nod and looked over at my mom. "We're a little tired from traveling, but we wanted to stop by here first," he offered. "We'll come by again tomorrow." My mom nodded and watched my aunt and uncle depart the room. She decided to take advantage of the quiet time and read through all the documents and medical reports she had been given. She sat next to her brother and sipped on a cup of water.

"Oh my God!" The unmistakable yelp made my mom pop her head up from the binder. My Uncle Frankie sat trembling against his chair. His eyes were glued to his phone.

"What's wrong?" she asked.

Frankie held his phone in front of my mom's face. A vivid picture of me sprawled against my hospital bed with a tube down a gaping hole in my throat was plastered across his Facebook newsfeed. My mom's face twisted into a glare as she walked towards the door and noticed my aunt and uncle who had just made it to the elevator. She and Tony stormed down the hall toward them.

"Why would you do that?!"

My aunt and uncle turned to my mom reluctantly.

"We haven't seen you in how many years and your first inclination is to snap a photo to share on your damn newsfeed?! How inconsiderate could you be? He's not some attraction that you can exploit. Take it down, now!"

"Whoa! Alright, we can take it down. We just wanted to give his family on this side an update of how he is doing."

"If the people on your side wanted to know how he is doing then they can drive up here just like everyone else," my mom fumed.

Tony remained silent as they argued back and forth. Finally, my dad's brother-in-law threw up his hands. He pulled out his phone and began to tap fervently on the screen.

"I removed it."

My aunt fell silent and shook her head.

"We are just going to g—"

The retreating footsteps of my mom cut her off. My aunt and uncle didn't make anymore appearances. From that point on, my mom and Tony kept a closer watch on my visitors, carefully scrutinizing anyone they were uneasy about. Other aunts and uncles from my dad's family came to visit and were very considerate. One aunt exchanged phone numbers with Tony and offered to assist whenever they would call her. She even thanked him for all that he had done. It was comforting to my mom to know that her ex-husband's family genuinely cared about me and wanted the best. Those people understood that there was no room for drama.

Over time, the doctors slowly weaned me off of the ventilator. They leveraged it to supplement my respiration as needed, but relied on my lungs to help me breathe. My body was starting to work again.

As my body healed, my family slowly began to head back home. Day by day, the lobby became more empty. My mom glanced over at Tony. It was time for a change. Morgan and Logan needed some semblance of stability.

"I'm worried about the kids..." her voice trailed. She took a deep breath and looked into Tony's eyes. "Specifically, Morgan. Regardless of what any of us tell her, she's probably terribly confused. Her older brother and her mother have been out of her life; and even though people have looked after her, it's not the same. She needs us. Not saying that you haven't been wonderful. They both just need consistency. On my part as well."

"The doctor has been pushing us to head home," Tony said.

My mom's face contorted, and she slowly shook her head solemnly. Tony could tell she was fighting a war internally.

"I think you should be here right now," he said finally. My mom stared back at Tony who gave her a smile. "I could spend a little more time at home. There's no other place you could be other than here." Tears flickered in my mom's eyes. Tony always understood. He was truly her anchor. She nodded in submission.

Tony made runs for meals and fresh clothes so that my mom could stay by my side. She'd update him on my condition and he would fill her in on what happened at home, at school and daycare, and with the construction of my family's coffee shop.

Things had a semblance of normalcy, but Morgan—who was in the fifth grade—was getting restless. Eventually, my mom would have to make a decision. Placating assurances wouldn't sedate Morgan forever. In the darkness of the cold hospital room, she tried to put the thought to the back of her mind.

My mom had taken back to smoking excessively again. She'd excuse herself downstairs to the atrium. Amidst craggy patients and weary visitors, she puffed on a cigarette--or two. It gave her minimal solidarity and temporary relief. The pleasant exchanges she had with the nursing staff helped keep her sane. The day-to-day silence began to smother her, but the staff's warm smiles and idle conversation urged her on. My mother silently thanked them for supplying my food trays each day. I was comatose, but that didn't matter. Even in the deepest slumber, I was still treated like everyone else in the trauma center.

Pepa made use of the trays when he visited. It amused my mom to watch him gobble up the heaps of gelatin and meats during their conversations. She was always tired, but for the first time in a long time, everyone came together to offer their support. That was enough for now.

RYAN TROUTMAN

Morgan crept into her mind frequently throughout the day. A pang of guilt struck her. She couldn't imagine how confused Morgan was in the midst of the calamity.

"She's getting impatient." Tony had relayed on more than one occasion. My mom rose from my bedside and headed into the hallway.

It was time.

"Forever an early riser, eh?" a voice chuckled.

My mom spun around and was greeted by Dr. Tepend's smiling face. He looked exceptionally tired.

"Do you know if the psychologist is available?"

Dr. Tepend's brow raised. "He is... Are you-"

"I'm okay. It's about my daughter."

"Your daughter?"

"She hasn't seen Ryan yet. I wanted to ease her into it. She's young."

Dr. Tepend nodded emphatically and studied my mom before speaking. "I could send him to Ryan's room to meet you. He tends to never be in his office, but I'll make sure he finds you."

"Thank you."

My mom sank into one of the cushioned chairs in the lobby. Her nerves were reeling. She wasn't sure how Morgan would react or if she was making a mistake. She raked her hands through her hair and waited an hour before deciding to return to my room.

"Mrs. Leon, correct?" a masculine voice asked.

My mom raised her head and glanced up blankly at the older, portly man. He was dressed in a dark gray suit and wore thick rimless glasses. His salt-and-pepper hair began just at the top of his head and tapered to his sides. My mom nodded tentatively. He smiled and extended his hand.

"I'm Dr. Rivers, the family psychologist here." He greeted jovially.

My mom took his hand and forced her lips to curve upward. He looked inviting enough. "Lisa."

RYAN TROUTMAN

The doctor released my mom's hand and motioned to the seat next to her. "May I sit down, Mrs. Leon?" My mom nodded and straightened herself in the chair. "So, Dr. Tepend tells me that you'd like some console in terms of conditioning your daughter for her visit with..."

"Ryan." My mom finished knowingly. "Yes. In your expert opinion, what would prepare her the most for seeing him?"

Dr. Rivers was silent for a moment. He shifted in his seat to face my mom before he spoke again.

"Every child is different. To be perfectly honest, I'd need to know what she already knows."

"She knows that he was in an accident. We told her that his body needs rest to heal."

"How is she handling home life?"

"Home life?"

"Her parents going back and forth between the hospital to clarify." Dr. Rivers must've noticed the shift in my mom's expression, because he quickly followed up his query before she could speak.

"Not to belittle the care and concern that you must have for Ryan. However, she is young I'm surmising, and children are prone to some difficulties during these trying times. How old is your daughter?"

"She's ten years old." My mom paused. The sincerity in the psychologist's twinkling blue eyes urged her on. "Her name is Morgan. I'm estranged from her father, their father... Tony, my current husband, has been taking care of the children mainly along with other family. Admittedly, I've been here looking after Ryan. I haven't been home muc—."

Dr. Rivers cut in. "Don't beat yourself up about it. I can tell from your tone that you are." His voice softened. "How about we have Morgan come in and speak with me and you, of course. We can explain what the machines are that Ryan's hooked up to before she enters the room and explain what his recovery journey will look like. Tony can help as well from home. He can share tidbits about Ryan's condition to give her an idea of what she'll experience. Just let me know when you'd like to have her come down here. Fair enough?"

"Y-yes." My mom replied in a near whisper. Her thoughts drifted to my battered body. In her mind she could see me lying motionless surrounded by bags of fluids.

"Mrs. Leon? Mrs. Leon?"

My mom blinked and turned back to the doctor. She hadn't realized that he was talking to her.

"I-I'm sorry...yes?" She faltered.

"This has been extremely stressful on you. I wanted to let you know that my door will always be open for you as well." Dr. Rivers smiled.

My mom didn't reply; she sat silently until Dr. Rivers left. She didn't want to talk about it anymore. She just wanted a sense of peace for everyone.

Dr. Rivers visited with my mom and Tony over the next few days offering guidance. It relieved and worried my mom simultaneously. In theory, his methods seemed advantageous, but how Morgan reacted was inevitably up to her.

MORGAN HAS QUESTIONS

"Hello? How is Morgan and Logan?" My mother asked Janet.

"They are doing fine. But Morgan is starting to ask a lot of questions and I just don't know what to say to her. She wants to see Ryan."

My mother let out a deep, long sigh. It was finally time to let Morgan see her older brother. "Bring her up here. I'll take her to Ryan."

"Alright, I'll drop Logan off at daycare and head that way after lunch."

Later that day when they entered the waiting room my mom looked at Morgan and began to cry. Her daughter looked so scared. Morgan was always, shy, and quiet. My total opposite. She and my mom walked over to an empty corner in the waiting room. My mom sat her down and told her I was in a very bad accident and that no one was sure what was going to happen but that everyone was working extremely hard to help me heal. Morgan remained silent but her tears streamed down her face. She looked up with big, watery eyes and began to let soft words trickle from her lips.

"Is he going to die?"

"No honey. No. The doctors are working very hard to make Ryan feel better." A feeling of guilt filled my mother. She had no idea if I was going to make it out of this alive.

RYAN TROUTMAN

A slight, pleasing smile crept across my sister's face. The thought of someday getting her brother back was all that she needed.

"I want to see him. A lot of other people already have."

"Honey, Ryan looks really bad right now. I am not sure if you would like to see him like this." This was a very hard decision for my mom to make because Morgan had been protected from agony all her life. She didn't want Morgan to be frightened and have nightmares after seeing me. But at the same time, my mom was thinking *God forbid Ryan dies and I never gave Morgan the chance to see her brother once more. I couldn't live with that guilt.*

"Alright. Ryan has a lot of tubes and machines hooked up to him that are giving him medicine to feel better. Before we go see him, I want you to talk to my friend who will explain things a little better." Mom prepared Morgan for the gruesome sight she was about to witness.

Morgan seemed to be fine with speaking to someone first but my mom could never tell. Morgan was the child who would internalize her emotions and opinions. All my mom could do was wrap her only daughter in a tight hug and hope for the best.

Morgan, Janet, and my mom sat in the waiting room for a while. This was one of the few opportunities my mother got to spend with Morgan and she did so by holding her. After twenty minutes had passed, Janet broke the silence by gathering her belongings and rising up from her seat.

"I'm going to go pick up Logan from daycare. I'll bring him and Morgan back later this evening."

My mom softly nodded and returned to my room. I was still very critical and unstable but family, friends, neighbors, co-workers and kids from my school kept visiting throughout the remainder of the day. The nurses said they would allow a few people in the room at a time to see me. It was all very somber. My mom allowed a few of my close friends in to see me because the nurses really didn't expect me to live much longer.

RYAN TROUTMAN

Jordan, Oliver, Nat, Andy, and Caroline visited me as if they were saying their final goodbyes. Jordan was a kind, loyal friend all through my school years. Oliver, Nat, and Andy were my classroom comrades. And Caroline was my high school sweetheart for two years. Caroline's parents forbad her from seeing me regardless of my medical condition. They felt I was a bad influence and that she didn't need to worry about boys and instead needed to focus on her schoolwork. All of my friends drifted pass my mom who hadn't slept. She simply couldn't no matter how hard she tried. She couldn't even eat. The thought of food made her sick and although she would close her eyes to rest, sleep would never come. My mom stayed at my side in a broken recliner, watching my monitors which still showed no improvement.

Later that night, my mom received a phone call from Caroline's parents. They found out their daughter had come to visit me. Caroline's mom began to scrutinize my mother on her parenting and said that she needed to stop hiding Caroline. This was literally the worst possible time she could judge my mom and her parenting skills.

"Are you kidding me?!" my mom retorted. "My son is laying in a bed on life support nearly dead and you think I'm worried about hiding your daughter? If anyone needs a lesson on parenting, it is you. Keep up with your kid." She said before hanging up.

Morgan's Day

Morgan tiptoed through the hospital's double doors, stepping in out of the rain and clutching Tony's hand nervously. Morgan slowly eased into the noisy lobby and glanced around. Tony recognized the sense of urgency in her movements.

"Where's Ryan?"

"He's upstairs. We're going to have you meet Dr. Rivers first like we talked about," he replied gently. "Your mom will meet us down here."

Morgan's face brightened. She always loved seeing our mom. Her eyes danced around the lobby expectantly and then stopped on the outline of a petite woman with long brown hair.

"Mom!" she bellowed.

My mom turned in their direction with a warm smile. Morgan released Tony's hand, ran toward my mom, and enveloped her in a tight hug. "Hi, sweetie!" my mom said, gently rubbing Morgan's back. She choked back tears. Even though the children had come to the hospital before, Morgan's slender frame was such a welcoming comfort.

"I missed you, Mommy," Morgan whispered. My mom kissed her forehead and released her from the embrace.

"I missed you, too," she breathed, smiling down at Morgan. "I've missed you so much, sweetie." Tony joined them. My mom turned her gaze to him. Nowadays, he always looked tired. She imagined she probably did as well, but she wondered if he was even able to rest. At two years old, Logan was hard to put down at times. She felt guilty again.

"Were you able to sleep at all?"

"Logan fussed a little last night, but this one helped me get him to bed." Tony playfully nudged Morgan. My mom's eyes narrowed at him. "I got a few hours," he confessed. Before my mom could counter, Tony patted Morgan on the head and kneeled down to her.

"I'm going to leave you here to spend some time with your mom and Ryan, ok?"

Morgan nodded with a smile and hugged Tony's neck. Mom's face tightened. She knew Tony needed to go back to Logan and let Janet go home, but she was terrified.

Tony stood and lightly kissed mom. "It'll be alright."

My mom nodded, but doubt filled her mind. They both watched Tony leave and then head to the elevator. She asked Morgan about school and Logan as they ascended. As she answered, my mom reveled in the sound of Morgan's voice. The slight lilt in her soft voice calmed my mom's nerves. She missed their exchanges, let alone holding her daughter close.

A grin slid across my mom's face. Dr. Rivers' was waiting for them as they neared his office.

"Hello," he greeted warmly. "You must be Morgan," he extended his hand and Morgan timidly shook it.

"It's okay, sweetie. This is one of Ryan's doctors. He's gonna tell you some important things."

My mom stayed closely behind Dr. Rivers and Morgan as he led her into his office. The room was relatively small with gray walls and medical machines scattered about. Morgan sank into one of the chairs in the middle of the room, glancing around. My mom allowed Dr. Rivers to lead the conversation, chiming in sporadically only to affirm his statements. He showed Morgan several photographs of the machines I was connected to and took the time to slowly explain each machine. He patiently elucidated what I could and could not do as result of the accident.

Occasionally, Morgan nodded and asked questions. As the exchange continued, my mom's face softened. Her mind ran back to medical school. In one of her classes, they spoke about the awareness of patients in comas. Sometimes all it took was touch or sound to ignite activity in the body. She smiled solemnly and glanced over at Morgan. Maybe Morgan's touch could help, she thought. The room fell silent and Dr. Rivers eyes turned to my mom in silent entreaty. She exhaled and nodded.

It was time.

"Let's go see Ryan, sweetie."

Dr. Rivers led them to PICU. Morgan got to my door and froze. She began to cry. She was afraid and didn't know what to do.

"It's okay to be upset, baby," my mom said while wiping her own tears. Dr. Rivers gave Morgan a reassuring smile and offered his hand for comfort. She took his hand and walked in the room. She passed slowly through the doorway and reached back to clutch my mom's hand. Her eyes fell on me. She froze. Her eyes scanned over the blood-stained bandages covering my body and the hole housing the trach in my neck. She erupted in tears.

"Mom!" she cried and turned into my mom's arms. Her small body began to shake. "W-why i-is he l-like t-hat-?"

"Oh, honey," it tore my mother's heart from her chest.

"T-there's a h-hole," Morgan cried.

My mom pulled Morgan close to her and rubbed her back. "He was hurt really badly, and he needs that to help him breathe, sweetie," my mom explained softly.

Morgan didn't speak, she continued to cry. She stepped closer to me and touched my hand lightly. "I love you, Ryan," she whispered, crying and falling over into mom's arms again.

"Let's go, honey," my mom whispered. She walked out of the room cradling Morgan. "Come with me, sweetie."

Morgan again said nothing but began to walk in step with my mom down the hallway and into the elevator. Mom studied

Morgan. She lifted her face gently and bore into Morgan's hazel eyes.

"I cried, too," she said.

The elevator dinged and the doors opened. My mom led her toward the back of the hospital and stopped in front of a glass door.

"When I need a moment and can't take it anymore, I come here."

Mom gripped the handle of the door and pushed it open allowing Morgan to exit first. Morgan ran her eyes across the lush garden and stone pathway. It was a small space where a few oak trees and wooden benches were scattered about. It was encased with glass.

"This is the atrium. Let's sit down," my mom sat Morgan down on one of the benches and moved next to her with a deep sigh.

"I was scared of this moment," she admitted. Morgan blinked up at mom with a twisted expression. She wiped her eyes. "You get scared?" she sniffed.

My mom chuckled lightly and wrapped her arms around Morgan. "Yes, even grown ups get scared. I've spent a lot of time scared lately."

"Is he gonna be okay? He wasn't moving."

"He's fighting to be okay. His body needs a lot of rest so that he can move." Silently, my mother decided to keep Morgan away from the hospital. Seeing her crumble at the sight of my body wounded her. Morgan was a child. She needed some stability.

She held Morgan for a while before walking her back to the patient waiting room. My grandparents stood awaiting them. Morgan ran into their arms and was consoled by light kisses and encompassing hugs. My mom was met by a representative from Kyle's insurance company who wanted her to sign papers for a $10,000 payoff and to agree that she would not sue the company for more. Crushed and vulnerable, my mom agreed and within a matter of days a check was delivered directly to the hospital as part of the stipulations. She had not determined how the family would survive financially and she was not concerned or focused with money or hospital bills. My mom had only one concern: me. Sadly, she had no idea the financial devastation that would come from being by my side and not working.

As the days passed, my mom became a shell of herself, quiet and despondent. Dr. Rivers implored her to talk about her feelings, but she recanted and recoiled back into the chair next to my bedside. The days began to become monotonous.

Eye Never Saw It Coming

After a month of me being non-responsive, Dr. Vetarve asked my mom to hold my hand and call my name. The doctor told my mom to squeeze my hand and see if I squeezed back. She clasped my hand but it resulted in nothing. No response, no tension, no jerking. Nothing. Each day Dr. Vetarve would come and they would try once more. After so many failed attempts, my mom was desperate. She was begging for some form of improvement. She would squeeze my hand and tell the doctor that she felt something. Both of them knew that was nothing more than an empty hope. A lie.

Janet, Tony, Pepa, and Ms. Rae were frequently in the room to witness mom's sad attempts at squeezing life out of me. Everyone knew I wasn't responding but my mom was desperate. She didn't want the hospital staff to give up on me or tell her that I wasn't going to make it.

"Please," my mom would whisper.

Dr. Vetarve would always say, "It's ok, Lisa, we will try again."

Everyday they would ask her to take my hand and squeeze it. I would never respond. All of me would remain motionless. As my body fought to revitalize itself, the doctors would whisper in my ears for me to try to raise my eyelids or move my limbs. Again and again, my body was motionless. Only, my breathing was improving. The doctors changed the cannula tube of my trach to a smaller one. My mother was told to enter the room and speak to me in the hopes that I would come out of the coma. My response was always the same. I'd lie still upon the bed, despondent. Eyes closed.

"It'll take some time, Lisa."

My mom shook her head vehemently. *How much time?* She wondered. This had gone on for way too long. Her eyes drifted over to a calendar hanging loosely on the wall. She began to lose track of the days. It was Sunday now. The end of the month. Dr. Vetarve came into the room and encouraged mom to try waking me again. "This time, talk to him a little more. Squeeze his hand."

"Ryan," my mom moved next to my bed and sat down beside me. Tears began to spill from her eyes. She grasped my hand tightly.

"Wake up, Ryan. It's time to wake up. Please! Please, wake up!"

After a month of motionless silence, my eyes began to crack open. The beaming light above me pierced my slightly visible pupils. My mother's eyes bulged and a wide smile pierced across her mouth.

"Ryan!" she breathed and started crying heavily, "it's me, Ryan! It's me!" She resisted the urge to pull me into her arms. I wasn't showing the same level of excitement. My eyes blankly stared at the ceiling and I made no sounds. I had no idea where I was or who any of the people standing around me were. I made no notion that I even knew they were in the room.

Dr. Vetarve smiled and said that this was certainly a good thing but still cautioned my mom and wanted her to still understand the magnitude of the situation. That although this was certainly good, I was still in a very critical condition. I suffered a severe traumatic brain injury and no one knew the extent of the damages. I was breathing somewhat on my own but still had an external source of high flow oxygen should anything go wrong. I still had a long way to go to get to full recovery.

RYAN TROUTMAN

Early the next morning, my team of doctors met to discuss treatment now that I had awakened. The first plan of action was for a physical therapist to try and sit me up in my hospital bed. I had been in a coma for a month. Even though my eyes were open, I could not speak nor respond. Watching the physical therapist sit me up was one of the many painful things my mom had to endure. Every attempt to move my body caused tears to roll down my face. My mom could not stand to watch me trapped in a painful body. The depressing look on my face made my mom feel light headed.

"Stop! You're hurting him! Look at him!" she cried.

The nurses and therapist tried to comfort her and let her know that this was going to be a tough time but it needed to start right away. Dr. Tepend walked in the room while the therapist tried contorting my limbs.

"It's time to transfer Ryan to a rehabilitation hospital," he said with finality.

"He isn't ready! He hardly has his eyes open!" my mom refuted.

A stern grin crept across the doctor's face. Tony and my mom glanced at each other, bewildered. They didn't know how to respond. It almost made them angry.

"How can you sit there and sm—"

"Your boy is a fighter, Mrs. Leon. However, he can only win half of the fight here."

"But—"

"He's ready, trust me. We need to start all the therapies immediately with Ryan, especially cognitive therapy. We have to get the brain working."

My parents fell silent in defeat. A resident soon came in with a nurse to downsize my trach. He had boxes with a few different sizes and had to decide which was the proper size. The resident removed the inner cannula from my throat. Instantly, my body struggled for oxygen. This caused the resident to begin feeling nervous and confused on which cannula he had chosen from the boxes. He suddenly began yelling at the nearby nurse as if it was her fault. She did nothing but hand him the proper piece he needed. This caused my mom to sink in sorrowful tears. There wasn't enough time to worry about blaming someone for a mistake. She wanted them to get the job done and get it done fast.

Although it was agonizing to watch me on life support, the few hours I had been awake were much more taxing. The hardest part of my recovery was coming. My mother certainly did not realize how hard it was going to be.

Dr. Tepend walked into the room and told my mom that they would not place a feeding tube in my stomach as long as she was certain I took in at least three cans of nutritional shakes, like Ensure, every day. My mom nodded. Each day, she had to slowly feed me small amounts of Ensure through a syringe. When it was time for me to eat, she would slurp up the liquid into the syringe and squirt it into my drooping mouth.

It wasn't long before I was set to transfer out of the trauma hospital. Mom, Tony, Pepa, and Ms. Rae began packing up the things scattered around the room that was my home for the last thirty days. Ms. Rae and Pepa loaded their car and drove to the rehabilitation hospital while my mom and I were transported in an ambulance.

As the paramedics hoisted me onto a stretcher, my limbs began to flail involuntarily. I simply didn't know what was happening or where they were taking me. The paramedics gave me a shot to stop my swinging arms and calm me before easing me into the vehicle.

My mom held my hand in the back of the ambulance. She tried talking to me but I made no sounds. I stared straight with a spaced out expression. I was in a wakeful coma. My mom felt sick to her stomach. She was a ball of nerves and shifted uncomfortably in her seat. Everything was suddenly moving so fast. So fast that it scared her. But she resigned herself to optimism. This was a defining moment in my journey. It was the opportunity everyone hoped and prayed I would get. Things were still very ambiguous. The possibility of me making a full recovery was slim. But, it was still worth celebrating. Life had squeezed me.

And I squeezed back.

RECOVERY IS DISCOVERY

The rehabilitation hospital was considerably less chaotic than the trauma hospital. I was carefully placed in my new room. It was relatively small with cream-colored walls and a small window overlooking the street outside. My bed lie in the far corner.

A nurse lingered in the hall before approaching my mom and Tony. She was a tall woman with a slender build, pale skin, and wavy blonde hair that stopped at her shoulders. Sincerity flooded her azure eyes as she spoke.

"I'm Sandy," she informed them with a smile. "We rotate here so you may see one to four of us at any given time cycling in and out to care for Ryan."

"I'm Lisa," my mom replied, "and this is my husband, Tony."

"Alright," Sandy said. "The receptionist told me that you wanted to stay here with us, Lisa. The couch folds out into a small bed. Feel free to use that."

"That is wonderful," my mom answered back.

Sandy began to give my parents an overwhelming amount of information on traumatic brain injury recovery. She handed my mom a large, three-inch blue binder with numerous pages of information that would guide my mom for the next eight weeks while I lived in the rehabilitation hospital and for the remainder of my life, it seemed.

"I want everyone to rest for today. I'm sure you both could use it. Get familiar with the place, and we will get started on therapy tomorrow," Sandy continued.

My mom and Tony exchanged glances.

"What type of therapy will he begin tomorrow?" Tony asked.

The nurse gave a gentle smile. "Everything," she said. Her eyebrow raised in inflection. "Ryan will start working on all aspects of his body tomorrow. We'll stop by at eight A.M. to get him started." She collected her clipboard and badges off of a nearby table. She looked up at my mom and Tony with soft, sympathetic eyes.

"Alright, I'm going to leave you guys to it," she smiled and left the room. My mom closed the door behind her and looked at me grimly.

"I think he'll be okay here," Tony yawned. My mother nodded with a faint smile.

This first day was quite emotional as my family had to leave the comfort that they had worked to build at the trauma hospital.

"What's worrying you?" Tony asked.

"I don't know how to explain it. I guess it's that we had just formed bonds and trust with the staff over in trauma and now we're here so quickly," she struggled with her words. "They are special, you know? I mean, they were the ones who brought our son back from the dead. Now I will have to trust that these new people here can bring him back to life."

Tony listened and waited for her to finish.

"And now I must learn to trust this process, but with a watchful eye. I just got my son back and I'm not about to let him go! I will be right here by his side every step of the way, and I will be here to be sure he receives the very best care!"

"Yes you will," Tony said. "Yes, you will; and Ryan will be okay."

She allowed him to hug her and she closed her eyes long enough to enjoy his comfort. "I better go get the kids," he said.

"Okay," she replied.

RYAN TROUTMAN

My mom hugged him once more and watched him depart the room. After a few hours, Tony returned to the hospital room with Morgan and Logan. Ms. Rae and Pepa also came by to check on us. They sat with the lights out and blinds drawn in order to decrease as much stimulation which would easily get me riled up. I hated any soft sound or glimmer of a light. It was like I was a vampire with overly sensitive hearing.

Sandy returned with blankets and a pillow in tow. My mom went to her side.

"Let me help you."

"Pish posh, you relax! I imagine you've done a lot of helping."

My mom took a step back ruminating on Sandy's words. She didn't feel helpful at all. Her son was still struggling to pull through and she was condemned to watch helplessly.

"It's all pretty for you!" Sandy beamed.

My mom glanced down at the makeshift bedroom. The bed made from a couch looked fluffy despite its size. The bright orange pillow and blanket made the dreary space more inviting. Sandy gestured toward a cabinet attached to the wall.

"There's extra blankets in there. If any bandages come undone there are spares in the one on the left." Sandy's finger shifted to a red button on the wall. "Or you can page us if you need assistance of any kind with Ryan."

"Thank you, Sandy," my mom said graciously.

Sandy bowed and winked at my mom. "No problem. Try to have a good night, Lisa." She left the room and my mom stood silently. Her gaze ran to the small cabinets adhered to the wall and then to the window. This room felt more homely than the last and even though it was small she secretly praised the lack of sub zero temperatures in the new residence.

She imagined that tomorrow would be a long day. They all needed rest. Tony walked over and kissed my forehead before saying goodnight. He held Morgan, then Logan, up to kiss me their good nights as well. Pepa and Ms. Rae followed.

RYAN TROUTMAN

I was trapped inside my body. My eyes were opened but I was still unresponsive. I just blankly stared off into space. I had repetitive motions, restlessness, anxiety, and I was unable to communicate any of my needs. I was unable to walk, talk, use the restroom, or feed myself. I was a 120-pound, sixteen-year-old baby. I needed my mom and Tony to do everything for me. Similar to a newborn, they fed me, changed my clothes, and repositioned me in my bed. Everyone was a stranger to me. The nurses explained to my mom that I was trying to process the world at the speed of light. That my brain was on overload and that it was difficult for me to process what was happening around me. One nurse said I wasn't aware of my surroundings or who I was. My Mom thought through the details of all the conversations and caveats she'd heard from the first moment she saw me in trauma, but tonight was different.

He opened his eyes.

My mom smiled to herself and turned back to me. My chest steadily rose and fell as my monitor chirped softly. She nodded to herself, content with my state and lowered herself down to the makeshift bed.

It was more comfortable than her trusty chair back at the trauma hospital. Her body melted into the mattress. She was so tired.

"Goodnight, Ryan, I love you," she whispered. Her eyes began to close as she pulled white sheets around her. "I'll be right here if you need anything." My mother heard no response. She didn't fully expect one, but a slither of her being dared to hope. I lie motionless. My eyes blankly stared off into space. I didn't sleep that night.

Time passed and my mom couldn't fall asleep. Instead she laid there in the dark, thinking, thankful that I was alive but wondering, *Will I ever get my Ryan back, the boy so full of life, emotion, and love? Will I ever get to hear those exciting, over-exaggerated explanations and rationalizations that only Ryan could do so well?* Her thoughts drifted to a memory of me as a young toddler, always trying to bargain, rationalize, and make a point of why I should have my way. *Sure, he'll be back. Ryan has too strong of a will and conviction. This isn't any different.*

She decided to not fight back the tears overflowing inside of her. She sobbed quietly but with such force she had to take deep breaths to calm down again. *I'd give anything to hear his voice, have him talk non-stop trying to argue his point, right now. I'd give anything to hear him say 'mom.'*

She sat up with her face in her hands, quietly contemplating things. My body began growing more and more restless, and the sleeping giant inside of me awoke. Still incognizant, I began flailing, trying to roll out of bed, pulling at the trach. My mom caught my hand and tried telling me to stop, calm down, and that everything was okay. I could not comprehend anything she said. My body shook against the bed violently. Concerned that I would hurt my head or succeed at falling out of the bed, my mom climbed in my bed and held me down until the nurses ran into the room. One nurse gave me a stiff shot of medicine to quickly calm my body. It would settle me for just a very short time before I was back at it again. Another nurse offered a net bed—a standard hospital bed completely covered in a plastic white net that zipped closed. Since my mom was a pediatric nurse, she had to use those all the time on little kids.

"No, I don't want him to be scared," she replied. This decision forced my mom to stay awake and hold me tight, trying to keep me safe from myself.

A few hours later my mom woke to the sounds of my violent thrashing and guttural moans. She jumped up from her bed and raced over to me. I was grabbing at my trach and I.V,. trying to rip it all out.

She made a mental note to tell the doctor about it in the morning. After taming my body, she lowered herself down uneasily onto my mattress. My monitor normalized before she reluctantly closed her eyes.

RYAN TROUTMAN

Morning finally came. For my mom, it felt as though daylight would never come. She looked over by the door and there sat a reclining wheelchair with a therapy schedule. Sandy tapped lightly on the door. My mom clumsily picked herself up and wiped her eyes. The sun colored the room with a warm carmine tint.

She slunk to the door and opened it. Sandy stood in the doorway, wearing a wide smile.

"Sorry for waking you."

"It's fine," my mom garbled. "What time is it?"

"7:45 A.M," Sandy answered.

My mom's eyes bulged. "I didn't mean to over—"

"You're perfectly fine," she chuckled. Sandy moseyed into the room and looked at my monitor and I.V. She scribbled on her clipboard and faced my mom. "Let's get him started."

Three other nurses filed in and began getting my bed ready for transport. As they wheeled me in the hallway, my mom followed closely behind. It was early morning, so many of the rehabilitation hospital's residents had not yet begun moving around, although breakfast was being served in the north wing.

They got on the elevator and rode to the first floor. It was just a few floors down. Once again, my body was flailing around in the wheelchair. I kept slinging my legs out of the leg lifts and swinging my arms frantically. Mom tried pushing me in the wheelchair while trying to hold me in so I don't fall out. To make things worse, I still kept trying to pull my trach out. The day had just started and my mom was already in tears.

As they came out of the elevator and rolled me to a waiting area for my therapy, I cut my leg on the side of the wheelchair. Blood dripped down my leg and onto the tiled floor. My mom plopped down on her knees and did everything she could to stop the bleeding. While trying to clean me off she had to hold me down in my chair so I wouldn't fall out. She stared around the room. She was distraught, crying, and desperate. Salvation came when her eyes locked onto Tony, Morgan, and Logan.

RYAN TROUTMAN

Their arrival to the hospital couldn't have been at a better time. She quickly stood up and hugged each of them.

"He keeps trying to climb out! He didn't sleep last night! I don't know what to do!" my mom cried to Tony.

"You can do this. We can do this. Look how strong you have been for him. I know you will only get stronger," Tony calmly responded.

I was sitting in a wheelchair unable to walk, wearing diapers and constantly had to be changed. The diabetes insipidus caused me to urinate constantly regardless of how little I drank. All day and night I had to have my diaper and clothes changed after getting soaked. I still couldn't even sit up in the wheelchair. I would constantly droop down into a painful posture. Mom, Tony, the rest of the family, and nurses would have to reposition me everywhere I sat. I was nothing more than a beat up life-sized doll.

Finally, I was rolled into a medic room with bright floor mats, hand weights, and a massage table. The nurses lifted my back and head to a sitting position. I offered no response. My eyes glared straight ahead emotionless. My body was there. My eyes were opened. But my brain remained comatose; I was alive but unaware.

The first day of physical therapy was a series of gentle let's-see-if-he'll-react-to-this attempts at getting my limbs to move. My mom watched in silence. Thanks to her years as a nurse, watching the therapists work on her oldest son wasn't as unnerving as she thought it would be. But, the pain swelling through my body was brutal and unforgiving—and she knew it was.

I could not actively participate in any of the therapies. Every therapy involved me just sitting in the wheelchair with a blank stare. The physical therapist in the room worked my extremities since some of my muscles were contracted from being lifeless for so long. Even though I could not speak, everyone could see the look of fear, pain, and distress in my eyes.

RYAN TROUTMAN

They were attentive and careful with me. My unresponsiveness didn't faze them. Their retort was always the same: "We'll try again tomorrow." Then, the nurses would wheel me back into my room. My mom helped them secure me and let herself plop down on her small mattress near my bedside. She was thankful that none of the attendants cycled in and out as they did at the trauma center. The added privacy gave her time to rest, sob quietly, and think—especially when reading and re-reading my medical records made her weary.

My mom still had to feed me nutrition supplements through a syringe. Throughout the day she had to make sure I got enough calories. If I did not, she knew the doctors would restrict me to a feeding tube.

At the end of the first full day of therapy, my mom telephoned Tony and filled him in before asking to speak to Morgan and Logan. Logan playfully babbled into the speaker of the phone. Morgan went on about school and some new toy she'd gotten. The sound of their voices made her smile and stilled some of the restlessness coursing through her.

She hung up the phone and looked up at my bed. "I love you." The words almost sounded melodic as she laid down against the mattress. Her stomach growled, but she ignored it. The room was wonderfully quiet. No one was shrilly shouting demands nor were a trail of obscenities being echoed down the hallways as it had from time to time at the trauma hospital.

The welcomed silence began to lull my mom to sleep. But, the moment was short-lived. Once again, I flailed around, yanking at my trach and shifting from side to side. My mom rushed over to restrain me. Her breath was ragged as she steadied my hands. My hollow irises stared up at her. Tears began to stream from her eyes. Her voice was soft and broken when she spoke.

"Ryan, please hear me. I need you to calm yourself," she repeated, "be still," until I settled into a sleepless stupor. My mom sank back onto the mattress. Her eyes were heavy with fatigue. She pulled her phone out of her pocket and glanced at the time. It was one in the morning now. Even so, she needed someone.

She flipped open the phone and began to scroll down her recent calls seeking out Tony's name. Her finger lie still on the ENTER button. It was really late and he'd have to be up early to get the kids ready for school and then head to the coffee shop. She didn't want to bother him. She shook her head and exhaled. Janet's name lie right under his. My mom clicked on her name and placed the phone close to her ear. The phone only rang twice before Janet's yawning voice came onto the line.

"Hello?"

My mom wasn't able to stop herself from sobbing. "I'm s-sorry for c-calling so late."

"Don't be sorry. Is everything okay?" Alarm spilled into Janet's voice.

"He keeps trying to pull his breathing tube o-out. H-he hasn't been s-sleeping. E-every night he has fits. What if I can't w-wake up i-in time one night and he—"

"I'm coming down there," Janet said decidedly.

"But—"

"I'll help you with him."

When Janet arrived, she stayed for three nights and each night ended up the same. No changes and no positive sign of recovery at all. With each rising sun came another round of therapy. I was taken to a friendly older woman who would attempt to test my cognitive functions. She would move her finger from side to side to see if my pupils skipped while following her motion. I was made of stone. My brain consistently triggered waves of excruciating pain through my body. But I was trapped. I was at the mercy of the nurses and could only thrash about to resist when my appendages were disturbed. My mom would steady me and place her warm hands on my shoulders until I ceased my struggle.

Daily, my mom would slurp Boost and Ensure though a thin straw and carefully release it into my mouth, past my chapped lips and decayed teeth. The nurses offered to assist, but my mom was adamant. This was her duty.

My family and friends popped in sporadically to check in on me. With the exception of Kirsten, Jordan, Kyle, Daniel, and Ben, visits from other friends and classmates had long ceased. Lights distressed me so their visits were conducted in dark and silent reflection. My nightly thrashings continued.

HOUSTON, WE STILL HAVE A PROBLEM

Tony, my mom, Ms. Rae, Morgan, and Logan walked downstairs for coffee one morning and out the backdoor by the cafeteria to smoke. Pepa was in the room watching over me. Nobody expected anything to happen in the ten minutes they were gone. But when everyone entered the room they saw a look of panic in Pepa's eyes. He was laying on top of me in the bed, trying to contain my agitated body. There happened to be two strangers in the room. While Pepa was wrestling my thrashing limbs, they stood in the room to tell my mom their story.

Jim and his mother calmly stood off to the side. He was a former patient who also had a traumatic brain injury. His mother was a member of Mothers Against Traumatic Brain Injuries. The had visited my room to speak to my family about Jim and how well he was doing. It seemed like a motivational speech. Jim was twenty-three years old and was acting like a toddler. He repeatedly tapped his mother on the arm and interrupted her speech.

Repeatedly, the man would shout, "Mom, mom, mom, mom, tell her, tell her, tell her!"

"Wait a minute!" she commanded.

Her forceful tone made Jim angry and he shouted and cursed.

My family was in shock. The mother told my family that this sometimes happened to people after a traumatic brain injury and prior to this Jim had an expansive vocabulary. She even said people could become combative and uncharacteristically angry. The message she tried to deliver wasn't received very well. *Is this how Ryan will be? Will he forever remain trapped in there somewhere? Will we be taming a wild child forever?*

During the first two weeks at this rehabilitation hospital, I had extreme pain and discomfort in my right shoulder. Even with all of the flailing, I tended to not move that side of my body much. After my family brought this to a doctor's attention, he ordered an X-ray to determine if any damage had been done.

Fortunately, the rehabilitation hospital was connected to another hospital through a long hallway. This is where I was rolled for my X-ray. My mom had to stay in the room to hold me down. Once the X-ray tech noticed me trying to sit up, she put her hand across my chest and pushed me back down.

"Lay down! Be still! Be still!" she yelled.

My mom grabbed the tech's hand and got in the woman's face. "Take your hands off of my son. He has a traumatic brain injury. He doesn't even know what you are saying. Get someone else in here to do this X-ray because you WILL NOT be touching my son again!" my mom demanded with a sharp, cutting tone.

The tech stormed out of the room and switched with another older, male tech. After my scans were taken, I was rolled back to my room where I would once again get little to no sleep.

The nights were long. I was still just "there." No communication, no eye contact, no deliberate movement, no smiles. Nothing. It seemed like each day was the same: therapies all day with no noticeable progress and long, restless nights.

Each day, Tony, Pepa, Ms. Rae, and Janet would get off work, come straight to the hospital and stay late into the night. Janet and Tony had a routine for alternating care of my siblings. Their presences were my mother's saving grace. She was alone all night when everyone would go home and was very thankful when they returned the next day. She needed them. Even though she tried to never show her vulnerability, she needed their support. This was an entire family affair. It took each and everyone of them playing their own unique, intricate part in the journey. Everyone altered their lives and their schedules to be there for me. I was very lucky to have such an amazing family. The staff upgraded me to a larger room once I got acclimated to the rehabilitation hospital, but it could have truly been because of the family present daily.

For weeks, each therapy proved to be ineffective, and I still wasn't acknowledging the right side of my body at all. Day after day, the specialists and nurses continuously entreated me to do a variety of painful movements. All they knew was that I could not move; they had no indication of how much pain each motion caused.

One day, my mom and I went to cognitive therapy, the therapist asked, "What are some things Ryan liked to do? What were his interests?"

"Well, he played video games and liked to write on this website called Althenex. It was a website where people start a story and others keep adding to it," my mom answered.

"Okay," the therapist said. "Let's try something."

She pushed my wheelchair up to a computer sitting on an otherwise empty desk. I sat in the wheelchair staring ahead emotionless. The therapist pulled up the website and she and my mom waited to see what I would do. The therapist noticed a change in my eyes. I blinked and seemed intrigued. She smiled at my mom who held her breath. I began to inch my hand closer to the keyboard, and to their surprise I typed in my username and password.

The therapist quickly stopped my mom before she could cheer and celebrate.

"Wait," she whispered. My mom was amazed. I sat my hand on the table and stared at the monitor. I had returned within my self, dazed and unresponsive.

"How can he remember a password when he really doesn't know who he is or what's going on?" she whispered to the therapist.

"The brain is amazing," she tried her best to not raise her voice beyond normal.

"Wow! Lisa, this is a wonderful sign! A positive sign that maybe just maybe, we are finally starting to see a glimpse that Ryan is there and trying to find his way back to us."

My mom was overjoyed.

I Always Did Like Rollercoasters

One day, an occupational therapist came in to help with my dressing and grooming. She put me in the wheelchair and rolled me into the bathroom and up to the sink's mirror. She basically had to teach me all the things I learned as a child. She started by making me wash my face, then handed me a toothbrush to practice brushing. These exercises were uncomfortable, painful, and exhausting.

"Alright Ryan, you're doing great. Let's try to raise our arm and get a good brush in," she softly said.

My mom stared at my stressful face and heard me shout, "Mom! Mom! Moooom!"

She had waited what seemed like eternity to hear my voice again. But what came next made her cringe.

"Mom, mom, she's a fucking bitch!"

Out of all of the things I could've said, I chose that. My mom's eyes grew wide. Her jaw sank to the floor as the words replayed in her mind. She was mortified.

"Ryan!" she scorned.

I continued on like this for the next couple of weeks. It was the most I had ever swore in my life. My mom hated my awful behavior—cursing and shooting my middle finger. But, inside she was glad to see some progress.

"Yesterday there was no response and no talking. I'll take what ever I can get! I want my boy back!" she later told Janet.

RYAN TROUTMAN

But, finally one day, Tony put his foot down. He walked up to my bedside and told me he would no longer allow me to talk to the staff in such a manner and I'd better figure out another way to express myself.

I was beginning to find somewhat of a larger vocabulary, but I still couldn't walk. I would lay in bed and make grabbing hand gestures and yell out, "Mom! Mom! Mom! Thirsty! Thirsty! Thirsty!" I did this over and over and would not stop until I got a drink.

Then, only minutes later, I was doing it all over again. Every drink I was given had to be mixed with a thickener to prevent liquid from entering my lungs and causing me to aspirate. I still wasn't fully aware of who anyone was and it didn't really matter just as long as someone got me a drink.

I still continued letting everyone I came in contact with know that I was ready to go home. I had enough of my hospital getaway and I just wanted to return to my bed, video games, and home cooked meals.

But I still had a lot of recovery ahead of me.

———

One day, I was awake and rambling in my bed. My family decided to wheel me downstairs to the courtyard. The light hit me with a fierceness once I exited the double doors.

I suddenly jerked my hands around to show my discomfort.

"I am cold! I am cold! I want to go inside!" I commanded.

My family obeyed and wheeled me back inside. My journeys under the sun continued on to the point that I was noticing the same, usual faces. My family would roll me out in my wheelchair as I pulled a thick blanket tight around me.

A tall, slinky man with a thick mustache and a worn baseball cap was always standing near the exit each time I would roll out. Finally one day, I watched him light up a cigarette and take a deep puff.

RYAN TROUTMAN

"You should not do that! You are going to die!" I shouted.

"Hey, let's go inside. Your therapy is starting soon," my mom said shushing me. She turned the wheelchair towards the door and quickly rolled me to the physical therapy room.

"Hey Ryan! I'm glad you made it! We are going to jump right into it and get started!" the therapist exclaimed.

Using a brace, I could stand on my feet but I didn't have the ability to lift my legs and move forward. I just didn't know how. While I was in the physical therapy room, I saw a young girl who needed assistance getting back up onto her feet. So I began reaching around on my wheelchair trying to grasp something sturdy enough to hoist me out of my seat. I wanted to help her. My attempt was quickly halted by both my strength and the therapist who was helping me up towards a pair of rails.

These were two handrails that were right beside each other. The objective was for me to grab onto the rails and let them assist me moving my feet. I had to use these rails in order to re-learn how to walk. Multiple staff members would hold me up and rely on my legs to do the rest. My biggest problem was that my right leg wasn't cooperating. Every time I would attempt to move it forward in hopes of taking a step, it would get tangled and cross over my left leg. I would get angry and tearful. What was supposed to be a simple task wasn't simple at all. It was only up to a minute or two before becoming too weak. The therapist would sit me down in the wheelchair only for a moment before standing me up to try to make the connection and walk again.

My mom talked with the therapist trying to understand if my body could remember how to use its own muscles again, "I can't imagine how painful this must be for Ryan," she said. "He's had his head and body bounce off the interstate road at more than 100 miles per hour. He's been in bed—in a coma, and now without his own capacities, he is awake but not that long. He still has road rash from head to toe with deep wounds on his leg still trying to heal. His muscles and brain have atrophied, and now he must push through all this pain and find that will to recover and walk again. Can he really do what you are asking him to do right now?"

The well-trained therapist nodded his head while she expressed her concern.

"We have to push Ryan to try. We can not determine if his brain will catch up." He seemed stern and uncaring. "But, we owe it to him to try our best."

My mom agreed.

One day my cognitive therapist gave me a piece of paper that had a star and a heart drawn on it. The symbols were scrambled and mixed up across the sheet of paper. I was instructed to circle all of the hearts and ignore the stars. I held the marker with ease and stared down at the paper and very easily distinguished what was a heart and what was not. I quickly made my circles and handed the sheet back to the therapist proudly and non-verbally signifying that I needed something a little more challenging. The therapist looked down at the paper and grinned. Nothing on the right side was circled. It was like half of my body was shut down. She shared the paper with my mom and made notes in my folder and encouraged me to continue working so excellently.

All of my therapies continued their usual rhythms. I would excel with some and drastically fail with others. My speech therapist would task me with repeating the sound "duh" as many times as I could over and over. The therapist would lead by example and say "duh duh duh duh duh duh" with such precision, articulation, and expertise. When it was my turn, mine sounded a lot like "duhhhhhhhhhhhhhhh…duhhhh..duhhhhhhh." My tongue, mouth, and vocal cords were still reeling from the accident.

Still in a Galaxy Far, Far Away

After a month had passed at the rehabilitation center, my patience with the cumbersome trach had long passed. It was time to see an ear, nose, and throat specialist. The doctor entered the room and explained that he would place a long scope into the trach opening and guide it down to examine my trachea to see if my airway would work properly on it's own once the trach was removed.

Immediately, the ENT doctor checked inside my throat and cleaned the airway before deciding to remove the trach. Trumpets might as well have sounded out the joy I felt. It was going to be so nice to have a neck again! One that I could call my own and wasn't being leased out by a piece of plastic.

The old Ryan shined through me once again when I turned the trach removal into a comedic act. Once they moved the plastic tube, I had an open hole in my neck that was simply covered up by a bandage. When the bandage wasn't on, I could take a couple of fingers and rest them over the hole. I would begin breathing heavy and feigned a deep encompassing tone. Once Tony, Morgan, Logan, Pepa, and Ms. Rae came up, I decided to joke with Tony.

Trying to talk like Darth Vader, but breathing funny, I managed to say, "Luke, I'm your father!"

The lack of my trach didn't still my thirst nor did it improve my ability to sleep. Everything I said was still excessively repetitious. You could hand me a spoon or fork and I would bang it around on a tray like a toddler. The reality of the situation caused a few of the remaining friends to cease coming to see me. I was no longer the miracle survivor but a reminder of what a simple, errant decision—like not wearing a seatbelt—could cause.

While all of these things were going on with me, I still had to continue following orders from the nurses and therapists. The nurses would walk me around the facility to help me relearn how to take steps and manipulate turns. Three people had to hold me up while I tried walking because I kept letting the right side of my body droop. It took so long for me to relearn how to do something as simple as moving one leg in front of the other. Imagine living sixteen years of your life and obviously doing quite a bit of walking throughout that time. Then one day you wake up and nothing works. Your legs don't have the strength or coordination to complete a step and your mind is still too checked out to remember what it took to walk.

This was one of the most defining times because now I was truly digging myself out of the pit that I had fallen into. There was still so much work left to do. And I still was only a teenager.

Each day I walked a little further with help. Each day I was pushed harder than the day before. I was even communicating a little more each day. I still had a blank look in my eyes, still said things repetitiously, and still got annoyed by everything but I was understanding a little more each day.

Mental challenges became just as problematic as physical ones. I still wasn't really aware of my surroundings or who people were, I didn't know what happened to me or why I was wearing men's diapers. During this stay, I was having multiple loose stools. The medical staff tested a specimen and found out I had C-Diff. This was a bacteria that was caused by all the medications and antibiotics I received during my time at the trauma hospital. C-Diff was highly contagious through contact with the stool. Since my mom lived in the room, cleaned me up, and shared the same bathroom, she had to be vigilant and wear gloves. She had to constantly clean the room and bathroom.

When I would yell out, "Mom! Mom! Mom! Bathroom, Bathroom, Bathroom" she would press the nurse call button. Sadly, all of them knew my mom was a nurse and lackadaisically responded. They knew my mom wouldn't let me sit there unattended.

"Alright, let's get you to the bathroom," she whispered.

She grasped my body and hoisted me into the nearby wheelchair. My mind had not returned to me and so much of my actions were uncharacteristic. It caused my family to wonder if the extent of my injury had permanently disabled me intellectually.

I was able to stand on my feet but couldn't walk, so as long as she was able to carefully maneuver my dead-weight body, she could take me to the toilet without the help of the nurses.

"You're doing good. Just turn a bit and I'll help you off—," I swiped my hand across her face. For some reason, I decided to reach down into the stool that filled my diaper and coat my hand in my own feces. I then painted my mom's face like I was some clown at a kid's birthday party. Except I was working with only one color.

We never made it to the bathroom that night. There was poop everywhere. My mom's hands, body, and clothes were all covered in my artistic poop-painting. Talk about having a shitty day. Knowing the risks of C-Diff my mom went into emergency clean up mode and immediately cleaned her face and hands then laid me down and began taking the dirty clothes off of me. Ms. Rae walked into the hospital room and gasped at the sight and smell. My mom turned and stared at her with the widest eyes swollen with anger and confusion.

"It's okay, Lisa. It's okay," Ms. Rae said, quickly removing her purse and sweater. "Let's just get him in the shower and get him cleaned up."

RYAN TROUTMAN

After they got me cleaned up, my mom took a shower and threw away our clothes and towels. She got dressed and walked back into my room where Daniel was standing. I'm sure he could tell by the half-tamed look on my mom's face that something had just happened.

"How is he doing?" Daniel whispered from a nearby seat.

"He's fine. We just had a little incident," my mom left out the finer details. Daniel nodded and made his way toward my bed. He worried about what he would do in the event I needed to use the bathroom.

"H..hey man. How are you feeling?" he asked with hesitancy. Like every visitor, he stayed aware of his voice's volume to prevent upsetting me.

"Bathroom, bathroom, bathroom!" I began shouting. Daniel's face went pale. He didn't know how to get me off of the bed and was not looking forward to wiping me during my diaper change.

"Watch out. I'll take care of it." My mom spoke like a true pro. "Alright, let's try this again," she said giving me a stern look as she began the process of getting me into my wheelchair. She let out a deep sigh of relief when, in one swift motion, I successfully transitioned to my wheelchair without the urge to be an artist.

"You did it!" she yelped.

This would've been an appropriate time for a brief applause but the room remained silent. My mom began wheeling me towards the bathroom as I began mumbling and making a sad attempt at uttering words. The things I said made no sense and I spun off any sentence that popped into my clouded mind.

"You know what I wan—," my poor articulation was cut short. My head cocked to the side and I blankly stared off into the distance. Daniel and my mom looked in horror. She knew I was having a seizure.

She jumped to my side and kept mashing the nurse call button but wasn't getting a response. Sadly, I was having a focal seizure and needed medical attention as soon as possible.

"Go get help, now!" she ordered Daniel.

"Ryan! Ryan! Can you hear me?!" my mom cried, searching my hollow eyes. My deep, blank stare continued off into the distance and I made no sound. It must have been like going to a wax museum. I looked and felt real but at that moment I was about at lively as Madame Tussaud's version of Michael Jordan.

Suddenly my eyes flickered. My head snapped upwards and I began mumbling mid-sentence as if nothing had ever happened. Mom didn't acknowledge how awkward the experience was. Her only concern was that I was safe.

Hours passed before a nurse showed up to do an electroencephalogram to detect abnormalities and record my brain's wave patterns; but, it took so long for the orders and testing to be completed that they weren't able to see whether or not anything was going on with my brain. As a precaution, the doctor prescribed a seizure medicine to decrease the chance of it happening again. Up to this point, I was dealing with diabetes insipidus, a broken jaw, inability to walk or talk, damage to my right eye socket, and mild amnesia.

My future wasn't looking too bright.

I'M WALKING ON SUNSHINE

Soon after my seizure scare, the occupational therapist felt it would be good to begin reintroducing me to society. She recommended we take a field trip to a Walgreens so that I could practice counting change and interacting with a cashier. At the time I didn't know what was going on but if I was aware, I would have felt severely embarrassed. I would have felt belittled or less of a person. While all of my friends were in their classroom taking a trigonometry test, I would be rolling around a Walgreens trying to find something I wanted to count coins towards. The part that was hardest was not knowing if I would ever have the opportunity to be myself again.

While at the store, I chose to purchase extra-strength hair gel. My hair has always grown very quickly and after this much time in the hospital, it was pretty bushy.

"Oh, nice," my mom said, even though she stared at the hair gel with a confused look on her face. There were so many other things I could've practiced my money spending on. Maybe a pack of Skittles or a bag of beef jerky. But nope, for some reason, I wanted hair gel.

Surely, I had something else in mind. For about a week after that field trip, I decided to gel my hair up into an excessively long mohawk. Every bit of my shaggy hair was plastered to a point that spanned from my forehead to the back of my neck.

RYAN TROUTMAN

Around the same time that I was flaunting my new hair style, I began talking better. As you would expect, I didn't say the friendliest of things unless it was to ask my family and friends to bring me food from different restaurants. The hospital would drop a tray of food off every night but I would never touch it. Instead, I lived the life of delicacies by asking for food like sushi, wings, and seafood. It soon became routine for me to order up food from a restaurant in town then kick back in my hospital bed and watch a movie.

Everything seemed to be going smoothly until my dad and his girlfriend surprisingly showed up at the rehabilitation hospital at ten o'clock one night. This was the one and only time he came to visit me in rehab. During his visit, my dad gave everyone a much needed laugh when he walked outside to smoke a cigarette and ended up locking himself out. My mom watched as the two of them walk through the door knowing they wouldn't be able to get back inside. It just seemed to always add drama to an already stressful situation when family feuds would match up in my hospital room.

To make things even more eventful, my uncle and his wife announced they were going to have a baby. To be honest, it felt like everything life had to offer waited to show up when I wasn't able to enjoy experiencing any of it.

Although life events carried on regardless of whether or not I was healthy, it never stopped my family and friends from doing everything in their power to help me recover. Even after a full day of therapy, my family would still challenge me to speak correctly or focus on controlling the right side of my body.

Eventually everyone was contributing to my mental health. I needed to be prepared for life after the hospital and the only way that was going to happen was through working with the people who would be a part of my normal life. The hope was that I would return to a somewhat normal life supported by accommodations and safety precautions.

RYAN TROUTMAN

My uncles even participated in this family rehabilitation by rolling me outside to play wheelchair basketball. Each of them would hop in a chair and roll around the court with me trying to block shots and steal the ball. I couldn't stand being outside under the hot sunlight. But all they were trying to do was show their support and love. They were not playing ball as a way to poke fun at me.

I would've been ferociously laughed at if I weren't surrounded by people who loved and cared for me. I was rolled up and down the court and handed the ball to take a shot. The only problem was that I wasn't able to shoot the ball higher than the top of my head. I never let it bother me because I was about as skilled at the hospital as I was when I tried out for basketball in middle school and got dropped on the first day of tryouts even though we didn't even see a ball. It was strictly a day of running, push ups, and jumping. At least now I could say I made it on a team and was the star player. This hour or so of gametime showed me that I wasn't any different from the friends and family surrounding me.

I may have faltered in wheelchair basketball, but I was the rehabilitation ping-pong champion. I fell in love with failed attempts at hitting a little bouncing ball across the net. My body simply wasn't cut out for much of anything except trying to correct all that was wrong with it.

Things were starting to look up. I was playing basketball and ping-pong, watching movies, and hanging out with people that loved me. You could almost say it felt like I was away at a summer camp with a bunch of other injured people. While that feeling was accurate, it had an expiration date.

I was nearing the end of my stay at the rehabilitation resort. Only a few more check-ups and therapy sessions stood between me and the outside world. Days after my wheelchair athletic event, Ms. Rae and mom took me to the trauma hospital to visit an oral surgeon for a follow up on my jaw just to ensure all of the metal plates inside of me weren't hurting and that I was able to chew food and talk with no problems. This was major because it was the first time I had rode in a car since my accident.

"Alright, sweetie, let's get you buckled in," Ms. Rae said. The sunlight I had come to hate shined down through the car window as if it was a spotlight for what was going to be a main event. My fingers were restless and my body was jittery. My mom and Ms. Rae would glance back to see how I was doing but all I wanted them to do was focus on the road and not get us killed.

Getting in a car was something I had never planned on doing again. Even to this day I get nervous when other drivers whip through lanes at high speeds. No matter how carefully these people would drive and regardless of how much I trusted them, all of the horrifying outcomes of a car ride would flash through my mind.

Once we made it to the oral surgeon's office, I was barraged with questions. The man had a series of things he needed to cover before I could leave the room.

"Do you ever feel any pain?" he asked.

"No." Besides the numbness, my jaw didn't bother me. The surgeon reached over and ran his fingers down my jawline. His fingertips floated across the bolts, screws, and metal plates that were planted beneath my skin.

"Have any trouble eating?"

I shook my head to let him know I wasn't bothered. Besides feeling like I was a cyborg, everything appeared to be normal. He skimmed through my records and took a quick scan of my jaw before sending us on our way. On the return ride to the rehab room I now called home, I realized I had forgotten what it felt like to have a normal body—one that didn't have a numb jaw, limp legs, and a struggling brain.

"See, that wasn't so bad!" my mom tried to reassure me but I just wanted to get back to bed. The one I lay in all day, every day. Once I was snuggled up in my bed sheets, my mom flicked on the television. This had become my sanctuary of routine and peace. I would lay there, watch the same movies, drink the same flavor of Vitamin Water, and listen to Jack Johnson's "Banana Pancakes" as if I had never heard it before. The same people would come to visit and they would say the same things: "I'm so glad to see you!" or "You look great!"

My family, friends, and the medical staff eventually broke this routine and truly challenged me to use my brain, no matter how damaged it was. When I was thirsty, which was all the time, Tony would have me recite lyrics from the song "Paul Revere" by The Beastie Boys. I used to work with Tony's construction company and we would sing this song at the tops of our voices on the way to job sites.

In a poor, non-rhythmic voice, I would quickly murmur, "Now here's a little story I've got to tell about three bad brothers you know so well." Tony would smile at the memory only he and I shared.

"Here you go!" he would say and hand me a drink.

"One lonely Beastie I be / all by myself without nobody." I would sing and take a sip from my cup of Vitamin Water. "The sun was beating down on my baseball cap / the air is gettin' hot / the beer is gettin' flat." This went on for a while until I was almost able to recite the song from beginning to end.

On a daily basis, Tony would drop my siblings off to school, do some side construction jobs in order to get enough money to buy food and pay bills, then hurry to the hospital to work with me on my recovery. He also managed to make time to work with the construction team hired to build our family's coffee shop.

One day, a woman walked into the room. She wasn't family and was too old to be a friend of mine. Her tall, slinky body was cushioned with by the folders, pencils, and markers she carried. She smiled at my family before turning to me.

"Hello, Ryan. I am one of the hospital's teachers," she calmly announced. My heart sank at the sound of those words. Not only was I a typical teenager who disliked school work, but I was also a kid with a traumatic brain injury and was still trying to figure out what had even happened to me.

"We're going to do some educational activities together to help prepare you for your return to high school!" she said with excitement.

Nothing she said sparked a glimmer of joy in me. The thought of going back algebra, literature, and biology made me sink into my mattress.

"Let's begin with a simple activity today to help us gauge what kinds of activities we should work on going forward." She was talking to my family more than she was to me.

The teacher helped me sit up in my bed just enough to slip a piece of paper onto my serving table. Because of the cognitive therapy, I knew I was struggling intellectually, so when she pulled out the paper, I expected to see something like "Solve 2x - 121 = 0" or "Where are chromosomes located in the nucleus?" Surprisingly, I saw neither of these questions nor anything even close.

"Now, we're going to start with numbers, colors, and coloring," the woman softly spoke. I didn't know whether to jump with joy or feel offended. I could just breeze through these simple exercises enough to get her up and out of my room. I wanted to return to watching more television programs and chanting Beastie Boys.

I would write my numbers, label my colors, and color pictures in a coloring book like I was a toddler.

"Alright, Ryan, way to go! I'm going to have a word with your mom and dad outside. I will see you tomorrow," she said, then signaled for my mom and Tony to follow her.

"We've got a lot of work to do," she whispered and showed my mom and Tony the coloring I had done and my poor attempt at transcribing numbers onto paper. If I wasn't able to do simple things like color inside the lines, I would be a big joke back at school. "I would like to set up a time for you to meet with Ryan's guidance counselor at the school," she told them. Until then, she consistently worked with me on academic exercises. It didn't take long for her to see that I was going to need extensive assistance.

"We recommend that Ryan come back to school in the Exceptional Student Education program. Based on our evaluations, Ryan would have a hard time obtaining a diploma if he remains in standard classes," a doctor soon told my mom.

He and the rehabilitation teacher thought I would never be able to function as an adult, get a decent job, or live a productive life. It was as if they wanted to discount my life just to help me get through it. My mom declined the ESE program and knew I had the potential to excel in normal classes and return to a normal life.

"Alright miss, if you want your son to remain in standard classes, I recommend setting up at time to meet at his school and discuss his accommodations," the doctor concluded.

The meeting with school officials eventually took place and the things that were said were not what my mother wanted to hear. It was a roundtable discussion between my mother, my guidance counselor, a social worker, a school board official, and a neuropsychologist. Other than my mom, the only other person who advocated for my potential was the guidance counselor. She comforted my mom by telling her they would find a way to make things work out for me. They were going to put me through the same schooling that all my non-brain injured peers were experiencing.

These meetings, educational exercises, and therapy activities were the few remaining things to complete before I was released from the in-patient rehabilitation hospital. But before leaving, the therapist wanted to take me on one more field trip. It would expose me to the real world before my release. My mom, Tony, Logan, Morgan, Ms. Rae, Pepa, and Aunt Chris were my entourage of support, and together we visited an outdoor mall near my home. It was the farthest I had been away from the hospital and would expose me to many more people.

RYAN TROUTMAN

This was my last hoorah before leaving the comfort of my hospital bed and 24-hour medical support. My family brought a wheelchair to the outdoor mall but I did not want to use it. I was motivated and inspired enough to try walking on my own.

While we were inside Abercrombie and Fitch, a few teenagers maniacally laughed at my struggle to walk. Out of all of the stores we could've went to, I am not quite sure why we chose one filled with the "bros" who are too self-involved to consider other people's walk of life. They made faces and said mean things. They cackled and made comments that labeled me retarded. I can't imagine how sad my family felt to see some random kids harass their helpless son, nephew, and grandson. I didn't acknowledge it, of course, because I had enough on my hands with trying to stay balanced and not cross my right leg over my left.

"Please take him outside," Tony requested. While my grandparents and aunt helped me step outside, my mom and Tony remained inside the store, staring at the group of kids with piercing eyes. I won't go into all of the details but let's just say my mom and Tony said firmly "you have no idea what he has been through." This sentence was surrounded by a lot of words that began with the letter "F". It was almost as if my aggressive, "F-bomb" phase was contagious and mom and Tony had been afflicted by it.

The kids stared back at my parents with fear and slight regret. They never expected my parents to confront their laughter and insults. Those shamed kids half-stepped backwards and bolted away from my family in an attempt to hide the regretful scene they had just caused.

Who's embarrassed now?

Surprisingly, I didn't pick up any hair gel that day. My mohawk phase had come to an end, and I was just happy to have made it through the day. All of the time I spent in the rehabilitation clinic was finally complete. I made significant progress recovering, and it was time to reintroduce me to the world and expose me to my new life. Before I was transferred to the out-patient clinic, the doctors approached my mom and asked, "So, what exactly do you want Ryan to be able to do before he is finished in out-patient?"

My mom's confused face squinted at the question. "What do you mean?! I want him to be able to do everything! I want my son to be himself again!"

Those were the last words my mom said before I was set free. As the doctors and nurses waved goodbye, I hobbled out of the rehabilitation hospital and back into the real world.

RYAN TROUTMAN

LIKE-MINDED

Walking out of that hospital was somewhat invigorating. I would alternate between slowly pacing my walk through the parking lot and sitting down in my all-too-familiar wheelchair.

"We're going to get you home and settled in," my mom said. I glanced back at her with a mixed expression of relief, excitement, and absent-mindedness. I wheeled closer toward the four-tire chariot that would carry me home. My heart began beating faster, and my breath grew short.

"It's ok. Everything will be ok," she comforted me while opening the car door and hoisting my frail, brittle body into the vehicle.

SNAP.

The seatbelt clipped shut and was securely fastened across my chest. My mother climbed into the driver's seat and cranked the ignition. This sound sent shivers down my spine. I wasn't mentally capable of understanding what exactly was going on, but somehow my body knew to grab the door and middle console for safety. The wheels slowly began turning as we strolled down the parking lot aisles. My mom drove deliberately and patiently.

The car ride home was smooth and much safer than the one that got me into this dilemma. After a few stop lights and seamless turns, we arrived back at my lollipop-shaped neighborhood. The house I grew up in was guarded by three boys and my sister, all cheering and waving their hands in the air. Kyle, Daniel, Ben, and Morgan had hung a "Welcome Home" banner above my garage to celebrate my return to home. *Was this what it was going to be like? Will everyone celebrate my release from the hospital like its a birthday party or big anniversary? Will everyone continue to celebrate me?*

"Welcome home, dude!" Ben shouted from the driveway. His oversized Nirvana t-shirt fluttered freely in the wind. The towering figure next to him raised a finger to chime in.

"Hey Ryan! I'm so glad you're home!" Daniel cheered.

Kyle peered down the driveway at my still-mangled body with a sigh of relief. I can't imagine the pressure that was lifted off his shoulders when I pulled through in the trauma hospital and now seeing me in front of my own home, alive, and almost well. His smile stretched from ear to ear and he, too, was jumping up and down celebrating.

After the cheering stopped, the three brothers returned to their home and I was able to walk through my own home and into my bedroom for the first time in more than three months. I stretched across my bed in total darkness. This moment was a major step toward the life I was preparing to begin.

The next morning, we went to my grandparents' home to celebrate. Ms. Rae and Pepa were throwing me a Coming Home Party. We celebrate everything at their house. Every birthday, holiday, and every life moment was celebrated with a huge Italian dinner, coffee, and pastries. My entire family would sit around the dinner table to laugh and enjoy their time together.

All of my family and many of my friends came to see me and to celebrate. I wore a "Back By Popular Demand" t-shirt, befitting the occasion.

Ms. Rae enjoyed crafts and had a whole room in her house dedicated to sewing and knitting. So, I didn't find it odd that little white cloth squares were stacked high on the dinner table surrounded by colored markers. She wanted everyone to grab a square and write or draw anything they pleased on it as long as it offered a message of love welcoming me back home. On some of the squares, my friends made corny pictures of a seatbelt or phrases that only a gamer would understand. Of course my parents wrote heartwarming messages. Many others wrote things you'd see on the inside of a Hallmark card.

Ms. Rae would later weave all of those memories together into one blanket. Around each square, she'd add borders with bold phrases like "Roads to Travel," "Dreams to Live," "Choices to Make," and "Second Chance."

Two diamond patterns were etched across the middle. The outside diamond was designed with camouflage squares and the smaller diamond inside was made with black squares covered in red writing.

Some time after the accident, Ms. Rae got my clothes from the paramedics and started sewing them into this amazing blanket that I have never let go of. The memories, the messages, and the love in that blanket will forever be with me.

I was surrounded by all of this love and compassion but still wasn't cognitive enough to really soak it in. I was still behaving like an irritated toddler and couldn't really process anything going on around me.

Can you imagine what that must be like? How could a person go to such a happy, positive celebration and not be able to recognize that it was all for them? Well, I was that person. My ability to remember things still hadn't recovered and my absentmindedness and erratic outbursts prevented me from being able to be socialize with others.

My mom and Tony had many discussions about what the rest of my life was going to be like. I was still a teenager. I hadn't truly experienced any major events like going to college, getting married, and becoming a father. They were all hidden in my obscure future. At this point, I might not graduate with a high school diploma. No girl would find me attractive because I acted like a zoned out toddler. My friends will all have moved on to experience the finer things in life while I sat back still trying to figure out who I was or what had ever happened to me.

Throughout my entire life, I had planned to grow up and become a successful medical professional. Like any other teenager, I dreamt of driving a fancy car and living in a mansion with a supermodel of a wife. I wanted money, friends, and an abundance of materialistic things. I wanted to grow up into some showstopper of an adult.

But, my brain injury changed everything.

THE MIRACLE MILE

The Monday following our celebration was my first day at the out-patient rehabilitation center. A weekend had gone by and allowed me to become settled in and re-familiarize myself with the house I grew up in. I still had some noticeable issues. For example, I would go into the kitchen to cook something but I would never turn the stove off. Or I would wander into the middle of the living room and just stand there because I forgot what I was trying to do. I still wasn't trusted to be on my own and I guess I can understand why. My little sister and I would fight but I'm not sure how comparable it was to usual sibling bickering.

For some reason, Morgan and I would get into a shouting matches over the stupidest of things. She would run into her room and lock the door. I saw that as an opportunity to hold the door knob and not let her out. She would have to climb out of her bedroom window and circle the house to find unlocked doors. Our screaming became so ferocious at times that the neighbors would hear us and would call my mom.

"STOP!" Morgan would scream. I made no response and was simply too busy annoying her to shout back.

"I'm calling mom!" she added. I didn't flinch. I knew she wasn't going to call mom, because I had all of the telephones. After a brief period of silence, I would hear the window opening inside of her room. I knew it was time to quickly run towards the backdoor and hold that knob shut just as tightly. This feuding was a daily occurrence.

Now that I was home, it must have felt like house training a new puppy for the rest of my family. They had to help me do pretty much everything and always had to keep an eye on me to make sure I didn't get into trouble. If it wasn't for their watchful eyes, I'd leave the stove on and burn the house down or slip and fall to never wake up. I had heard stories of people in their forties who were still living at home because they couldn't take care of themselves. Every time I was told stories, these people had a traumatic brain injury.

Honestly, I would've been scared to live on my own at this point. I wasn't thinking clearly. I walked in my sleep. I would even sink into a horrid state of depression. There were nights when I would break out in tears at what had happened. And even nights where I would cry for no reason. You would think that after getting through the hospital and all of my rehabilitation I would feel happy. But no, having to be hospitalized was an excuse. It was a justification for me to act the way I did. All of my disabilities were masked by uniform hospital gowns and hospital bracelets. I blended in with those people. They were my friends.

Now, I was out in the real world getting exposed to everyone at every different level imaginable. This made my deficiencies stand out to both me and everyone around me. But at the same time, it really shined a light on everyone's best qualities. I would watch my friends and family do quick math in their head while I had no idea where to begin. Some of my friends would throw perfect spirals with a football while I had trouble just getting the ball into the air. I knew people who would sing loudly to songs in the car while I still had trouble pronouncing words.

In fact, I had no independence. My mom still chauffeured me around everywhere. She would stand at the door while I attempted to bathe myself then she'd help me dress. When she had to run an errand, I was under the supervision of my little sister. I couldn't be left alone. My brain couldn't be trusted.

Yes, I was out of the hospital. But, I wasn't done recovering. It wasn't over yet.

Similar to a regular school day, I had to go to the out-patient rehabilitation center each weekday. I would move from treatment room to treatment room completing different therapies. My mom would drive me to the center and walk me inside like a third grader on his first day of school.

"Hello. I'm here with Ryan," my mom would tell the receptionist who sat just beyond the sliding glass doors. I guess I was the only Ryan in the system because routinely, she would click a few buttons on the computer and direct me to the waiting lobby for my classes to begin.

The first day at this place was quite interesting. I was surrounded by brain-injured patients all waiting to continue their journey through recovery. Each person had their own unique walk of life and everyone was injured in the craziest of ways. We all sat beside each other, blankly gazing around trying to take it all in. Each of us would take turns poorly introducing ourselves and trying to convey our life's story.

One woman had gotten kicked in the head by a horse. She was a southern lady with cowboys boots, a plaid button down shirt, and no sense of who she was or what was happening.

Beside her sat a young guy with a clean-trimmed hair cut and a muscular physique. He was a soldier who had a grenade explode close behind him. The force of the grenade caused a near-fatal injury. He was a man of few words and sat quietly in the corner.

The quietest classmate—if that's what you want to call them — was a stout Black man who was a detective prior to his injury. He had severe trouble speaking and, like me, he wasn't able to clearly express his thoughts or demands.

Sitting next to him was a sixteen-year-old boy. I imagined he would become my closest comrade since we were both teens. One night after some underage drinking and drugs at his friend's house, the boy chose to walk—actually stagger—in the middle of the road rather the sidewalk. The road was poorly lit by the worn streetlights and the faded lines barely distinguished the two lanes. He was plowed into by a car going forty-five miles per hour and was catapulted down the street. Like me, he laid paralyzed and moments away from death until someone found him. Now, he was plopped down in a wheelchair and much of his cognitive abilities had diminished.

Then, there sat a man in his mid-forties who had been driving down the interstate when his car ran out of gas. He rolled the car safely to the side and began walking towards the nearest exit. His plan was to get enough gas in a container to return to the station and fill up. While he walked toward the nearest exit, a truck spun out of control and collided into his back and skidded over his torn body. His ribs were crushed. His hip bone was broken, and one of his lungs collapsed. He also suffered a traumatic brain injury that caused him to behave younger than any of his three children. His mental capacity and intellectual strength was broken down to its most rudimentary stage. Flashing lights and beeping sounds made him jump with joy.

We were all sitting at a long, rectangular table that resembled a conference room more than a therapy or class room. An older, Spanish guy sat across from me. He was an aviation engineer in the U.S. Navy until one day he fell head first from the top of a ladder while working on an EA-18G Growler aircraft.

My eyes scanned from person to person. I wanted to know them all even if I wouldn't remember them until months later. I noticed a older woman who had a stroke and just wasn't able to fully recover. She too was very quite—almost like the sweet, calm grandmother or grandaunt we all have in our families.

I looked throughout the room, assessing everyone there. Not necessarily to understand our issues but because I was fascinated by the different faces gathered in one place. I noticed a younger guy in his mid-twenties with long dreadlocks who decided to take his motorcycle downtown one night. He visited the strip of bars and drank all through the night. When the bars made their last call and lights were shutting off, he hopped on his motorcycle to ride home. Of course, that was the first problem. The second much larger problem was that he decided to speed down the road as fast as his sport bike could without wearing a helmet. After his motorcycle sped out of control, he slammed head first into the gravel.

Beside him sat a younger guy whose sinus infection traveled to his brain causing a traumatic injury.

Lastly, there I sat. A teenage boy who drew the shortest straw on a car ride home. For a while, these would be the people I would work with to get my life back.

My mom sat near me at the big table and learned about all of the types of therapy I would endure: cognitive, physical, speech, occupational, and sleep therapies. Yes, I even had a class where the goal was to teach me how to sleep right.

"Alright everyone, I am excited for us to begin our therapy sessions! We're going to have a lot of fun!" a therapist spoke cheerfully from the end of the table. No one responded.

The first couple weeks at this rehabilitation clinic took some getting used to. Every day around noon, my brain-injured buds and I would gather in the neuropsychologist's office to talk about our feelings. It was almost like I was in a movie. Every time we would share, the psychologist would mumble "mhmm, mhmm" and jot down notes on a piece of paper. He walked in pen and pad in hand.

"Hello everyone. How are we doing today?" he asked, leaning back into his soft, cushioned computer chair. He readied his pen to take notes on all of the crazy things we were about to unleash. Everyone in my group therapy found their favorite chair and raced over to it. For some reason, we each became enamored with certain areas in the small office. Some of us wanted to sit right next to the neuropsychologist so they would get the most opportunities to speak. Others tried to hide out in the shadows of the cluttered corners.

"Anyone have trouble with therapy today?" he asked.

Everyone remained motionless and silent. He began to scan the room looking for the weak one of the pack. That person would be singled out and asked the question directly. We all knew this was happening. Each of us gazed off at different areas of the ceiling as if we had become preoccupied by a piece of sheet rock.

"Alright then. What about you?" he pointed at the sixteen-year-old boy who thought he was the Real Slim Shady or a seasoned Eminem.

"Man, I 'unno. This therapy stuff stupid any..anyways," he shouted with a tempered, over-exaggerated voice. "I'm ready to hop out 'dis joint and smoke some bud with my boys."

On command, the neuropsychologist jotted notes on his yellow note pad and robotically muttered, "Mhmm, mhmm. I see."

We were helpless. Here he was, someone who was brutally injured and managed to stay alive only by a miracle. He ignored the therapy he received and only looked forward to returning to the same ignorant activity that got him brutally injured.

But there was nothing anyone could do to change that. We all thought up wild things or would get furious or depressed at the drop of a dime. It was like we were trapped in a foreign body that was partially functioning. For all I knew, that boy had no idea of the things he was telling us. The only thing we hoped for was time and support. The more these therapists and nurses worked on us, the more our brains were fit to begin recovery.

Although I was out of the hospital and seemed much better off than some of my therapy mates, I still had many issues going on inside my head. My words were repetitive, and I was impulsive with no filter. I would shout whatever was on my mind regardless of how atrocious or inappropriate it was. I had little to no patience. I wanted everything right away. Interestingly, I still act that way today, but in a good way. I still have little patience but fortunately it's focused on impatiently accomplishing goals and progressing in life. I have grown into a man who instead of trying to cure his waiting patience by screaming "I want it now! I want it now! I want it now!," I now work harder. I exhaust myself towards accomplishing the goals I've set. But, I'm still that brain-injured teenager with zero patience. Only now, I call it "hungry." I'm always hungry for more. A better life, a better experience, a better me.

For months I wasn't allowed to leave and be off on my own. My patience ran thin on days I would want to leave and hangout with my friends. It was almost like everything I had worked towards in the realm of independence had been washed away, and I was back to holding my mother's hand everywhere I went.

We would stroll around town together and when people would look and stare, I would become enraged. The hateful words would hang loosely on my lips and were only halted by my mother's calming presence.

On one occasion, a girl who I had never met before somehow found out about my story on Facebook. I have no idea why, but this girl decided to rant and rave about how disabled and broken I was in what was a lengthy status update. She called me names, said I was retarded, and would specifically make fun of my inability to walk or talk correctly. I had never even met her!

She set me off. I was like the game Jenga, and this girl pulled the wrong block. I searched around on the Internet to find her phone number. I gave this girl a call and screamed at the top of my lungs. My hands were trembling, and my entire body was shaking. Beads of sweat and tears rolled down my face. My little sister listened from behind her bedroom door. She was scared and had never heard me react to anything so hatefully. My next door neighbors heard the shouting and called my mom at work.

"Lisa, you might want to call the house. Ryan is really upset about something."

"Alright," was all she said before calling. No matter where she was, she was always trying to protect me. After a few moments of ringing, I answered the phone in a huffing, panting cry.

"Hello?!" I shouted. My articulation was worse.

"What's going on? Are you okay?"

I rambled on about the girl and what she had done. Emotions and impulsivity were always on high alert since getting a brain injury. I exaggerated my feelings and made choices without thinking of the effect it would have on me or other people. My mom continued listening to me shout through my tears. She was waiting to interrupt me and calm me down.

"Alright well just try to calm down. Let Morgan know that Tony or I will be home shortly." She ended the call. A moment of silence floated through the speaker before she added, "Hey! Cheer up, someone has a birthday soon!"

Even after hanging up the phone, I kept thinking, *Why would someone do something like that? Why did it make her happy to say those things?*

The way I screamed at this girl was the way I felt inside. I felt alone. Abandoned by all the healthy people around me. It's a feeling I never want to experience again.

––––––––––

Have you ever felt ostracized by those around you? Has there ever been just one distinguishing factor that separated you from the rest? I have felt that feeling quite a bit since my accident and over time I began learning how to use it to my advantage. I let my biggest life story empower me to become the person I am today.

––––––––––

With all of these obstacles and situations going on in my personal life, I had to remember to stay focused on therapy. I still had a long road ahead of me. One that seemed like it would take a lifetime. My body experienced pain when a therapist twisted and turned my limbs. I still couldn't quite articulate my words, and my overall awareness was not where it needed to be

—especially if I were to get to the level of success I had aimed for in school and in my career.

Me, Myself, and My Money

Not long after that phone call my mother came dozing through the front door. She wanted to make sure I was still safe and that I had calmed down enough for her to talk to me about a call she received.

"How are you feeling?" she asked as I trotted through the kitchen in silence. Before I could respond, Tony walked in the front door. He could tell by the awkward feeling in the air that something was going on.

"Hey! Answer your mother," he said sternly. Sometimes I needed to not be so cushioned.

"Im fine," I muttered back.

"Tomorrow morning we need to drive downtown to the bank."

"The bank?"

"Yes. My insurance is writing you a check for the accident so you need to be there to sign some paperwork."

Because of my mom's insurance plan, the company agreed to write me a $25,000 check. When she told me this, the wind was knocked out of me, and everything around me stopped. All that was in my mind was what I could buy with $25,000.

"Ryan!" my mom brought my attention back to the present.

I went to sleep that night dreaming of a life full of riches. At my age, $25,000 was like winning the lottery. I could buy a car, new games, or even a new computer. I stayed awake in bed budgeting my future all through the night.

I woke up the following morning with baggy, restless eyes that declared my excitement. Mom and Tony were dressed in nice clothing and both had their hair neatly combed. They were much farther along in their morning routine than I was.

"Ready?" Tony asked.

I wasn't even changed out of my basketball shorts and oversized t-shirt but I nodded in response. My sleepy index finger rose before his eyes to signal that I needed a few minutes to change. I don't think any of us knew exactly what we were about to encounter. Surely they were more prepared and would lead me in the right direction as any loving parent would. I expected the ride downtown to be filled with a strategic discussion on how to get the money and run.

"Alright, so what do I say to these people?" I asked from the backseat.

Mom and Tony pondered the question. "There isn't much to it. Just sign on the dotted line, and they'll release the funds. We'll make sure they don't talk you into signing up for anything else," Tony responded.

The remainder of the car ride was silent. My eyes connected with the same blurred buildings it did the night of my accident. I didn't quite know how to react. My mind tried retracing itself to that night but nothing surfaced. Once our car was underneath the shadow of the bank's towering building, mom turned to me once more.

"You okay?" she wanted to see how I gauged the trip.

"Yes. I am fine. I am excited," I replied. My body was still very weak.

Soon after parking the car next to one of those coin-slot timers, we walked into the magnificent lobby of the bank.

"Good afternoon!" a well-dressed man initiated as soon as we entered. He looked like a fraternity guy that finagled a free college education and finance career out of his wealthy father.

His slacks had poorly hidden wrinkles and the smell of salt and vinegar potato chips lingered around him.

"Please, take a seat and get comfortable," he pointed to the cushioned chairs in front of his desk.

"I'll have you start by filling out a couple of papers," he slid a thick packet of paper in front of me. I took a few moments an flipped through them to get an idea of what I was agreeing to and if anything odd would jump out at me. It seemed like the appropriate thing to do even though I wasn't totally trusting of my own comprehension.

My handwriting had always been sloppy but after my hand-eye coordination suffered from my injury, it was almost illegible. To make things even worse, my hand was trembling at the idea of $25,000 instantly dropping into my account. I kept asking myself what would I do with it all. My pen struck the paper and ink bled out the nam: Ryan Troutman.

"Alright, you're all set!" the banker said while pulling the papers away from me. "The money has been transferred to your account, Ryan. Good luck."

He seemed to be a little too friendly. *Had the insurance agency tipped him off and told him to play along? Did he honestly just not care and had to paint a smile on until he could clock out and go home?*

The conversation on the drive home was one giant strategy, well, at least for me it was. The idea of buying a new car around my seventeenth birthday drove me wild. I still wasn't outwardly conveying my emotions but inside my entire body was a celebratory party.

"The first thing I want is something to drive."

"Alright, we'll go take a look at cars soon," Tony declared.

"You're not even allowed to drive yet, Ryan." My mother called out from the front seat. The tone of her voice made it apparent that she didn't like the idea of me getting my own car.

"But I—"

"But you still need to finish therapy. Don't think you're going to be driving all over town once you get a car. You're seventeen years old. I still make the rules," she got motherly with me.

"You just wait. Once I hit the big one eight, I'm going to decide what I'm doing and when I am doing it!" I snapped back.

My parents and I are not perfect. Every mother and child has talks like this. You know the ones where the kid is talking all high and mighty, and it's only a matter of seconds before the mom lays down the law.

After returning to our home and parking in our driveway, I crawled out of the backseat with a dulled excitement. I was ecstatic about my newly acquired treasure, but my body was still worn. I still had physical limitations that bound me and, on top of that, my age constricted me.

The following morning, I returned to therapy. No matter how much money a person has, they still need to take care of themselves. I soon realized that just because the dollar sign in my checking account got larger, didn't mean my brain injury got smaller.

My physical therapist would discuss my therapy plan and all I would do is stare from across the table with a look of hatred. All she was trying to do was stop my body from experiencing pain but I seemed to ignore her knowing that every therapeutic exercise was nothing short of agonizing. Then there was my speech therapist who would have me do exercises to help recover my ability to annunciate words. He would say, "Alright, Ryan, I'm going to have you say the sound BAH as fast as you can over and over."

Like always, I would stare back with discontent and confusion. The speech therapist would even give me an example of the sounds I was to make. That was the point when I began losing hope but at the same time gaining confidence.

I would clear my throat and began "bahb..b..bahhhh..bahh-hhhbahhhbahh..bah..bah." My mouth just wouldn't function the way I intended it to. He would sigh and softly smile before saying, "Alright, we didn't quite do it there. Let's try again. Remember it sounds like bah bah bah bah bah b..ba..bah..b."

Every time he would give me an example of the repetitive sound, he would slip at the end as if mimicking the poor attempts I had made. I knew all he wanted to do was help, but I thought, "if this guy can't make the sounds, how in the world am I supposed to?".

At the same time I was losing hope that he would fix my voice, I gained confidence knowing that non-brain-injured people truly weren't the elite perfect people that I was beginning to feel they were. Of course, I had to work harder than the therapist did, but it was nice to see that I wasn't the only one who had trouble with the activity.

My experiences with the occupational therapist were different. She had impactful activities that demonstrated my strengths and areas of opportunity. She would have me sit at a table and complete a very simple worksheet. The door was intentionally left open, and the therapist would casually stroll past the doorway and lock eyes with me as my head would shoot up to see who was passing ny.

In a positive, humorous kind of way she should tell me, "Ryan! Keep your eyes on your paper! Don't worry about me or what is going on outside the doorway."

This activity determined my ability to stay focused, and it was not easy. Every time she would walk pass the table, my head would jolt up to stare at her. Surprisingly, I would quickly whip my head towards the door even though I knew what was about to happen and who was going to pass by. This is a great example of how my brain triumphed over my mind. It is the same feeling as an addiction. You can tell yourself all day long to do or not to do something but sometimes your body makes the final decision. In my case, I was having a lot of trouble grasping control over my own body.

While in the weekly therapy sessions, one of my favorite times of the day was lunch. Each of the patients would gather in the lunchroom and glance around at where to begin.

"Go ahead and grab a plate," a server would direct us. Everyone would quietly shuffle over to the plastic plates and gaze in wonder waiting for the next step. We all seemed to have trouble forming a line, and we might as well had been sitting in a high chair having food spoon-fed to us. We would eat at different paces and in different manners. I would shovel my food down and head to the gym so I could spend the remaining time working on my strength.

One day, the former detective left the lunchroom to go to the restroom. He walked out of the room and froze as if he had been teleported to another planet. After wandering to the end of the hallway, he found the restroom. The detective must have lost his strong investigation skills because when he walked out of the bathroom he had no idea how to get back to the lunchroom. It's crazy to think that we were only a hallway away but he just couldn't remember or process how to trace his steps back.

Each day had its own complications and challenges, but the therapists made sure we always completed the total sessions. I would get to the rehabilitation center and complete hours of physical, cognitive, occupational, and speech therapies each day—just as if I we completing classes in school. But the most unusual part of my day was right at the end when we would all huddle our way into a dark room filled with cushioned recliners to work with the last therapist.

He called himself the sleep therapist.

He was an older gentlemen, bald, who always had a wise, calming grin resting across his face. He would instruct us to lie down in our large recliners and close our eyes. The soft sounds of stringed instruments would begin playing from a stereo that sat on a small table near his recliner.

His job was to pop in a CD and close his eyes just as we closed ours. We would all sit in silence for a while just listening to the sounds. Some of us would drift away, others would just stare blankly at the ceiling.

This session was meant to teach relaxation strategies but, for me, it was always a mind-racing session. On some days, I was able to relax but a majority of the time my attention would dart around in the darkness and my mind would stay busy juggling all of its random, hallow thoughts.

Have you ever tried just breaking away from reality for a bit? For some of us that seems nearly impossible but you wouldn't believe the benefits. The purpose behind this therapeutic activity was to teach us how to take a break and create mental clarity. At the time, I had many frustrating and depressing thoughts running through my mind. I wasn't able to do much of anything but I had recovered enough to realize that I was in an onerous situation, and I might not come out of it the way I'd like.

Regardless of how long the road ahead of me would turn out to be, I felt I couldn't give up. I was given the opportunity MANY people never get: the opportunity to still be alive. Unlike many others who died in a major car accident, I was still able to become depressed at my disabilities. Unlike them, I still was able to fail miserably at therapeutic exercises.

I bet the thousands of people who die each year from a traumatic brain injury would sell their soul to be able to not talk right or to sit in a wheelchair—but still be alive. All of those people who had their lives taken from them in an instant would dream of walking out of an in-patient hospital and be chauffeured around by a loving mother.

It was time to move things under my own control. This entire recovery journey had been a handholding experience but I was never going to return to my old self if I continued to let others guide my life for me. While in the outpatient rehabilitation clinic, I made the promise to never give up on anything. Not even myself. I knew I could be a better person. I wasn't as broken as everyone liked to think. I could grow up to be the kind of person

I always wanted to be. No brain injury was going to stop me from being me.

Think about it.

There are countless people around the world who are healthier, younger, or just plain luckier, than I am. A lot of those people died the instant that their accident occurred. But here I was, sitting in a classroom recliner surrounded by a dozen other survivors, with the lights out, listening to a soothing violin music. *What did I do right? Why was I one to make it out alive? What do I need to do now that I've been given an opportunity to continue living my life?* Those are questions I still ask myself. They are the driving force behind my constant motivation. I am personally responsible to live my life to the absolute fullest. While I'm here, I want to do good. Help others. Continue surpassing the boy I once was and recover two hundred percent.

I couldn't imagine how selfish I would feel if I wasted away a gift many people never get a chance to have. So while I was at this out-patient center, I did everything I could to overcome my traumatic brain injury and the disabilities it left me with.

This constant struggle of hard work and intense effort was exhausting. At times I didn't know if I was getting anywhere with the therapy activity I had completed. It became depressing at times to imagine never gaining back any of the basic life skills I had lost. Day after day, I would devote my time to activities at the clinic, but I needed a break. I needed some indication that showed me everything would be okay. I hoped that something would let me get away from all of the stressful situations just long enough to catch my breath.

Then one day I was surprised when I was told I'd be given a "dream".

RYAN TROUTMAN

I'M NOT DREAMING

"Hello," my mom answered her cellphone.

"Hello, Lisa! My name is Beatrice. I'm with Dreams Come True. We heard about what had happened to your son, Ryan, and wish to give him his very own dream."

"Wow! He will love that!"

"Yes! We're here to create a memorable day for him and his family. Ryan can choose whatever unforgettable experience he'd like! For example, he could go on a shopping spree and you could spend all day with him while he picks out all of his cool new gadgets!"

"A shopping spree would be fantastic!" My mom exclaimed.

"Fantastic! I will call you back, and we can set up a day to meet."

My mom happily agreed and ended the call. Less than two week later my mom and Beatrice had made all the arrangements to give me the surprise of my life.

On the morning of my dream, I was picked up in a limousine and driven to the first store of my choice. I walked down the isles pointing at items to be added to a shopping cart. This trip helped me exercise my decision-making ability. Up until that moment, everyone had made decisions for me. I simply waited for my next instruction from a therapist or my parents. But Dreams Come True gave me the power to make my own decisions and rediscover my own interests.

RYAN TROUTMAN

I would ride around in the limousine, smiling and laughing with my family and telling the driver where I wanted to travel to next. This was such a magical break away from everything I had been through. It was one full day where my family and I could forget about anything that happened to me. For that day I wasn't depressed about my slow recovery or dim future. I wasn't screaming uncontrollably at my family for reasons I couldn't explain. No, it truly was a dream that made me smile the most since the day before my car accident.

I still have and use many of the things I purchased that day. But the joy and quality time I gained during that dream was priceless and it remains one of the shining days of my dark time through the hospital and through rehabilitation.

In fact, I appreciate Dreams Come True so much that I now volunteer to create memorable dreams for children who are going through tragedies. I like to think that children are comforted once they know I was once a Dreamer. I connect with them on a level not many other volunteers can. In addition to creating a memorable day, I tell them brief stories of my time pushing through recovery. They smile and tell me about times they've had to stay strong and fight through an illness. I'm always taken back and reminded where I once was.

The young Dreamers I've met have been the most humble, appreciative people I've ever had the chance to work with. It's organizations like Dreams Come True that are doing something really great for my community, and I feel honored to be able to volunteer my time to making the dreams of children come true!

But before I could go on to volunteering at places like Dreams Come True, I had to first make it through my own recovery. Towards the end of my time at the out-patient rehabilitation center, I had to take a driving test to have my license reinstated. The state requires a therapist to medically approve me for driving privileges again to ensure that my disabilities won't cause a danger to others on the road.

RYAN TROUTMAN

Luckily, the rules of the road were still very fresh in my mind. I was a teenager who had just become old enough to sit behind the wheel and drive alone. Regardless of the fact that I remembered the mechanics of driving, my body didn't cooperate too well with operating a vehicle.

The therapist to approve my driving was a skinny, pale woman. Her low profile eyeglasses sat just below her short, black hair.

"Hello, Ryan! Today we are going to test your ability with some minor driving exercises," she explained. My eyes grew in excitement. Was this the first step to me becoming normal again?

"But before we get into the car, you'll need to go through some simulators," she added.

I nodded my head eagerly. I didn't care what I needed to do just as long as it ended in me driving again and possibly buying my own car. This simulator was just like playing a racing game in an arcade. Only, this time I was driving the speed limit and using blinkers to merge between lanes.

"Alright. Nice work! Let's move on to the next step," her words caused a nervous smile to streak across my face.

We headed outside to the front of the center and walked through the parking lot. We approached a typical family sedan. When I sat down behind the wheel, the therapist instructed me to practice making slow and steady turns.

"Alright, now, let's start the vehicle and drive up to that stop sign on your left and turn on your blinker before taking a right," she ordered.

I remembered my driving days prior to my accident. Back then my turn signal was used just about as much as my seatbelt was: never. I took special care to buckle up, check my mirrors, and start up the vehicle. I eased out of the open parking space and deliberately followed her instructions at five miles per hour. She then instructed me to continue driving around the perimeter of the parking lot, signaling each turn, and parking at the entrance doors.

"You're doing great!" she celebrated.

As I was driving, I thought to myself. *Is this really the freedom I was looking for? I'll never make it to the beach with my friends with right-hand turns and neutral coasting.*

Patty had a very motherly personality. She wore a stern face that was weathered by all of the responsibilities she took on each day. Her voice was soft but strict. This lady was going to be my ticket to feeling a little more like an actual teen, again.

"Lisa, Ryan did alright on today's test," she said, "but he needs a lot more practice. We would like to take him out on the road to see how he interacts with other drivers. How do you feel about that?"

My mom's face became pale. This was the first actual time I would be behind the wheel of the machine that almost killed me.

"A..alright," my mom murmured. When she finally told me I'd be behind the wheel, driving near other cars, it excited me while shaking me with fear. With my minuscule driving experience and downgraded dexterity, I felt as if I would surely do something wrong. Something that wouldn't give me a third chance.

I laid in my bed that night and dreamt of all the places I could travel, friends I would make, and experiences I would have. In all honesty, I wanted to cry for help. I had no idea what my future looked like to the point that I didn't even know that the next day held. If I messed this driving test up, I would not be able to drive. People who can't drive have a hard time meeting up with friends. Therefore, to not drive would make me lose contact with a lot of people. If I lost contact with my friends, I'd feel lonely—lonelier than I already felt. There would be no job or school to occupy my time because I wasn't smart nor capable enough to have either.

The next morning, my mother drove me back to the out-patient center for my driving test. The slick family sedan I was scheduled to drive had been modified with an emergency break pedal on the floorboard of the passenger's side in order to ensure that all passengers were safe and that the therapist could be in control at all times during the drive.

"Alright, Ryan. You've been doing great. Let's knock this test out together," Patty said. If I didn't relax and drive right, the only thing I would be knocking out was us. I turned the key and heard the eco-friendly car's engine trickle.

"Remember, seat belt first," Patty said with glaring eyes. It almost offended me that she would even say that. You would think that after all I've been through, I'd remember to do the one thing I didn't do that night after The Empire. I tauntingly snapped the seat belt already strapped across my chest.

"I've had it buckled since we sat down," I said. I guess I was a little edgy about the whole thing. I didn't know how I was going to do and even if I thought I did well, the final say so was all up to her and her evaluation chart.

As we pulled out of the parking lot and onto the road, my heart began pumping like I had just ran a race. I felt that icky feeling you sometimes get with a fever. My body felt cold as if I was naked in an igloo, but beads of sweat were pooling between my back and the seat. No matter how enticing this drive was going to be, I had to remain calm. I had to portray to this lady that I was an able driver, not another car accident just waiting to happen.

We made our way down the road and my fingers began to loosen on the wheel. I felt a sense of comfort and my body began to sink further into the cushioned leather seat. Each time I made mistakes like that, she would make marks in her small book. I would do my best to glance over at the writing, but I needed to focus on the road. And besides, my peripheral vision was almost non-existent. After a deep, stressful sigh, she glared at the side of my face.

"Whew, let's get this car parked," she said with a cheerful but concerned voice.

At this point, I had no idea how truthful her cushioned words really were. I parked the car and went back into the main lobby while she and my mom talked privately in an office.

"Lisa, thank you for waiting," she said in a professional tone, "Ryan had a few issues while driving that I'd like to review with you." My mother's eyes grew with anticipation. She braced herself to hear that I would always be medically restricted from driving and that I would be a danger to myself and others on the road.

"Ryan had a few instances where he would flick on his turn signal and attempt to merge onto another car in the lane beside him. I had to continue breaking and reminding him to check his blind spot," she continued.

"But, rather than denying him driving privileges, I will reinstate his license only if you agree to ride with him until he becomes more skillful at the the things we've talked about today."

My mother's countenance filled with excitement. I would be able to drive and it was the hospital's orders for her to hang out with me every time.

"Alright, thank you! I will supervise him until I feel he is driving properly."

That meeting ended my rehabilitation and was a milestone on my road to recovery. Not only was my hospital and rehabilitation time completed, but now I was transitioning back into the real world. Trained nurses or therapists would no longer guide me through every step. I would now have to begin doing more things for myself. I would return to living and controlling my own life—creating my future.

THERAPEUTIC DAYS AND TALLADEGA NIGHTS

Soon after completing the out-patient program, Tony and I drove to a small, family-owned car lot in a bad neighborhood, on the wrong side of Jacksonville. We pulled up to the lot and approached a crummy trailer. Wrinkled button-down shirts and stained khakis paced back and forth through the window. A tall, slinky man emerged from the rusty trailer door.

"Good morning, gentlemen! The name's Ricky. Who do I have the pleasure of doing business with?" The man gazed at us with piercing eyes.

"Tony," my step-father spoke with a manly, brute tone. Apparently, you couldn't show signs of weakness in a place like this. These guys will tear you apart. "This is my son, Ryan."

"Well hey, buddy!" the man over-enthusiastically shouted.

I looked up with annoyed, excited eyes. "Yo."

"So what are we looking for here today?"

"We just want to take a look at something safe," Tony knew how to deal with the roguish car salesman.

"Alright then! Let's go over here and take a look at this SAAB," the salesman directed us to a dirty corner of the lot that had been consumed by weeds and tainted with chewing tobacco.

"No," I instantly replied. I could see the piece of junk that he was leading us to, and I would never waste my newly acquired money on it.

RYAN TROUTMAN

"Eh... ok," the man was stripped of his only showcase car. Everything else was F-150 trucks or El Caminos. There was one shiny silver exception that instantly caught my eye.

"That one! I want that one," I commanded. Throughout my childhood, I always tended to get overly involved with things, but after my injury things just consumed me.

"Alright, man. Chill! Let's take a look at it first," Tony hushed me. I didn't care. That's was the only car I wanted. The glistening silver Mazda 6 had slick dual exhaust and quite a sporty look. Much more appealing than the dumpy SAAB.

"Want to take it for a test drive?" The salesman asked.

My head lunged up and down at the idea of driving my brand new toy. Tony opened the back door and climbed in. The salesman buckled into the front passenger seat. I ran my fingers across the smooth hood before plopping down behind the wheel.

"How does it feel?" the man asked. I could see the greasy large pores pooling out of his cheeks and nose. His unclean, nappy stubble was his poor attempt at a clean-shaven beard. Sunlight shined through the windshield and inflamed his beady pupils. This guy was not someone I wanted to pay commission to but unfortunately he held the keys to my freedom.

"Crank her up," he encouraged.

"Yeah, let's go," Tony added from the back.

I turned the key and felt the car rumble. The engine's soft purr was calming and the air freshener dangling from the rear view mirror had a hurry-up-and-buy-it scent. I pulled off onto the road and began coasting down the lane. I still wasn't the greatest at driving but at least I remembered the basics. One thing I surely remembered to do was wear a seatbelt.

After strolling up and down a few nearby streets, I returned to the junk yard of a car lot. The feeling was invigorating. It gave me a a hopeful assurance that I was heading to my own promised land. This car would be life changing. Just as soon as I could drive it on my own.

RYAN TROUTMAN

"Alright, so it looks like this is the one for you!" the man cheered. I don't know why he was trying so hard. This would be the easiest sale of his career. I'm sure no one has ever walked into this place as desperate as I was. This guy's colleagues all peeked over at his desk to see if he could close the sale.

"So, would you like to take a look at financing options or have you already been approved by your ba—."

"Cash," I interrupted. "I'll buy it cash." The power I felt saying that was short lived. The odd salesman almost put his hands together in a thankful, submissive praise. His eyes widened and his beady pupils were dilated with joy. Tony smiled at me. He knew how it must have felt for me to finally have an opportunity to make a decision for myself.

"Alright then! She's all yours!"

The dead, brown grass beneath my feet crackled as I shuffled towards the driver's seat. This was my moment. I was finally beginning to feel my age. I stuck the jagged key into the ignition and cranked on the engine. A powerful energy surged through my veins. It felt like I had finally tamed the animal that nearly killed me.

"Hold up, man!" Tony yelled over the engine's four-cylinder purr. "You still have to pay the man. And, you can't drive that thing home by yourself. Let's wait for your mother to get here. I'll drive my car home, and she can ride with you."

I shrugged with the idea of waiting any longer. The impatient salesman had a vein bulging from his forehead. We walked inside his dingy trailer and sat at what may have someday been an office desk. With a few short signatures, initials, and checked off boxes, I was set. This guy got his money and was now ready for us to leave. "Is there anything else I can help you with?" his voice trailed off.

"No. We'll wait here. His grandmother and mom are already on the way up here and should arrive any minute," Tony sensed the eagerness in the salesman's voice.

My face had become red with anger. I was tired of needing a guardian in the car while I drove. "Why can't I just drive?! Nobody is going to pull me over and ask if I'm a medically restricted driver!" I scoffed.

Tony knew this was agonizing but didn't want me to get into any more trouble than I had already experienced. "Chill. Your mom will be here any second. In fact, here she is now."

Ms. Rae's vehicle coasted up behind me just as Tony had finished speaking. I could hear mainstream pop music escaping from her red Avalanche. The tires on her car were bald. They needed to be replaced long ago. As they came to a stop, trash, debris, clay dirt, and dry weeds floated around us.

"Heeeey!" Tony shouted jokingly at the car while swatting the dust away from his face. It was nearly impossible to not stir up this place's uncleanliness. The car salesman blushed in embarrassment and glanced out onto the main road to ensure no potential customers saw the dirty display.

"Hey, sweetie! I love your new car!" Ms. Rae shouted from her driver's window. My mom hustled out of the passenger seat and hurried over to me.

"Let's hurry. Janet is at our home watching Morgan and Logan," she said with a bit of urgency. I once again returned to my new prized possession and cranked the ignition.

The drive home with my mom was silent. My eyes were trained on the road in front of me and my mother ensured no distractions would divert my attention.

"Mom," I began. She instantly rose a finger to her lips to signal my silence.

"Focus on the road," she instructed. The worn expression on her face told me she didn't ever want to go through another hellish night like the one on February 18th. Minutes passed and I was on the last street that led to my neighborhood.

"I made it!" I shouted.

My mom's eyes eased in a relaxing way. "Pull up on the curb." My mom turned and locked eyes with me. "I wanted to wait until we got home. But, just so you know, all driving will need supervision. We can try taking the test again in a couple of months."

I didn't know whether to get mad or excited that I would soon have another chance at taking the test. The pupils of my eyes were filled with an energetic hope that I would finally break free from the grip this injury has had on me.

Janet glanced through the kitchen curtains and saw us talking. She decided not to interrupt and instead waited for us to enter. The front door opened and cool air flooded in along with us. Janet heard our footsteps rounding the corner and soon locked eyes with my still concentrated face.

"I like the car! It looks very nice," she complimented.

My mom smiled at Janet's comment. Everyone knew how excited I was to get a car. Janet walked towards the front door and waved. "I'll talk you soon, Lisa. Congrats again, Ryan!"

"Bye!" my mom yelled. "Go ahead and get cleaned up for dinner," she said while pulling pots and pans out of a cabinet.

The remainder of the night wasn't too far from normal. We ate dinner using our TV stands and tuned in to all the latest updates on SportsCenter. My mom and Tony were chipping away at their steaks while I pushed lima beans around. I was still consumed with thoughts and questions that were left unanswered.

"If I were you, I'd get some sleep tonight," Tony advised.

I nodded in agreement and went to scrape my remaining beans into a nearby trashcan. Mom and Tony stared me down in a loving way. They both were proud and glad to finally see me feel excited about the future.

"Alright. I'm going to go lay down. Thank you again for everything today. I love you, goodnight." I announced before heading to my bedroom.

"Goodnight, we love you, too!" my mom exclaimed as I exited the living room.

THIS WASN'T AN EPISODE OF GLEE

A month after completing rehabilitation and buying my car, I returned to high school. Because I missed a majority of my junior year, I had to take eleventh and twelfth grade classes simultaneously in order to graduate with my original class. This meant waking up every weekday morning and going to my school for my senior classes then riding the bus home so I could hop online and attend my junior classes.

I did not use the individual education plan I had received from the school district and therapists. Instead, I trudged through two classes of science, math, English, and history, along with a course which prepared students for the workforce. These all were required courses. I had no exceptions nor special provisions because of my brain injury, and I wasn't going to let it prevent me from challenging myself the same way my fellow classmates did. This would soon become the toughest year of my schooling.

I had a simple routine. I would always rush home in order to quickly transition into a virtual student. I would greet mom and Tony. while grabbing an unhealthy snack or something quick to throw in my mouth like a bag of Sour Patch Kids or a Fruit Roll Up. Then, I would head to my room to attempt the math I hardly understood. I conveniently attended my junior-level algebra class online shortly after I got home from completing senior-level algebra at school.

RYAN TROUTMAN

Math was never a strong suit for me and after the injury, it became tougher. If I couldn't grasp high school algebra, I was going to have a tough time finding a successful career—or so I was told. Still to this day I can feel my mind trying to chug through any kind of mental math. But, fortunately for me Tony always had a knack for mathematics. I would listen to him rattle off fractions, percentages, and values while he would sit in the living room and mark up my paper with a sharpened pencil. Not only did I not understand the calculation portion of this math, but I had just following along on what numbers moved to where was difficult.

"Real simple, man. Just take this number, stick it there, and multiply it by that number," he told me confidently.

I would nod my head as if I knew what was going on, then, I would run off to my room to keep working only to return moments later needing more help.

"Can you help me with this one?" I scurried out into the living room flapping a paper in Tony's face. A deep sigh crept from his throat. The dimly lit room had a surreal ambiance to it that was always disrupted by my continuous nagging. Tony would extended an arm waiting for me to place my scratch paper in his hands. We both would quietly glance through my chicken scratch trying to see where exactly I messed up.

"I told you, man! You have to carry this number or it isn't going to work!" Tony let out.

"Thank you!" I rejoiced before returning to my hideout. I still had trouble remembering all of the steps in the equation and would very easily get confused and disorganized. Mathematics was my worst enemy. The creative thinking mind inside my head had trouble logically placing numbers in their proper places and routinely carrying out the steps of a function.

I sat in my room and tried working on the next problem. It was literally the same type of equation just with different numbers. I would try to replicate the same steps I watched Tony do but eventually my mind would wander off onto a more interesting topic. Sometimes it would even just go blank and I would awkwardly stare off into space for long periods of time.

"How's it going in there?" Tony would call out.

"Great! Almost done!" I responded. He had no idea that for the last fifteen minutes I had been practicing my meditation skills. Finally, after numerous failed attempts, I rushed back into the living room waving my partially completed paperwork. "Can you help me with this one?" I would ask.

No matter how irritating or hard to believe things got, Tony always remained calm and helped me through my next problem. This went on all year. Honestly, my high school diploma should be in his name. He was the most impactful person leading me to my high school diploma. To be honest, I wouldn't be too offended if the name on my diploma said "Ryan Troutman. In Partnership With..." then a dreadfully long list of parents, friends, teachers and tutors who helped make it a reality.

"Done!" I shouted after watching Tony make the final mark on my paper.

"You're all set, man. But you really need to spend some time mastering these skills," he said, then ended with, "You're going to use them all throughout life."

Was I really going to use this math all throughout my life? With my current debilitated state of mind I didn't even know if I was ever going to succeed in college or if I would ever grow up and get a decent career. I felt so incapable that the idea of growing up and being a dog-sitter was more of a reality in my eyes. A reality that doesn't require algebra or geometry.

"Thank you again. I'm going to head to bed," I said while sliding back into my bedroom lit by my computer monitor. I had other plans for the night.

I stayed up all night for many nights looking for a way to tell my story. I began searching the Internet for free websites to start a blog. Once I found a decent site, I only planned to make one post that told my entire journey through this major life event.

RYAN TROUTMAN

I must admit, for someone with a broken brain, I was able to type up a pretty engaging story. In vivid detail, I described how my injury made me feel. I wrote about myself, others, and life. I reflected on what I remembered the night it happened and took readers through a tale of recovery and repentance.

I began my blog post with "February 18, 2007, was the day I died."

After I finished writing, I closed my eyes with a good feeling deep in my heart. I didn't have the money or knowledge to market my blog post nor did I have the time. But I just knew that some kid somewhere would be up one night aimlessly crawling around on the web. My story would hopefully inspire them to wear a seatbelt or choose not to speed, knowing what life could be like if things don't go right.

Over time, I would occasionally check the blog's stats to see that seven people viewed it over the last six months. While those are horrible numbers, it always made me smile. A handful of people took the time to read my story and not have to experience the pain and suffering I did in order to grasp the life lessons I was taught.

As the school year went on, I came to my senses more each day. I began acting more lively and was able to participate in group conversations without showing any signs of mentally lagging. But, I was still not my best self, yet.

One day at school my friends and I were sitting at our usual lunch table. I had just finished going through the cafeteria's line and began slopping through my packaged, microwaved slime. Everyone at the table watched in disgust at my lack of self-awareness. My friend Oliver was sitting next to me at the long table. He stared at my feeding frenzy with wide eyes before reaching into his lunchbox and grabbing a neatly made ham sandwich.

"So what's everyone doing after class today?" he asked.

"I gotta poop. So yeah, that's what's on my agenda," I thought this would make the table erupt in laughter. Oliver glanced over at me while I continued battering through a pile of mashed potatoes. Everyone blushed in embarrassment at the answer I gave.

If this was the Hunger Games, I'd be winning right about now.

Regardless of my social struggle, It seemed that everything was going in an upward trend until one day my high school sweetheart, Caroline, walked me out to her car during lunch. I didn't see her much after I woke from my coma and there definitely was a noticeable change in our relationship. It almost felt like the last time she cared about me was when she snuck up to the trauma hospital to stare at my motionless body. Caroline and I had been dating for more than two years and let's just say my accident didn't make me any more attractive. She told me that she tried her hardest but could no longer be with me. Apparently, I had changed.

"You're just not the same," she began.

"What do you mean? I'm the same person I've always been."

"It's just too much to handle. I mean, you are..." She tried explaining. At the time, I didn't know what she was talking about. I thought she was just embarrassed of me for having a brain injury. It made me angry to think that she didn't see the situation for what it truly was. I thought she was being shallow and just wanted to find someone else, probably a popular boy to date.

But to be honest, around that time, I still didn't quite know how to behave in most social circumstances, publicly or privately. My words still had no filter and the random, sometimes dirty things I would say left her embarrassed and ashamed.

Back when I was in the trauma hospital, Caroline's best friend Mack decided to capitalize on my absence from our relationship. He would comfort Caroline through her sadness and offer a warm hug to ease the pain. They seemed even closer than they were prior to my car accident. While I was in a coma, the entire high school came together and made a huge banner to hang in my hospital room. Students who had never even met me would walk up and jot down a few nice words.

My best friend, Kirsten, watched from the other side of the table as Caroline and Mack wrote their messages. They would flirtatiously poke around at each other in a playful, loving manner. It made Kirsten furious to know that at that time I still could die at any moment, and the way those two showed their respects was by queueing up their inevitable future relationship.

Everything that went on around this time made me feel helpless. I knew I had changed and a lot of it was for the worse. I had trouble controlling my emotions and the filter on my language was still missing. It felt like my injury was subtlety working against me in the background. I lost a lot of my friends, my personality had changed, foods no longer tasted the same to me, I changed my opinions on certain topics, and now her. These were things I had no control over but had to live with every day.

Later that night, I was in my bedroom when I received a text message. I read the words that popped up on the screen and my heart sank. It wasn't a complex message that I would have trouble understanding. I knew exactly what I was reading but I didn't want to believe it. Surely this text message was meant to be sent to someone else. The sender must have typed in the wrong phone number. But, her name was in the message.

I slowly stumbled out into the living room where my mom and Tony were watching TV. My mom knew something was wrong by the terrifying look on my face. Wood burning in the fire place lit the room and casted a warm ambiance. I was interrupting them but fear was engulfing me.

"What is it? Is everything alr—."

"Jordan died," I blurted out before she could finish.

My mother's eyes grew wide in disbelief. Maybe I misunderstood something or could have dreamt about it. Everyone has nightmares that sometimes feel extremely real, right?

"What do you mean Jordan died?!"

RYAN TROUTMAN

I stood frozen. I couldn't answer.

Earlier that night, my mom was left to go to the grocery store and as she was turning out of our neighborhood, she looked left and saw blinding cop cars and ambulance lights. That was nearly three hours since the accident occurred. In that moment she connected what she saw to be the truth of my announcement, She could see the confused, solemn look on my face. *Why did things like this happen? Why was life so cruel?* We both asked subconsciously.

Jordan lived two neighborhoods down from me and would jog after school. There were even times she would text me to see if I wanted to run with her. Back when I returned home from the hospital, Jordan would constantly try to involve me in activities or would come over to my house just to hangout and to be what she had always been to me—a true friend.

One afternoon, she laced up her shoes and began jogging down the road. Like most people, Jordan had a route she enjoyed running. This routine path required her to cross a busy road that lined all of our neighborhoods. Reggae music was pumping through her earphones and beads of sweat began to dribble down her forehead. As usual, she approached the large black pole and pressed the button to allow her to cross the intersection. Occasionally, Jordan would jog in place to keep the blood flowing as she waited for the cars to stop and her signal to cross.

When the bright icon switched, Jordan began to cross the road. All cars had come to a complete stop as she made her way through the lanes.

And then it happened.

Just as she was making her final stride across the street and onto the sidewalk, a large truck piled into her. She died instantly.

One of my friends died and her killer will continue through life, free of any punishment.

I was slung out of a vehicle at more than one hundred miles per hour and landed head first. But, why was I given a second chance and not Jordan? What had I done to deserve keeping my life? It really makes me stop and think about all of the times I maybe wasn't the nicest person to my friends and family. Or times I would slop my way through something instead of doing my best. I thought about these things and compared it to everything I knew about Jordan. She was an amazing person in every manner. Kind, selfless, extremely positive, and genuine.

Stop for a second and think how that makes you feel. Does it hurt? What questions would you have if this were your friend? I sure know how it makes me feel and all of the questions it makes me ask. But in all honesty, have you ever stopped and wondered why you're not one of the horrifying stories on the news, or why you're still alive?

Jordan's death really put things into perspective for me. It helped me to realize that I was given a very special opportunity. One that should not be wasted or forgotten.

She is one of the people who I am living my life for right now. It's people like her who drive me to be twice as productive and to live my life with double the gratitude. I don't know if other people who have had a experience similar to mine feel this way, but I can't understand why people like her weren't given the second chance they deserve. I feel it is almost an obligation to live an impactful life, as a tribute to the one they lost.

The pressuring question that drives me to be a better person is never knowing what people like her would've done with their lives. Jordan, patients in the trauma center, and people all around the world have their lives taken from them instantly. Do you know how guilty I would feel if I was lucky enough to get a second chance, but horrible enough to waste it? Who knows what all of these people could've turned out to be. What if they could've found the cure to cancer or invented the next great gadget. They may have found a way to change the lives of millions of people or make the world a happier place. We'll never know. This is why I feel I have to be the best person I can possibly be. It's the respectful, right thing to do. But no matter how productive, successful and happy I am, I will still always ask the question: Why me?

You Can Always Dig a Hole Deeper

From this point on, things started sliding down a slippery slope. To be honest, I couldn't tell you what inspired me to take a complete U-turn on the progress I was making, but I did. My girlfriend dumped me; I felt limited when compared to my friends; a girl I knew and loved like a sister had died; and I still had this debilitating condition controlling my body. A condition that I constantly had to battle. Was it the money? The fame I felt from telling my story? Did I think I was invincible? I truly don't know what stopped me from the positive momentum I had going for me. And to make things worse, my life had become an aphrodisiac for accidents. The car I purchased had become even more broken, worn, and damaged than I was. Especially one evening when my mom and I drove to the store to pick up gifts for Morgan's and Logan's birthdays.

"Ready?" my mom asked from front door of our home.

"Yes. Can I drive us?" I begged.

My mom's face squinted in hesitancy. She would much rather be the person behind the steering wheel but at the same time I needed more practice. If she never gave me an opportunity to improve, I would forever be a danger to myself and others.

"Fine," she responded sharply.

I floated past her at the front door and into my driver's seat. The metal key in my hand was glistening from the setting sun.

After mom climbed in the car I buckled up and instructed her to do the same. We slowly coasted away from my house and onto a busy street. To her surprise, I was driving great. Blinkers were utilized and side mirrors were being checked. I never took my eyes off of the road or let things inside the vehicle like the stereo or my phone distract me. This smooth, controlled ride continued all the way to the superstore that housed gifts for my siblings.

"Alright, just drive to the back and park somewhere over there," My mom pointed to a part of the massive parking lot that was far from any other cars or objects.

"Look! Let's get that one!" I shouted after seeing a car pulling out of a parking spot closest to the store's entrance. The available parking spot had a car to the left and a grassy curb with a new fire hydrant to the right. I was confident in my ability to slip between the two objects and slide right into my premium spot.

"Be careful," she instructed.

I eased my car's hood into the parking spot. The neutral coasting I did wasn't quiet getting me into the spot fully so I decided to tap the gas petal just a tad to nudge myself into the parking spot. Now, it's common sense to think that the next step is to press down on the brake petal and turn the car off, right?

I wish things went that way. I really do.

Instead of braking, I forgot to take my foot off of the gas petal. When I went to mash down on what I thought was the brake petal, I caused the vehicle to huff forward with a fast jolt. My car punched forward but I was able to whip the steering wheel to the right just in time to avoid crashing into the parked car in front of me. The fire hydrant wasn't so lucky; it took all of the impact. The underbelly of my car crinkled over the yellow hydrant and water began rushing out. Although I was furious at the mistake I had made, I did envy my quick reaction time. At least now you could say I was even closer to the store's entrance.

"Ryan!" my mom screamed.

RYAN TROUTMAN

I was silent.

Inside my head I was throwing a tantrum. If Patty found out about this, I would never get another chance to take that test. I lunged out of the car and began stomping around in a furious frustration. My mom watched as I felt that my world had ended. She reached into her purse and called Tony.

"Hey. Come up to Target. We got into an accident."

Tony's heart began pounding, "Is everyone alright?! Are you safe now?!"

"Yes. No other cars were involved."

"So…" Tony awaited a full explanation.

"We drove over a fire hydrant. We're sitting on top of it now. It's spraying us with water."

"I'll be right there."

Tony arrived minutes later and got out of his car far away enough to avoid what was now a growing puddle. He stared at my face and could see the ballistic temper I had burning inside me.

"You get a car and the first thing you do is take it out on the water for a quick sail?" He tried bringing humor to lighten the mood.

I found nothing funny. What seemed like a brighter future was now floating right past me. I would now have to get a ride from everyone for the rest of my life. The idea of this made my blood boil even more.

People around me began to stare at the mess I had made. A nearby woman dialed the non-emergency police phone number and ordered an office to come check out the situation. Mom and Tony were frustrated but knew things could've been much worse. The people around me had no idea of my background. They didn't know that I had just ruined my ability to take a driving test at a rehabilitation center where I worked on my recovery for eight long weeks.

The officer arrived and was amused. His stout mustache hid his inevitable smile. As long as everyone was safe, it seemed like a joke. Well, at least to everyone but me. I was still parading around the massive parking lot kicking things and flailing my arms around angrily. Tony marched over and told me to calm down. He told me I was going to get a ticket but that is going to happen whether I liked it or not.

"DON'T TELL PATTY! PLEASE!" I screamed.

"Dude, I'm not going to tattle to Patty. You're safe, this situation is getting taken care of, and your car will get fixed. Now get back over here so we can finish up and leave," he ordered.

I followed him back to my mounted car where the officer had finished his work and left. My mom was pleased Tony was able to bring my emotions down and stop me from parading around the parking lot. Since Tony ordered me to end my tantrum, I switched to being completely silent and shut in. I made no sounds or notions to anything going on around me. Not even when the store's staff were leaving and loudly singing, "row, row, row your boat gently down the stream."

The following day must have been an act of rebellion against life. My car was in the shop getting fixed, the parking lot I ruined was still drowning underwater, and I didn't know what to do with myself. High school wasn't all it was hyped up to be and I was being smothered by one stressful situation after another. The slippery slope I mentioned was getting slicker. In fact, I was so gullible I would let anyone talk me into doing anything. But the worst was being convinced to do something I would've never imagined doing. Reflecting on this time of my life I can point to decision after decision that began with just that—me being gullible and convinced to do something dumb.

"Hey man, want to skitch near the beach?" my friend Tanner texted me one weekend morning.

His question had just awakened me to an activity I had never heard of before. The word "skitch" had to be somewhere on the Internet so I decided to lunge out of my bed and into my computer chair for some serious research. Google's powerful search engine not only defined the word but it also posted videos of kids my age making dumb decisions. Decisions, which at the time, totally enthralled all of my senses.

Skitching involved hanging onto the back of a moving car while riding a skateboard. Sounds like the worst possible risk I could take knowing all of things I've been through, right? Well, I stupidly texted back, "Yes! Let's roll."

We drove to a quiet two-lane road closest to the ocean. Palm trees lined the curbs and offered shade to the sleeping homeless. Strong gusts of wind combatted the bicyclists and skaters trying to get in their daily exercise.

Tanner's tall, slinky figure towered over his lowered street car. He had a knack for cars, and his Scion was one that had been greatly transformed. An important part of the exhaust that regulates the toxic emissions had been removed to give it a raspy, race car sound. The interior's bucket seats were weathered and smelled of cheap fabric. The sunroof was slightly jammed and let in droplets anytime there was a thunderstorm. Although the makeshift customizations didn't make the car very appealing, there was one thing it surely was able to do and that was drive.

"Alright, dude. You wanna go first?" he pressured me. I didn't quite understand why Tanner was so eager for me to unsafely soar down the road without a helmet. And, I never chose to stop and ask why.

"I guess," my voice was uncertain. It shook with hesitancy. The idea of hitting the ground head first flashed through my mind over and over again.

I planted my feet onto the long gravity board and grasped onto the trunk of his car. There wasn't any handles and certainly not a seatbelt or airbag. Just me, a board with wheels, and a whole lot of speed. The neon wheels began rotating beneath me.

"Hang on! Here we go!" he shouted out the driver's window.

The car gradually accelerated. Local beach dwellers stopped and stared at the entertaining stunt. As bad as it may sound, they wanted me to fall. Sort of like when you see a clown taunting a bull. While the running and dodging is mildly amusing, its horns driving that silly clown in the air and against the railing is exactly what you paid to see.

My board was swiftly coasting down the pavement. I began to experience speed wobbles and gripped a spot on the trunk even tighter. A spot that if anything was to happen, it would just be me and the open pavement.

God only knows how fast I was going. I knew if I came off of the board, I would be dead. My body surely couldn't take hitting another hard pavement. If I fell, there would be no way to cover my head; it was bound to hit the concrete.

"Yo! Slow down a bit!" I screamed back.

"Alright, little baby. Want me to hold your hand and roll you down the road?" he popped off at me.

I didn't appreciate his sarcasm. Or anyone's to be exact. How did he not see this through my eyes? The better question was why did I try this in the first place? If I would've fallen off that board, I'd have nobody to blame but myself and I would have made my family revisit the most horrific time of our lives. Many times, the hardships we face are results of our own actions and warped decisions. I honestly have no idea why something like skitching never registered as an extreme sport—entirely too dangerous to consider. Thinking back, I am ashamed that I would gamble the miracle of my life that I so graciously was granted not once but twice. Would anyone else in the trauma hospital make a poor decision like that? I think back to the boy who died from the same brain injury just across the hall from me in the PICU. Had he survived, would he carelessly believe he was invincible like I did? Or would he remember that one poor decision that cost him his life? For me, the question is would I remember that car ride home from a night of fun that could've ended my entire life? Now I was doing stupid action stunts like skitching. Why? What was I thinking? Who was I trying to become other than a better version of myself?

I guess I still hadn't learned my lesson.

What was my life becoming? Clutter everywhere, constant risk taking, unhealthy friendships, on top of piss-poor decision making. That's what. Aside from making one of the dumbest decisions I possibly could, I figured the remainder of my day would go as normal. Video games, junk food snacks, and TV shows. All in the comfort of my safe little bedroom.

I wish things were that simple. Because the next day after class, I noticed a message appear on my computer screen. Surprisingly, it was from Oliver. One of many people who had seemed to had lost interest in me once I opened my eyes at the trauma hospital.

I read his message: "Hey, dude. What are you up to tonight?"

He must have exhausted all options before contacting me. I didn't want to tell him what I really planned on doing. It may have excluded me from whatever his plans were. Imagined if I responded with, "Probably playing World of Warcraft until my mom finished cooking her awesome country fried steak then going back to my games until my eyes pop out." I surely would lose any cool points I had remaining.

Instead, I slyly responded, "Not much. What are you up to?"

I stared blankly back at the screen waiting for an answer. I had no idea if he was even in front of his computer but that didn't matter. I needed this. You can only cast so many spells or adorn new armor in a video game before you realize that you're still lonely. The people I had hung out with up to this point weren't filling my void of friendship.

Minutes passed and I saw no response to my message. I worried that I was too late. I waited too long because I was stuck in a classroom learning about people's hobbies. All I wanted was a life. I didn't care about sharpening my grammatical skills or improving my vocabulary. Sure, I wanted to be a better person but I felt that started with an active, social life.

RYAN TROUTMAN

How can I be a better person and do great things, if no one ever notices me?

My excitement sank when the screensaver danced across the screen. I fell backwards into my bed and imagined taking a course on how to get friends. I began thinking about all of the ways I could've ended up. There wasn't much to complain about. I could've been a vegetable or died the moment I catapulted into the wall. There was even a possibility I'd have to lose a limb. But all I really lost were friends and a social life. My thoughts deepened before getting interrupted by a buzzing alarm. It was my computer!

I raced over and shook the mouse to dismiss the screen saver. I got Oliver's response, and it was the one I had hoped for. The small beady font read, "Oh, I was seeing if you wanted to hang out tonight. Me and a couple of friends are going to the hookah lounge."

I froze. Should I really be smoking tobacco? I was still early in my recovery stage and felt that huffing smoke would do nothing but slow my success. But, I let the idea of friendship consume me—again. I needed to do this.

Thinking quickly, I ran into the living room and made a request. "Hey, ma. My friend invited me over to spend the night. He just got a new game and wanted me to check it out," I lied. It didn't feel good lying to my parents but at the same time I felt it was a necessary evil.

"Who's picking you up and where are you staying?" The parental interrogation began. I glared back at my mom with the softest, sweetest eyes I could muster.

"Oliver is picking me up. We're just going to his house right down the road. He has a new game we're going to play."

My mom hesitated.

"Alright. But I want to know when you get there," she replied. She wanted to give me my freedom but, at the same time, she was scared for my life. Letting me out of her sight was nerve-racking.

"I will. Thank you. I love you," I ended with kind words.

A race to my room led me straight to the computer keyboard. "I'm down. You cool with picking me up?" I asked in the coolest way I could. Instantly, a response shot across the screen.

"Yeah, I'll be there soon."

I expected that night could have been the start of the new me. Having friends was so important to me because it told me that I wasn't odd. I wasn't the abnormal kid that was too strange to find similarities with a normal person. I honestly would've been fine playing video games, but this new experience could be the missing piece to my puzzle. What would my neurologist think, if I told her I'm about to go stay up late into the night and inhale carcinogens? What would my family think of me? But, more importantly, what I didn't ask was how should I feel about this.

Moments later, I heard a stern knock on the door. It was him. My admission to a more social night had just arrived.

"Hello, Oliver! It's been a while since we've seen you. How have you been?" my mother opened the front door and asked. Oliver was wearing a backwards black baseball hat, khaki shorts, and a slim fit t-shirt that had a catchy band name in bold font.

"I've been good. How has everything over here been?"

"Hey, dude!" I shouted as I rounded the corner of the hallway.

"You ready?" Oliver asked.

I nodded my head and grabbed my backpack. It was filled with clothes, my toothbrush, and deodorant. In all honesty, a giant smoking device would have better prepared me for the night ahead.

"Alright. Let me know when you get there. Be safe. I love you." My mom demanded in her loving way.

I gazed up in embarrassment. "I will," I whispered. All she wanted was to know I was safe. Sending me off on my own still scared her. I understood and respected her concerns but I had just wished it wasn't done in front of my friend who lived a life that better represented his age.

Many of my friends had the freedom to come and go as they pleased. Why didn't I have all of that? Probably because they didn't lose their autonomy as a result of a bad decision like I did.

When we walked out the house and onto the front yard, I saw his car. It reminded me of the slick metal monstrosity I sat in that nearly ended my life.

"You cool with riding?" he hesitantly asked. He didn't know if I was still fearful of sitting in a vehicle.

"Yes," I replied confidently.

The drive was short. He lived with his parents just down the road. After we arrived, his mother was looking out the window. She cracked a slim smile and waited for us to enter.

"Hey, Ryan! It's so good to see you! I'm so happy to see you doing so well!" she said.

"Thank you! I'm excited to spend the night." I responded.

Oliver waved me down towards his bedroom. "It was great seeing you!" I added before making my way from the range of parental supervision.

"Alright, man, we'll head out soon," he instructed.

I nodded and took a seat near his computer. "So, who's all going to be there?" I inquired.

"Just some friends of mine," he said. I didn't really care who it was. I doubt I would've recognized anyone. Oliver gathered his things and shut his bedroom door. "Let's go," he added before we made our way back to his car.

The drive to the hookah lounge was one filled with blaring music and wind swiftly invading through the rolled down windows. I didn't even know what a hookah really was or how it worked.

As we approached the lounge, I noticed that the door was propped open and people were lined up waiting to sit.

"Is it always this busy?" I looked at Oliver and asked.

"It's like this pretty much every night," he softly answered.

We joined the back of the line. Soon we would talk to the host and see how long the wait was. People in front of us would shrug their shoulders or huff and sigh at the lengthy wait.

We were next.

"Hey man! How's it going?" the host excitedly shouted to Oliver. The Arabic music inside the lounge drowned out the host's words.

"He said something to you," I nudged Oliver.

"Oh, sorry, dude. I didn't hear you. I've been good," Oliver responded.

"I got you all a place on the patio," the host said. Apparently, the wait didn't apply to us. The people we were meeting had already been seated.

Thick clouds of white smoke limited our view through the lounge. Beer bottles clicked amongst the loud and sometimes odd conversations. There was a distinct smell coming from the tobacco's molasses. A man was stationed at a tabletop behind the bar. He was continuously pinching bright colored leaves from canisters and lighting charcoal bricks. The bartender was a stocky man in his mid-thirties. He was a very relaxed, joyful person who didn't seem phased by the bar's busy flow.

We strode through double doors and out onto a long, slender patio. Our table was filled with five other people who anxiously awaited our arrival.

"About time!" a red-headed guy joked.

"Sorry. I had to pick up my friend, Ryan," Oliver pointed to his left at my singled out body. I lifted my hand and gave a cracked grin to the seated onlookers.

"So, what are we getting tonight?" Everyone began scanning through the menu. The booklet contained a list of flavors. Mango-Tango or Blue Mist we're some of the pricier options while traditional strawberry and green apple were more inside my budget.

RYAN TROUTMAN

"Anything look good to you?" Oliver glanced over at me.

"I'm good with whatever," I replied partially because I didn't even know what any flavored smoke tasted like.

The waitress walked over and first took drink orders. She was a stocky woman covered head to toe in tattoos with massive gauges in her ears.

"What are you guys drinking?" she asked. This server seemed to know Oliver and his friends.

"I'll take a beer," a guy across the table ordered.

"Double that," Oliver chimed in.

She turned to me with inquisitive eyes. "What about you?" she asked in a more professional tone.

I didn't know what to say. Everyone around me was ordering beer and liquor. How would I look if I ordered a Dr. Pepper? I quickly tried to think through the situation but I froze mentally. Peer pressure was weighing on me. I gazed around the table at the waiting eyes.

"Triple that," I softly blurted.

She glanced over at Oliver as if to get a nod of approval. She wanted to know I was "in" and wasn't going to do anything stupid. Oliver confirmed my coolness and began discussing the next part of the evening's order.

"So what are we smoking?" he openly asked the table.

"Let's just go with green apple," a short, blonde haired girl announced from the end of the table.

"Sounds good to me," agreed a guy in his mid-twenties who sat cross-legged beside her.

The waitress nodded then left to begin our order. Everyone began talking about parties and wild stories of past drunken nights.

"I wonder how Party Fail Guy is doing after last night," the mid-twenties guy cackled.

The table erupted in laughter. I automatically chimed in with smiles and snickers as if I knew who they were talking about.

The server returned with a tray of mugs and a slender metal contraption.

The hookah had bright red coals stacked at the top that burned through to the wet, sticky tobacco. At the base was a glass vase that had bubbling water dancing through the pipe's thick white smoke.

"Thank you!" the girl spoke for our group.

The frosty beer in front of me sat idle while I contemplated drinking it. I wasn't stupid when it came to alcohol and my brain. I had heard countless times how my brain is in an important recovery stage. It's still healing and the negative effects of alcohol, drugs, and tobacco may hinder the recovery process. I was facing two of the three with a decision lingering before me.

Do I consider the long term effects and decline the beer and hookah or do I live in the moment and deal with potential consequences as they arrive?

"You can't drink it with your eyes," Oliver whispered.

Was I embarrassing him? I wondered if the people would still respect me had I chose not to drink. My trembling hand grasped the handle. My lips caressed the chilled glass and ice cold beer dribbled into my mouth.

I felt a nudge on my shoulder. It was Oliver holding a hose that was attached to the hookah. He had the tip wrapped around his knuckles.

"Here," he glanced down at the mouth piece.

By this time the thought of drinking beer had eased my anxious tension. I freely reached out at the hose but when I tried grabbing it from him I felt restraint. He wouldn't let go of the hose.

"You have to tap my hand twice before I hand it to you," he instructed. Apparently, this was common hookah smoking etiquette similar to the policing of anyone who had been hogging the hose. "Chiefing," they called it. I followed along and tapped his hand twice with my index finger. Oliver's palm flexed open and the hose came flinging out. It was my turn. The tip had small whips of smoke creeping out. How many people's mouths had been on this thing?

"Is there a mouthpiece I can slide into the tip?" I openly asked the table. A few people hid their smiles.

"No dude. Nobody uses a condom," Oliver responded. That appeared to be nickname for the hygienic plastic tips that fit the mouthpiece. The tips were available but it appeared to be un-cool to use one. So, I tightened my grip on the hose and brought it to my lips. One deep puff and the smoke filled my lungs. It had a sharp, overpowering taste—like black licorice. I belted out a series of dry coughs. From the end of the table, the girl comforted my coughing, "Don't worry. You'll get used to it."

"Yeah, it's an acquired taste," Oliver added.

We passed around the hose until the wet tobacco had be-come dry and burnt. Harsh, toxic smoke was all that was left after a night of hanging out with my "friends". Doing what friends do.

"So, what else is going on tonight?" I asked courageously. Everyone turned to stare at my hopeful eyes. All of this was so new to me. I stared back at each of them and caught a glimpse of where I was headed. Was this where I wanted to be? I felt guilty every time I took a sip of beer or a whiff of tobacco but the acceptance I felt from partying became addicting.

"Umm..there's a party going on at my friend's place," the girl responded. "All of you can come with me if you want."

Everyone nodded in agreement.

"It's looking pretty toasted," the server said.

"Yeah, we'll take the check. We're about to head out," the red-head announced.

"Alright then, I'll be right back."

The hookah lounge was beginning to clear out. I guess everyone had a party somewhere that requested their presence. I didn't know what it was like to be at an authentic house party. I honestly didn't know if it was going to be like some of the things

I saw in movies or if it would be a casual, laid-back atmosphere. Either way, Oliver's idle car was waiting, and I was ready.

"Alright, man. We'll hang out here for a bit then we'll come home and crash at my place," he said while keeping his eyes on the rear-view mirror.

The drive to the party was a short one. Once we rounded the neighborhood corner, rows of cars lined the streets. People were all piling into a small one-story house. It was around 11p.m., and families next door had all of their lights turned off. They were all probably trying to get a good night's sleep in order to make it to church the following morning.

"We're here," Oliver announced as he smoothly parallel parked between two beat-up looking vehicles. The house was just like something you would see on Adam Herz's "American Pie." The garage had two ping pong tables for the sole purpose of beer pong tournaments. All types of people crowded the driveway talking and joking. Two frosted kegs plopped in the grass just past the drive-way crowd.

"SHOTGUNNN!" a tall, muscular guy shouted to a surrounding crowd. Each person jabbed a key into their can of Budweiser and quickly consumed all of its contents. Through the front door, I could hear crashing cymbals and the tuning of an electric guitar. The people parading in and out of the house were just who I'd expected to see: slim guys with trimmed beards, buckled khaki shorts, a Ralph Lauren polo shirts, and boat shoes. They dressed their classiest to come to a sloppy event. Then, there were the girls who seemingly competed to see who could wear the least amount of clothing possible. Their shorts as they called them were as skimpy as the whitey-tighty underwear I wore in elementary school.

I must've stood out because as I slipped through the sea of clones, I got dirty looks as if I wandered into some enshrinement where I didn't belong. The important thing is that I made it inside without getting into a drunken fist-fight or cowering back to the passenger seat of Oliver's car. Inside the house, people were everywhere. They squirmed past each other in a kitchen that was way too crowded. Beer-soaked playing cards were slammed on to the kitchen table and quarters were being flipped near the stovetop. The scratchy guitar and cymbals were louder in this small space. I glanced over toward the living room and saw a band setting up between the couch and TV stand. I instantly thought back to the last time I saw a band setting up and the ending result wasn't one I was hoping to relive.

I glanced to my sides in search of Oliver. He was nowhere in sight. I now had to wager all of my awkward social skills and mingle with the crowd. Everyone seemed to be in hot pursuit somewhere other than where I was standing. I floated back towards the garage.

"Hey, man!" blurted a stout guy with shaggy hair. *Who was this guy?* I had never seen him before but he shouted at me as if we were old friends.

"Yo," I casually responded.

"You got next game?"

I glanced at the chalkboard mounted just above the beer pong table. The defeated opponents' names had been marked out. The guy was still looking at me waiting for a response. He didn't appear to have a partner. *Had he won all of these games by himself?*

"Sure. Care if I join your team?"

The guy's drunken glassy eyes coasted towards the ceiling while he considered his response. "Yeah, man! Come on!" He shouted and waved me over to the table. This guy had to almost scream over the band which had now began playing its first song.

He cleared his throat and focused on the speech he had queued up to deliver. "The rules are simple. You're going to take this here ping pong ball and throw it at them there cups." It was apparent he was purposefully trying to sound unintellectual. "If you get one in the cup, they drink the beer. If they get one in our cups, we drink the beer. If you bounce it in, they drink two. If you call 'solo cup' and get it....well..forget that. Just try to get the balls in the cups," he finished his referee-like instructions.

"Alright, let's play PONG to see who goes first," he shouted across the table. He leaned in and explained the rules behind PONG as if he was my official drinking game mentor. Each team would throw the balls at the cups while shouting the letters P-O-N-G. The first team to spell it out would get the balls first.

"You're up, my man," he declared while handing me a slick white ping-pong ball.

I trained my eyes on the red cups. My arm slowly cocked back ready to project the small ball towards its carbonated target. Just as the ball left my fingertips a scrawny, frail kid plunged out of the doorway. His face was painted in panic. Beads of sweat or possibly tears coated his cheeks.

"COPS!" the boy screamed.

Before I could even yell my first "P," red and blue lights surrounded the home. I had never seen a crowd disperse so quickly. It was like someone had found the Bubonic plague in one of their bottles. Every person in the garage scurried into the bushes nearby. Someone must've felt it was a defense tactic to close the garage. Bodies slid under the almost closed metal door. I managed to slip out of sight and onto a deserted street towards the side of the house.

"Hey!" Oliver screamed.

I praised the heavens and raced towards his car door. My hands were trembling and my heart was racing. After lunging myself into the passenger seat, I fastened my seatbelt. I don't care how risky things had gotten. I wasn't going to be stupid and fly out of another friend's car.

"Let's get home!" he ordered.

Those were just the words I wanted to hear. But why? After all I had been through, why in the world would I want some young, drunk, frantic kid to steer me to his parent's house? At this point, I didn't know what to think. I didn't know whether to be ashamed of the choices I had made or be proud of my new experiences.

The drive back to his house was quiet. I had my eyes focused on the road ahead as if I was in the driver's seat. No music played and we could hear each other's panting breath.

"Listen, when we get home. We're going through the garage. Don't be loud. I'll open the garage door a little and we can climb under it."

I nodded in response. This wasn't my first rodeo. Climbing under a moving garage door now seemed like a common occurrence. What started as a fun, energetic night had quickly been reduced to a night we nearly didn't escape. Oliver's neighborhood was dead asleep. Every house was pitch black. The headlight's of his car illuminated the shiny sedans as we rounded corners.

"Whew! We made it!" I tried to lighten the mood.

Oliver's stern face stayed locked on the task ahead. We crept up to the garage door's keypad and mashed in the buttons. I was paranoid that each button's beeping sound was a parental siren. The sound following the buttons was even more alarming. The giant metal door began folding up towards the ceiling.

"Hurry!" Oliver ushered me under the what had become a small opening between the moving door and ground. We both slipped into the garage, and Oliver raced over to stop the door from going any higher. In spite of our stealth-like demeanor, the door leading inside his house seemed to be the noisiest of all. The cracking, creaky sound of the door's hinges whined as we opened it to sneak inside.

"Hurry!" he whispered again.

We tip-toed towards his bedroom. Once inside, Oliver raised a hand and gave me a high five. His strict grin had now eased into a smile. I still didn't know what to think about all of this.

"We made it! You did it!" he said before climbing in his bed. I did the same by plopping down on his bedroom carpet. There were sheets that had been arranged into a makeshift sleeping bag.

All I could think was "what did I just do?"

PAYING 'RESPECTS'

"Hurry up and get ready. We need to leave. It will be starting soon," My mom softly instructed. She was dressed and ready to go. Her black attire was proper and respectful for the sad day ahead. It was the day of Jordan's funeral.

My mom and I rode in silence to the high school in a small town near the beach. Long stops at intersections intensified the uneasy feeling in the car. Her eyes darted over at the sad expression carved across my face.

"Are you going to be okay?" she worried.

"Mmhmm" I muttered.

Drivers in nearby cars would stare from their distant windows and—like my mom—saw a boy who looked terrified. A boy who felt guilty.

I would suddenly jolt my head up at them forcing them to shunt their gaze away and focus their attention on something less depressing.

Once arriving at the high school we passed endless rows of cars belonging to friends and family who came to show their respects. My mother came over to my side and held the car door open while I climbed out under the sun's beaming rays. My friend Ivan broke free from the crowd of waiting attendees and began making his way over to me and my mom.

"Hey man, how's everything been?" he whispered.

"Things have been great. Everything's been going good with school. It's been super busy but I'm hanging in there. Still haven't been back in the ocean yet, but I will be able to go soon. I can't wait to go surfing. My mom probably isn't too excited, but I am. I really can't wait. We'll have to hangout sometime soon. It feels like it's been forever. Maybe we could go grab a bite to eat or just hangout somewhere. What have you been up to? I think I saw you the other day," I rambled on and on about the most oblivious things. I was the happiest person you'd probably ever see at a funeral.

But I simply didn't understand. I didn't understand how I was being portrayed to others and that now wasn't the time to be loud and energetic. It was a time to show respects and think about the life of very a special person. I still didn't have a filter on my words so my mother was a little edgy to watch me spurt out whatever was on my mind. She hoped and prayed I didn't blurt out something inappropriate.

"Alright, well I'm going to head back over," Ivan awkwardly responded before tracing back his steps to the ceremony.

"Let's find a spot to sit," my mother instructed.

The presentations and speeches at the ceremony were powerful and truly acknowledged the great person Jordan was. Her closest friends and family recalled moments where she shined the brightest or they shared funny stories about Jordan to lighten the somber mood.

After the ceremony, everyone headed over to a nearby fishing pier to throw leis into the ocean in memory of Jordan. The rickety pier shot out past the shore into the dark ocean water. Mounds of sand were piled up against the splintered wooden columns. A thin metal fence was propped open to let attendees walk onto the pier without having to pay the daily admission fee. A woman was stationed near the fence to hand fishermen buckets of bait. Her face was drooped at the sight of the sad event. Hundreds of people were at the pier ready to participate in this special moment. Everyone was wearing bright, lively colors which is what Jordan would've wanted. Many people were surprised to see me there and that I looked to be doing so well.

I wore headphones that were connected to an MP3 player in my pocket. It was viewed as distasteful and disrespectful. But once again my social awkwardness prevailed. I had no idea how I appeared to others. To me it felt right. It felt like the best way to set the mood. I listened to one song and one song only throughout the entire pier ceremony. It was a song that truly brought emotion out of me and I didn't know why. Aerosmith's voice coursed through my body singing "I Don't Wanna Miss a Thing" and the powerful strumming of the electric guitar resonated in my ears.

Out of all of the songs I could have played. That was the song I chose to play on repeat while I thought of my friend and tossed my Hawaiian lei in the water. I stared at the waves crashing onto shore and listened to the lyrics vibrate within me. In that moment, as I thought of Jordan and paid what I considered to be my respect to her and her life, I thought those lyrics best described how I was feeling.

People would pass by and shake their head in disgust. Some people would stare at me in wide eyes of disbelief that I would listen to music during the ceremony. They may have thought I was jamming out to my favorite artist.

But, Jordan's death crushed me. I had no idea how to respond to the death of a long-time friend. Maybe I truly didn't want to miss a thing. Maybe it killed me to know that she was going to miss everything. That everyone would miss her.

This moment showed me that my second chance was not just for me. It was for everyone who had their life taken from them. Listening to Aerosmith at a very sad ceremony was such an awkward thing for me to do. But it reminded me of something.

It reminded me that I literally scraped the bottom life and somehow found my way out of a closing casket. People near and dear to me didn't get that luxury. It's so sad. This second chance I'm living means so much to me and all of the people in my life. Throwing a lei in the ocean is only a small way to pay respects to people like Jordan. But truly the only way I can feel deserving of this second chance is to do something with it.

Jordan's ceremony finally put things into perspective for me. If she were here today, I know she'd be off somewhere doing great things. It only seems fit that I do the same. To make her proud.

At the ceremony some of my friends would walk up and try and spark a brief conversation. I would take a swift U-turn on my mood and jump into an excited banter about completely random things. I just wanted to talk. I loved talking.

This was such a sad day but I was also energetic and talkative. I just didn't comprehend how to act or how to respond to the situation. I was still socially awkward and didn't behave appropriately. But more importantly I didn't understand what I did right to not have a sad day of my own.

Why not me?

The car ride home was quiet. Steven Tyler wasn't shouting in my ear and the rhythmic instruments were silenced. My mother could see I was lost in my thoughts. She wanted to do everything in her power to comfort me and tell me that it's going to be okay.

"Are you feeling alright?"

I didn't respond. I simply shoved the headphones back into my ear and scrolled through my music library for a touching song. Fortunately Aerosmith's set was over. I found a much more fitting song. A song that hit home even harder than the last. Why was I doing this to myself? Why was I finding songs that made me so sad? Songs that made me think hard about the chance I was given that other people weren't. I scrolled through songs that had the saddest titles. Choruses that made tears roll down my face on the ride home.

I pressed play on Puff Daddy's "I'll Be Missing You." I don't know why in the world I decided to download these songs in the first place but they were on my MP3 player when I needed them most. The songs I played were so sad. They seemed to be the types of songs you would hear in the background of a heart-breaking movie scene. As much as I didn't want to think about my second chance, I couldn't stop wondering why other people weren't given one.

I just didn't understand, and I don't think I ever will.

EVEN PHOTOSHOP COULDN'T FIX THIS

"Time to wake up!" my mom shouted behind my rattled bedroom door.

"Mhmmhmhmmm," I incoherently mumbled back. My mom swung open the door and grabbed my navy blue comforter. The fan above me would soon blow icy gusts of air causing a chill to crawl down my rigid spine. The look on her face was always alert and impatient. Any mom would agree that softly tip-toeing up to a teenage boy's sleeping body, kissing his cheek, and whispering "good morning my little boo-man" doesn't work. This was bootcamp.

My mother would march back into my room minutes later and raise her voice even louder. "I said, 'Get up!' I won't tell you again!"

Yes she would.

In fact I would intentionally fall back asleep knowing she had one more good scream left in her. Dreamy minutes would pass once again before she finally darted into my room, grabbed my jello-like body and stood me up on my own two feet.

"WAKE UP!" she was finally at her limit.

I slumped on a pair of wrinkled clothes and left my hair in its own mayhem. My backpack was a useless accessory as it never had anything in it of real importance. Fortunately for me, I only had to go to half of my classes today. We missed the senior

picture day for my graduating class due to a follow-up appointment with my endocrinologist. The school only allowed me one
day to go get my photo taken.

"You're not getting your photo taken looking like that" her
motherly voice inflected. "I'll pick you up a little earlier if I have to
so you can change and do your hair."

Score.

My grungy look shaved off even more time from my school
day. I was about ready to swan dive in my mud-pit of a closet to
see if I could skip the day all together. I winced at the foresight
of her licking her thumb and trying to rub something off of my
face that wasn't visible.

The ride to school was short; the class times felt even
shorter. All I could think about was dipping out of my mid-day
class just to go get a quick photo. The halls in my school were
bustling with my fellow graduates. Everyone seemed to be motivated by a different sense of urgency. Some of us were pacing
from one classroom to the next to catch the door before it shut
and locked at the sound of the bell. Others were just trying to
hurry through the remainder of the school year so they could
finally get the rest and relaxation they've waited twelve years for.
Unlike them, I was rushing to my guidance counselor's office so
my mother could check me out. After darting through a herd or
incoming students, I grasped my hand around the office door
knob and slung myself inside.

"Are you ready?" My mom asked while eyeing me from head
to toe.

"I couldn't be readier," my natural sarcasm was beginning
to flourish.

My mother drove me home and quickly started picking out
long sleeve button downs and dress slacks for me to wear. She
stretched out an ancient black tie that had been hiding in my
cluttered closet.

"Hurry up and change into these. I'll be waiting outside,"
she instructed while laying the clothes across my mattress.

RYAN TROUTMAN

After quickly changing my clothes and taming my messy hair, we returned to her car to drive downtown. When we arrived at the studio, my hair was slicked back and my slim frame was adorned in clothing that certainly looked as though it was rented. Interestingly, the photography studio wasn't too far from the wall I hit the night of my accident. It's old softening brick walls were dirtied with graffiti and the lighted sign hanging over the entrance had burned out.

"Hello. Welcome. How can we help you today?" A slim, depressed figure approached us. His all-black attire was decorated with pitch white bracelets and rings. Boring, right? This guy seemed like there was nothing colorful going on his life.

"My son is here to take his senior picture for high school," my mom answered.

"Cool. Let's get you over here so we can get ready," he instructed.

The studio was empty at the time. Towers of camera stands and lights were clumped into various corners of the studios pointing towards props and backdrops. The remainder of the staff all seemed to be on lunch break and gazed up at me with a disturbed look as I continued further into their personal space.

"Take a seat there. Put this hat on," the slim man said.

He would be my photographer today and didn't seem that enthused. His colleagues stopped biting into their sandwiches long enough to watch me pose with a smile. This wasn't exactly how I expected this fairy tale to play out. Like any other kid, I imagined today would be a day spent with my friends taking memorable photos, reflecting back on our school years together, and goofing off near camera equipment.

But, no. Instead I had to show up to the studio alone. My friends had come and gone just like they did at the hospital. I missed my big day by going to listen to a doctor tell me that the hormones in my body still aren't behaving correctly.

I had imagined what this moment would be like. In fact, a part of me had planned out the things I would do and say. I even daydreamed about all of the exciting twists this special day could bring. But,my tale didn't have quite an enjoyable ending.

"Smile," the photographer instructed.

I creaked my lips into a slanted smile and raised my eyebrows in strain and delight. My bottom lip was still numb from a recent surgery I had to take all of my wisdom teeth out and my medical braces at the same time. The surgeon performing the operation mistakenly clipped a nerve with his blade sending it into a numb, dull shock.

When I smiled, the left side of my lips wouldn't rise. I stood there, posed with my half-cracked smile. The photographer glanced up from his lens with a confused look.

"You going to smile or what?" he rudely asked.

At least it wasn't as bad as it could have been. If for some odd reason he wanted to photograph me eating, we'd be in a lot of trouble. Because of the numbness, I never felt when large pieces of food were dangling from that part of my mouth. So which would this guy settle with—a slanted smile or a full-sized pot roast tacked on to my chin?

"He's smiling." My mom defended.

The photographer mumbled under his breath and returned to his camera. The group of employees in the corner softly began to chuckle. I had been laughed at so many times before that it didn't offend me the slightest.

The camera made a few subtle clicking sounds and the large flash above me lit my face. The photographer taking the photo seemed impressed by the quality he was able to salvage.

"Alright, man. You're all set. We'll send your mom additional paperwork in the mail."

We left the studio that afternoon in silence. My mom knew I wasn't proud of the photo taken of me. But, I saw through the scars and marks all over my body or the dark blue spot on my nose. I saw a boy who may not have ever had the chance to have that photo taken.

RYAN TROUTMAN

Dead people can't smile either.

GRADE ME NOW

....

This vicious cycle of personality and intellectual changes continued as I persevered through two school years simultaneously
and without special accommodations. On the last day of school,
I brought home my final report card. Throughout the year, I had
earned A or B grades in all of my classes. This even surprised
me. It seemed there was a constant struggle between wanting
to be a better person and partying my days, nights, and life
away. I was being pulled in two directions and unfortunately I
never realized that I was the one doing all the pulling.

The grades blew my family, friends, and medical profes-
sionals away because all through my school years, I chose to
do average work and earn average grades. I routinely brought
home a report card covered in Cs with an occasional D or F that
would get me grounded.

But this time, I was a different person. I wanted to show the
little world I lived in that I wasn't debilitated in any kind of way
and that I could take on any challenge given to me. Tears of joy
rolled down my mother's face the night I handed her that report
card. Typically, each school year resulted in my mom asking
where my report card was. I would always respond with "they
haven't sent them out" and she would later call the school to
discover they were handed out three weeks prior. But this time, I
was proud to present that piece of paper to her. She gazed

RYAN TROUTMAN

down at all four nine-week grades and saw the hard work reflected in my above-average grades.

"You can have whatever you want!" she shouted.

My eyes widened after hearing that. The possibilities of exploiting that grand offer were endless. I could ask for a vacation somewhere or a trip to Islands of Adventure! Oh wait.. I couldn't ride any rollercoasters because the jerking motions could kill me. With theme parks out of the picture, I continued daydreaming about my reward until a light bulb flickered on in my atrophied brain.

"I want a tattoo," I cautiously murmured.

My mother let out a defeated sigh. She wasn't a fan of tattoos. We stood in silence and both thought about my request in different ways. I was only seventeen at the time, so it would be something that she would have to sign a waiver and authorize. I'm sure she thought about what other parents would think of her or what the family would think of her allowing me to get inked up.

On the other hand, I was envisioning myself as a tribal chieftain. Covered in blues and reds and oranges. The buzzing sound of a tattoo gun whispered gracefully in my ears. My mom might have thought that the pain would be too much, and I would settle for a tiny blotch of ink that is nearly impossible to recognize.

But, again, she and I weren't on the same page. The doctors told me that because of my brain injury, I would have amplified emotions and a propensity to addiction. This wasn't a result of either of those. I was simply excited to do something that no other person I know had experienced. I imagined myself walking into a tattoo parlor and walking out in what appeared to be a voodoo witch doctor costume.

"Okay," was all she said.

A few days later, we drove up to a tattoo parlor near our local beach. It was a small, tacky shop with neon lights and Harley Davidson motorcycles parked out front. At first, I couldn't tell if I was going to get a tattoo or into a bar fight with some burly dudes.

"Hey, how can I help you?" a canvased man rose from his chair and walked towards the front of the shop.

"I'm here to get a tattoo!" I shouted with excitement.

The man made no response and slumbered to the counter to routinely grab the proper paperwork.

"I need to see a driver's license, and I'm going to need your mom to sign here, here, and right here," he said as he robotically filed through cabinets to find the If-you-don't-like-the-tattoo-too-bad papers. "So what are you thinking about getting?" he continued.

Honestly, I hadn't put as much thought into it as I should have. Was I going to get H-A-R-D C-O-R-E tattooed across my knuckles? No, because that would be a D-U-M-B I-D-E-A.

"Uh... I want an octopus," I nervously replied.

My mom darted her eyes over at me wondering how in the world I landed on an octopus. The tattoo artist didn't seem too shocked. God only knows what crazy ideas he had etched onto people's skin for eternity.

"Alright, I'll go ahead and get started on drawing something up. Make sure you two complete that paper work," he said.

I began thinking what most people probably think about before they get their first tattoo. Would I regret it later in life? Would it prevent me from getting a job? Those questions and more raced through my mind as a futile plea to stop me from marking up my body.

All of these unanswered questions were silenced by the fame I thought I'd get from being a seventeen year old with a tattoo. It would make me stand out for something other than my injury and disability. It would be a big story that would hopefully quiet the one I had to tell to nearly everyone I met.

"How does this look?" the man said as he presented me with a marked up piece of paper. The octopus had its tentacles blossoming up around a skull which was the head of the octopus. "I figured a skull head would look cool so I added that in," the man said. My eyes were gleaming with excitement. It was everything I could hope to adorn my skin. The tattoo artist waited impatiently for my opinion to become vocal. My mom began biting her nails.

"I'll take it!" I shouted. The words erupted from my mouth, fueled by adrenaline and worry. How bad will it hurt? How long will it take? I asked these questions internally, careful to show no signs of hesitancy. Again, every question was muted once I reminded myself that I'd be the only student walking around with an A/B honor roll award permanently dug into his left leg.

"Alright then, let's get started," the tattoo artist said as he patted the chair, awaiting my arrival. "What colors do you want?" he asked before cranking on the rotary tattoo machine gun.

I shrugged my shoulders and responded. "I don't know, you're the tattoo artist. Do what you think looks the best." The man grabbed a few vials of ink and placed them on a metal plate near the chair.

"Here we go," he mumbled as his focused eyes honed in on the outline that had been pasted onto my leg. The needle dug into my skin. Although, I was able to tell the artist what I wanted, I was never really able to tell him or myself why. Just like the night at The Empire when I donned the X and attributed it to some fleeting lifestyle, I carried the octopus tattoo boldly without meaning. At least not at that time. Every day, three times a day I would coat it with a paste to prevent the ink from bleeding. I didn't want anyone to touch it or even look at it in the wrong kind of way.

The Monday after getting the tattoo, I returned to school. It was cold inside my school building but I was still wearing shorts. If available, I probably would've worn a neon arrow pointing down to my new accessorized leg. As I strutted down the hallway, students would glance down with wide eyes and then turn to whisper to their friend.

RYAN TROUTMAN

Regardless, I walked with a swagger from class to class making sure everyone knew what my reward was. I strolled into anatomy and physiology, proudly showing off my leg. My teacher wasn't amused.

"You're late," she said dryly. Mrs. Johnson ordered me to my seat. Many times, I would get caught passing around notes to other students. What made this teacher the worst was that she would catch me passing a note around and ask me to bring to her desk. She then made it a point to stand at the front of the classroom and read it aloud. She was only able to do this occasionally thanks to many of my notes having significant foul language and dislike towards the class, teacher, and school at large. I would pass notes poking fun at topics we discussed in class or write to my friends what I had planned on doing during lunch break. This teacher had to contact my mother numerous times to inform her of the crude notes I was exchanging with other students.

"Why were you passing notes and not doing completing your classwork?" my mother asked me that afternoon in a sharp tone.

I stared forward in silence, pleading The Fifth.

"I'm taking you to your scheduled driving test then we are going home. You won't be going anywhere or doing anything until you can figure out how to act right in class," she added with a shout.

Our drive to the rehabilitation center was filled with that eerie disappointed parent aura. A feeling that every child experienced at some point in their life. We continued driving until we arrived at the rehabilitation center. It was late in the afternoon and most of the staff had went home for the day.

"Hello. How can I help you today?" asked an assistant behind the front desk cheerfully. Her face was weathered and her body looked fatigued. She sat in her chair for eight hours and just wanted to go home.

RYAN TROUTMAN

"We're here to see Patty for Ryan's driving test," my mom replied.

"Yeah. So I can get my license and life back. I don't see why I was restricted in the first pl—," my mom nudged me with her right heel.

"Follow me. I'll take you to her office," she stood from her long idle sitting. I wouldn't have been surprised to hear a Velcro sound as she rose to her feet.

We followed the woman down the hall and past the rooms where I learned to speak, eat, walk, and function as a recovered human being. I looked into the eyes of newly admitted patients watching them go through the same exercises and fail just as I did.

"Ryan! I'm excited to try this once again. You were mighty close to passing the first time, there is just a few things I'd like to see you improve on. Ready to get started?" she asked from behind her desk.

"Yes. I'm way past ready!" My mom nudged me once more and gave me that familiar stare that told me to clean up my act.

"Does he need complete any paperwork prior to driving?" my mom asked.

Patty shook her head and continued walking to the test car. It was still just a basic, overly safe sedan that had been modified to ensure maximum protection against any sudden bad decisions or spastic movements. The car was cranked on and awaited its new test dummy.

"Alright. Let's take her out on the road," Patty turned to face my mom. "If you would like to take a seat back in the lobby, we will find you when we're finished," she said before taking a seat on the passenger side. "Put it in drive and ease your foot onto the gas pedal."

I jerked the knob into drive and leaned in on the gas pedal. The car huffed upwards in acceleration before I slammed my foot down on the break. That definitely wasn't the best way to start the test off. I glanced over at Patty's motherly face. She

RYAN TROUTMAN

was disappointed in my mistake but knew there was still a lot of driving ahead.

"Sorry. Must have slipped. That wasn't me." My excuse was weak.

She sighed at my poor attempt and cued me to try again. This time, I gradually accelerated and glided the sedan onto the main road with a soft right turn. Thankfully, the streets weren't too busy, and no drivers were feeling edgy enough to run a red light.

Unfortunately, the weather worsened. The last thing I needed was for it to rain. It would make the driving test harder than it already was and may even put the two of us in a heightened level of danger.

"Now, go ahead and merge onto this highway. We'll get off at the next exit and turn around to come back," she instructed.

I nodded in confirmation and began accelerating to sixty-five miles per hour onto the highway. The sedan's controlled momentum was exhilarating. While my friends were out racing their cars or stupidly hitching skateboards onto the trunk of a moving vehicle, I was feeling the safest rush of lawful speeds sitting next to the kind of lady who probably gave her kids coal if they were bad before Christmas. I wasn't on the highway too long before approaching the next exit where I would loop back around to the center's desolate parking lot.

"You're doing great," she encouraged me.

Was she lying? Maybe she was trained to blurt out motivating statements like that. But, there was always the chance that she truly meant what she said at that I'd be in my car sooner than I expected.

The center's stone white walls came into sight as I rounded the last corner. The end of the day was nearing, and there were no cars left in the parking lot besides Patty's and my mom's.

"Alright. Park it right here. I'd like to talk to your mom in private before you two leave for the day. Okay?"

"That's fine. Thank you for testing me again," I smiled.

The two of them scurried behind her office door and began to converse about my future. Patty grabbed a stack of papers and shuffled through them. My mother reached into her purse and check ed to see if anyone had called and left a voicemail.

"Ryan still has some work to do," Patty began.

My mother's face sank after hearing those words. While the idea of me driving still gave her nightmares, she wanted me to feel normal. My mom would do anything to ensure I was happy, and this appeared to be the most impactful way at the time.

"But, he still did good. A lot better than the first time. I'm willing to release Ryan if you're okay with it," Patty positioned.

My mom hesitantly nodded her head. The thought of me jumping with joy made her feel comfortable knowing I would make the right choices and drive safely. After completing their final deliberations they both turned to face the door.

"Ryan!" Patty shouted.

I weaseled my way into the small cubby of a room and stood at attention for my next orders. Both my mother and Patty looked like they had just seen a ghost. Their pale white faces told me they had just made a gutsy decision.

"You're released," Patty said.

My breath escaped from me, and my hands began to tremble. My whole future instantly changed with those two simple words. Moments ago, I didn't know if I'd ever be able to drive a car. I imagined a horrid future filled with pick-ups and backseat transportations.

But not now! I had a sporty car that wasn't too beat up, a driver's license that was no longer medically restricted, and about $20,000. What do you think a 17-year-old kid would do with that cocktail?

RYAN TROUTMAN

That Vitamin C Song Everyone Knows

There were only a small number of graduation ceremony tickets to give to my family and friends, and I chose to give one to my dad. I felt obligated to let him watch me walk across that stage. Everyone deserved to see that. I was so excited for them all to see me take hold of my diploma and life that I really didn't focus on the family drama that was bound to ignite.

I should've realized that my dad would be the only one from his side of the family present. That he would be lonely. My mother's side would naturally ostracize him and he would get to enjoy that moment by himself. But surprisingly none of that happened.

The day before my graduation ceremony, my mom was getting ready to take me to pick up my cap and gown. Although I had a car and license, she still wasn't allowing me to do much driving. Later that day when I had returned home, my dad drove to my house to tell me that he wasn't going to be able to make it to my graduation. He still hadn't found a job so he had to go searching. Apparently there wasn't enough time in the day to make it to his son's graduation and still be able to fill out a few applications.

Interestingly, he attended his second cousin's graduation earlier that day but managed to make it over to my house just in time to tell me how many interviews he had lined up the following day.

You could imagine that by this point, I was way past done.

RYAN TROUTMAN

His absence didn't ruin the day nor did it create a void in the auditorium's seating. Sure, one of my tickets was left unused but it didn't take away from the abundance of love and support I had ready to cheer me on.

I woke up the following morning with an excited smile stretched across my face. The sun's rays crept through my bamboo blinds and illuminated the joy that filled the air.

"Good morning!" my mother happily cheered from behind my bedroom door. She creaked it open and nudged her head through the small gap. The smile on her face matched mine, and we both fed off of each other's positivity.

"Ready to get up and have a great day?" she asked with an energetic tone that almost answered her question for me.

"Yes!" I shouted.

It wasn't the yes she was used to hearing. This time I sounded eager rather than drained. The day would be filled with family and friends focusing their attention on me but finally for the right reason. I wasn't lying in a bed nearly dead nor was I miserably failing at therapeutic exercises. Instead, today I accomplished something great. I powered through the toughest time in my life and came out victorious. This was a hardship that seemed to be everlasting. Many people who went through what I'd gone through resorted to giving up and becoming submissive to defeat. I couldn't become one of them.

I climbed out of bed and began combing my shrubbery hair and even chose to wear clothes that were clean and neatly ironed. I buttoned my shirt, tightened my belt, and whipped a glob of gel through my bangs. You'd almost think the hallway outside my room was a runway. Because when I trotted through it in a confident, proud manner I wouldn't have been surprised to see paparazzi's flashing cameras out the corner of my eyes.

This moment truly was mine.

So, who was I?

I was someone who saw the dark, bottom of life at an early age. A kid who took control during his teenage years after bouts with a few bad decisions and triumphantly began his upward momentum. While walking through the hallway, I passed the bathroom mirror and stopped for a quick glance. I wasn't touting my attractive good looks because they were non-existent. My eyes singled out the dark smudge on my nose and the scars on my neck and face. I was looking at myself in such a deeper manner. I saw something in me that I had never seen before. That something was a win. If my life was a boxing match, this was only round one. There would still be many battles in my future but the determined, courageous look in my eyes at that moment proved I wasn't taking the gloves off any time soon.

"Whoa! Who in the world is this?" My mom joked.

"You look very mature." Tony added.

I smiled at their compliments and took a seat on the couch. As soon as I did, a pack of three dogs sprinted over and lunged into my lap. They were our beloved animals and didn't know how to show their pride other can colliding into my clean clothes with slobbery faces and foul breath.

"GO LAY DOWN!" Tony thundered.

All three of the dogs cowered in fear. But I didn't really didn't mind. Nothing was going to ruin this day for me. I rose from the couch in defense and brushed the loose dog hair from my shirt.

"Ready?" my mother braced me.

I quietly nodded and began walking towards her car. I wasn't scared of vehicles anymore. The times I scared myself were gone and all the crazy paranoia I was told to worry about was absent from my mind.

The drive to the colosseum must've been down memory lane because we passed everything. The Empire, the parking lot where I lost a game of rock-paper-scissors, and even the wall where we collided.

"Alright, everyone should be here." Tony mentioned while whipping mom's car into a parking spot.

We hiked up to the colosseum's wide glass doors and turned in search of our kin. The families gathered outside were elated to take pictures with their beloved graduate. Kids dashed through herds of people to find their best friend or high school sweetheart. The sun was bright and the skies were clear. Nobody was raining on our parade today.

Through the crowds of people, I managed to catch a glimpse of a small, flashing red light. There is only one person who would begin recording my special day that far in advance and it was my aunt. Her short, curly hair was shining from the sun's light. The satchel strapped around her shoulder held additional camera equipment should there be a need.

"Hello! Hello!" she gasped while ducking under a burly man's swaying arm. At this point, her video must've looked straight out of the Blair Witch Project because the hurried, unsteady recording was bound to make this graduation ceremony look like it was a suspenseful, frightening one.

"Hey Aunt Chris! Over here!" I shouted from a distance. She has nearly all of my childhood captured on small cassettes, and I thank her for every one. Those short films were always a reminder of the happy people who were a part of my life. They showcased the times my family came together and loved one another. Videos like those were just a simple reminder that life isn't all that bad.

Pepa and Ms. Rae were close behind her. Their prideful looks could be seen from a mile away. They marched up the stairs and ran to me with open arms.

"Hey, honey!" Ms. Rae joyfully shouted. "You look so sharp!"

"Listen. Let's get this shit over with. I've got things to do." Pepa jokingly whispered. This made my family members erupt in laughter. He always had a knack for making a moment hilarious. Smiles danced across each of our faces as we looked outward amongst the crowd. One by one my family members broke free from the eager crowds and joined us at the top of the stairs.

The glass doors behind us began to open. A stampede of families bombarded through the doors like it was Black Friday.

RYAN TROUTMAN

"Ninety percent off a high school diploma!" They must've thought.

"Alright. You head that way and join the other students. We're going to find a seat." My mother instructed.

"See you soon!" I replied before hurrying off to the crowded line of graduating students.

The music began to play and students edged out of the curtains and walked to the rows of chairs. They lined us all up properly so that our names could be called alphabetically. The black fold out chairs weren't a king's throne but they were pretty close. The soft piano music echoing throughout the stadium began to quiet. The principal of my high school approached the podium wearing a ceremonial decorated robe. The French-looking hat on her head hid her dry hair that began graying from all the nonsense we made her deal with and stress we'd caused.

"Congratulations," she began. My graduating class erupted in cheer. We were about ready to throw our caps in the air at the sound of her first word.

"Hold on. Hold on. I know we're all excited today but I wanted to take a moment and recognize the hard work each of you have put in to earn you a seat here today."

I instantly reflected on the challenges I overcame. A prideful expression made its way onto my face. One that could be seen by my seated family. They all took notice of my response to the statement.

"The road hasn't been easy so far but I can promise you it's only going to get tougher."

Preach, sister, preach! I felt like her words were directed right at me. My head even began to nod in agreement after her last comment.

"Now listen, some of you want to go on to become surgeons, lawyers, business executives, or engineers. Regardless of whatever you choose to do, just know that everyone at this school and in your family believes in you. Nobody can stop you except yourself. Remember that. Now, I proudly congratulate you for all being apart of this school's largest graduating class!" she ended.

The music spiked in volume and choreographed the lines of students who began exiting from their row of chairs. This continued until everyone was eagerly waiting behind the main stage's massive curtain. I listened to the first name with an attentive ear while staring at the long, extended line of students ahead of me.

"You stoked?" a random kid turned and asked me.

"Yeah" I shortly responded. I had no idea who he was or what inspired him to begin a conversation with me.

"None of my family showed up. I caught a ride here with my friend and his family. They said that they can't wait to hear my name!" he admitted. Instantly I was taken back. I realized that having support from loved ones is a gift—one not to be taken for granted nor abused. I'm sure anyone would feel just as bad as I did for this guy. He was just as excited I was for this moment but had no one to share it with. I understand that many blessings sometimes go unrecognized. Having a caring, supportive family is definitely one of them. I couldn't imagine how hard everything would've been had I not had a family that dropped everything to tend to my health and education.

I dismissed the idea of asking about his family. Instead, I put an arm on his shoulder and let out a deep sigh. "It's all good, dude. You know what you accomplished at that's what matters the most. I'm happy and proud for you. Congratulations!" I tried comforting him.

His eyes lit up. The same way they would've had his family shown up like everyone else's. "Thanks, man! I can't wait to walk across the stage!" He seemed a bit more cheerful.

We stood and inched through the isles to take our place in line. We headed for the big stage. There were only a few people in front of us. A jittery chill started to creep down my spine. How would my family react when they heard my name? Would I be able to see their smiles? I quickly stopped thinking about myself and stared at the kid in front of me. He was staring forward out in the crowd but didn't fixate on any specific area. Because unfortunately, he didn't have one.

"Beau Trotherson," his name was sounded over the speaker. The crowd remained calm. A few sympathetic claps sounded through the arena like they were at a golf tournament. To improve this kid's one and only high school graduation, I quickly cleared my throat and erupted in a soft cheer. While clapping lightly, I continued to chant his name "Beau! Beau! Beau!"

He froze mid-way to his diploma and turned to see me. An appreciative smile blasted onto his face. His shaking hand rose and twisted into a classic thumbs-up. I watched his lips silently mouthed "thank you."

People like Beau will never forget the small, kind gesture I gave. If we don't put forth the effort to do good for others, opportunities like that are missed.

After Beau danced off the stage, it was my turn. The woman at the podium straightened the microphone and pulled it closer. She glanced down at the list to discover who was next in line.

"Ryan Troutman."

Before she could even finish calling my name, my family exploded in cheers and clapping. As I walked towards my degree, Tony began shouting. You know that one parent that completely disobeys the requests made by the school to limit loud celebration? Yeah, he was that guy and I loved it. In fact, my entire family completely disregarded the school's plea for controlled applause. They could care less what people thought of them or how they sounded.

Can you imagine what it must have felt like for my family to hear my name called and see me walk across the stage? It seemed like just before that I wasn't strong enough to stand on my own two feet or become mentally aware enough to respond when my name was called. Now, I was proudly walking across the stage, shaking hands, and strolling right into the next big chapter of my life.

RYAN TROUTMAN

Beer Basted BBQ

"Are you ready to go?" my mother asked.

"Yes!" I shouted with a hint of frustration.

My bedroom was half-way clean which made everything nearly impossible to find. Normally, I organized my clutter in piles. There was a pile of clean clothes near my bedroom door. I would rummage through this pile in the mornings looking for a somewhat matching outfit. Next, there was a pile of dirty clothes towering over the small hamper in my closet. That pile is where the dirty clothes went.

Between those two piles were stranded pairs of jeans, isolated socks, and wrinkled shirts that still had tags dangling from the sleeves. All of it was neatly scattered across my wood floor. If I ever needed to find shoes I would just visit a crate in my room that had a clutter of flip flops, dress shoes, and a sneaker spewing out from the top. Everyday I would blindly reach into the crate and feel around for two shoes that felt like they matched.

Seems about as disorganized as my life, right?

Fortunately, I never wore an embarrassing outfit nor mismatched shoes. I had become a pro at working my messy system. One that was being inflicted by my mother's recent cleaning.

"Ryan! Let's go! We're going to be late!" my mother's voice grew in anger.

RYAN TROUTMAN

I took one more dive into my crate of shoes and pulled out a winner. I slipped the matching sandal onto my bare foot and waltzed out into the living room ready to head to my eighteenth birthday dinner. My family and friends were all meeting at a nearby hot wings restaurant that had just opened. This type of food had become my favorite cuisine. Grease dripping, hot sauce slathered drumsticks and oily french fries seemed like the best meal for my initiation into adulthood.

"People are already there," my mother urgently said from the passenger seat of the car.

"Relax! Nobody is going to starve." Tony responded.

No other words were said before our short car ride led us to the restaurant's parking lot. My family and friends were crowded near the entrance's double doors. Some of them looked famished while others cheered and clapped at my arrival.

"We're here!" my mother turned to face me with excitement.

I unbuckled my trusty seatbelt and emerged from the backseat. Ms. Rae and Pepa were smiling and ushered me over to them while some of my friends stared down at their phone's screen. I hurried over to the waiting crowd and was quickly smothered by a swarm of loving hugs.

"You ready to eat?" Ms. Rae asked. The hunger growing inside me forced my head to jut up and down in response.

The restaurant had already pulled together a few tables to accommodate my large party. We all took our seats and began to order food and drinks. Some of us asked for a glass of water while others got a big gulp of sugary soda. No beer. At least not yet.

The dinner was what you would expect. Everyone told me that this was my birthday dinner and I can order whatever I want. Nobody wanted me to short-sell myself on the menu. They wanted me to get the grandest meal possible! I glanced down at the menu and saw:

Wings.

RYAN TROUTMAN

Wings.

More wings.

"I'll take some wings." I told the server. It felt like I made a solid choice. She glanced back at me with dumbfounded eyes. The look on her face screamed *I know that idiot. WHAT KIND?!*

Instead, she let out an almost kind, "Awesome! Do you know what kind you want? There are a lot of great flavors!" Her cheerful act was an attempt at protecting her night's largest tip.

"Hot! Really hot!" I ordered.

My family members glanced over with confused looks painted across their faces. They had never known of me to be a fan of spicy foods, but they kept their mouths shut and let me make my own choices.

The server soon returned and set a plate of wings on the table in front of me. The fiery smell of hot sauce radiated from the warmed plate. My eyes watered from the burning steam that sifted around me.

"Are you going to eat those?" asked my friend Nat.

I glanced up at him with defeated eyes and shook my head softly from left to right. The plate was taken from me and replaced with softer, easier to eat BBQ wings.

"I'm so pumped for the beach tonight!" Nat whispered in my ear. I pulled out my phone and switched the conversation over to text messages.

"Is everyone bringing stuff?" I typed to Nat.

"Definitely! We can unload the cars once we get there."

Our private conversation was halted from Ms. Rae's announcement.

"Time for presents!" she said while grabbing envelopes and boxes from beneath the table. A few of the boxes were the traditional clothes size which usually left me unexcited. But tonight marked the first night of my adulthood. I opened the boxes holding my new clothes, tore open the envelopes that housed gift cards and twenty dollar bills, and personally thanked each person for their gift.

RYAN TROUTMAN

The plates around us were beginning to pile up with chewed bones. Sauce covered napkins danced across the table and a few belt buckles unfastened to make room for full stomachs. I looked over at Nat and gave a slight nod.

"Alright. Thank you for this so much! I'm so happy everyone came to dinner! Nat and I are going to meet up with some of our friends," I spoke to the table.

My eyes scanned the table and watched as people signed their checks and gathered their belongings. After a few hugs and kisses, my friend and I set off toward the beach. Nat's car closely resembled the Camaro I almost died in. It's slick black hood and shining rims brought back memories of the night I rode downtown. A hint of nervousness wrapped around me but I was determined to enjoy my birthday as planned with my friends.

Once inside Nat's car, I buckled my seatbelt and checked the strap to ensure the restraint was working. No matter how eventful the night's plans were, wearing a seatbelt has become a permanent must for me. We drove over a small waterway and spotted the sparkling glimmer of the ocean from a distance. The car was drowning in loud, energetic music. Nat and I tried communicating about the night's event but were silenced by the resounding bass.

"We're here!" he shouted.

We ended up at a hotel overlooking the ocean. The seven-story building was slathered with a fresh coat of white paint and the drop-off area near the front door even looked like it was recently cleaned. Silhouettes of dormant cars filled the parking lot as Nat wheeled in between two white lines.

"Where is everyone?" I asked.

He smiled and looked past me at the oncoming herd of teenagers. I quickly turned to see many of my guests carrying brown bags full of liquor. A few of them had packs of beer huddled under their arms.

RYAN TROUTMAN

"Yo!" One of them shouted from a distance. The look on his face was that of an eager addict.

"Hey!" I openly welcomed the crowd.

The people joining tonight's festivities were people I would never imagine wanting to actually spend time with me. The kids standing before me had no common thread. Some were tall, slinky guys dressed in basketball shorts and a jersey. My hard-core-music-loving guests stood off to the side and the preppy ones stood in front of them; their bleach blonde hair slicked back with their father's finest gel. There were even people who I could've sworn had two kids and a spouse already. But everyone still found a way to party through a night with a kid they sort of knew from high school.

"Help me bring this inside," a girl asked from the trunk of her car.

I had no idea who she was but elected to cram bottles into my backpack at her request. All of us were geared up like alcoholic soldiers hiding our ammunition from enemy troops. Some of the guests wore tequila life vests while others were adorned in beer bottle utility belts. Regardless of our glass armor, we all hid the liquor well beneath our clothing.

"Alright, I'll go check in. Three people can join me. I'll text everyone the room number. Everyone just needs to slowly trickle in past the front desk. Don't rush in as one big group asking where Ryan's party is." I spoke to the group as if I was a commanding officer.

It kind of felt nice to grab the attention of others like that. I had become so used to being the famous "boy who almost died" or "that kid with the brain injury" that it was refreshing for once to be "a boy that had a genius plan."

The way my squadron and I rushed in to the lobby almost deserved a "GO GO GO!" We rushed up to the front desk and instantly found our composure. The lobby associate had a suspicious look on her face.

"Name, please," she asked robotically.

RYAN TROUTMAN

I pulled out my ID and slid it across the table. The three people standing beside me casually glanced around waiting to hear those precious numbers. Three simple digits that would tell us where the wildest part of this hotel would be.

"3-0-1," the associate said while sliding a key card over to me.

"Just go up this elevator to the third floor. It's the first door on your left."

"Alright. Thank you!" I shouted and hurried through the quiet lobby towards the elevator doors. The woman's stare pierced through our backs as we quickly tip-toed through the hall being careful not to clink any glass bottles.

Our hotel room was conveniently on the corner of the building, tucked away from nearby doors. I reached into my pocket and fished around for the sleek plastic card that would get us inside.

"Hurry!" my impatient comrade ordered.

"Relax! I'm working on i—"

The door creaked open and showed two beds plopped down in the middle of the room taking up nearly all of the floor space. There was a desk that had horrible packaged instant coffee and a small nightstand with an alarm that told you when you needed to pack up and leave.

"I guess we're going to have to get creative." I said while scanning the room looking for the best way to turn this place of sleep into a raging party.

It wasn't long before people started beating on the door. Groups would file into the room and start unpacking. In less than thirty minutes, I had thirty people in a room that only accommodated four.

"Yo! Drag that table over here. Let's get some pong going." A guy who I had never met shouted from the other side of the bed.

RYAN TROUTMAN

Who was he? Why was he so loud? How did he even get invited? I never stopped to find an answer. I just wanted to be here with all of these people.

My friends.

The night quickly got out of hand. Shouting, laughter, and loud music caused other hotel guests to call the front desk and complain. While other people were trying to sleep, my hotel room sounded like a rave you'd find in Las Vegas. The ringing of the room's telephone was the first of many party fails.

"Hello?" I grabbed the telephone. A quick silence crept through my hotel room. Everyone knew now wasn't the time to blow our cover.

"Hello. This is Dan from the front desk. I am the hotel supervisor and we received a call saying you were being extremely loud. If you are not able to remain quiet while our other guests are trying to sleep, I ask that you take it outside the building."

Clearly this guy knew I exceeded my four person occupancy. I smiled at the silent group hovering around me and nodded like I knew what to do.

"Alright sir. Thank you for letting me know. We'll be quieter." Then I hung up.

"What did he say?" a girl near the instant-coffee asked.

"He said we're being too loud and that we need to take it outside."

Everyone's eyes lit up with excitement. We were a few steps from the ocean on a narrow street in a small Florida beach town. I jumped the bed and ran to the door.

"Let's go!" I shouted.

At this point we didn't care. We grabbed plastic cups and poured cheap beer into them so we could slip past the front desk without a blatant alcoholic beverage in sight. Some people grabbed a backpack and filled it with a few extra beer cans and we made our way to the exit doors.

Once outside, we frantically ran around the hotel toward the beach, dancing in the cool breeze. The sky was illuminated by bright stars and the full moon shined a powerful glow on our unruly night.

"Come here! I spilled some beer!" Nat ushered me over.

"So, it's no problem," I said. "There's plenty more."

"No, dude! You need to snort that up! It's still good beer!"

"Yeah, man," others yelled.

Someone spilled beer and now everyone was cheering me to get on the ground and snort it up? Wait a second. Hold up.

"Yeah, Ryan!" They cheered and laughed.

Were they laughing with me or at me? I got down on the ground and felt the singe in my nostril as cheap beer bubbled inside it. The crowd standing around me erupted in cheer. I was so gullible that I did anything I was told without first stopping to think.

"Let's go to the sand!" a silhouette shouted as it raced across the narrow street.

Like sheep, we all followed. We crossed the street in a single-filed line like we were on Abbey Road. The sand was cool and soft. Everyone dispersed manically and shouted over the sound of crashing waves. We were free.

But this brief playfulness was soon halted by our intoxicated endurance. We were all drained of what little energy we had.

"I'm done."

"Yeah, me, too."

"Same."

Everyone agreed that the time for relaxation was long overdue. A tight circle formed and cans were passed around like it was show and tell. I could tell by the looks of people's darkened faces that they were ready to go home. It was late and we may have reached our limit on fun.

"Hey, man. Happy birthday. We're going to head out." Lance said while grabbing his girlfriend's hand and lifting her from the circle.

"I'm going to take off, too." Jack added.

The circle of friends broke and everyone went their separate ways. Some people climbed into the driver's seat of their car and fell asleep while others cranked the ignition and wrongfully drove home. A few others slipped back into the hotel lobby with me. Fortunately, there was nobody at the desk at the time we arrived which let us quickly return to the room.

"Alright. Let me pick the next song," I said with an open hand awaiting the MP3 player. The soft strum of an acoustic guitar painted confused looks across the faces of my friends. They did not expect for me to choose such a slow, depressing song. I thought they would've responded differently. I thought everyone knew this song. Nobody really knew how to react. It was such a buzzkill for me to choose this song that clearly wasn't fit for continuing a party.

But the lyrics were perfect.

I wrapped arms across the shoulders of my nearest pals and swayed rhythmically back and forth singing the song.

"Passed out / On the overpass / Sunday best and broken glass / Broken down by the bikes and bars / Suspended like spirits over speeding cars." I bellowed.

I tried to sing along, urging my friends to catch the chorus at least. They had no choice but to awkwardly join in on shoulder-supported swaying. Some people had never heard the song before but politely tried to mumble as if they knew what the next word was. Nat introduced me to the band, so he was the only other person who could sing along to the chorus. But his singing was choppy and reluctant.

"I'm gonna stay eighteen forever / so we can stay like this forever / And we'll never miss a party / Cause we keep them going constantly / And we'll never have to listen / To anyone / About anything."

The chorus was my favorite part. I sung it proudly as if it was written to the beat of my own story. But was that really the lyrics I wanted for my life? To think that I'll be like this forever.

RYAN TROUTMAN

The final strum of a guitar ended what had been an uncomfortable moment for everyone in the room. I still wasn't coping well with social situations. Things like singing that song played out so differently inside my head. I imagined everyone locking arms and singing loudly in celebration of my eighteenth birthday. Those lyrics meant so much to me.

In reflecting, I now know I should've been singing something like: "I'm not gonna be like this much longer / I know I've never felt more wronger / And I should have skipped these parties / Cause they are killing me constantly / I probably shouldn't listen / To anyone who says anything."

That's more like it.

Soon after singing my celebration lullaby, we all passed out on some portion of a nearby mattress. A few short hours later, I woke up from the sunlight and reflected on the night's activities. I started thinking about my near future. Would it be filled with routine partying and poor choices, or was I going to turn my life around? It seemed like after getting out of the hospital I was only digging my grave deeper with the choices I made every day.

MAN, I LOVE COLLEGE.

I started my first semester of college in August immediate following my high school graduation. Instead of taking a year off, I went straight into achieving a degree thanks to receiving vocational rehabilitation. At the start of the semester, I was scheduled to meet with my neurosurgeon for a routine check-up. After that appointment I planned to sit down with someone at a college where I could begin mapping out what has become a somewhat brighter future.

"Ryan, this is the last time you will see me," the neurosurgeon said solemnly.

"But, but, I'll need you." I responded.

The neurosurgeon let out a subtle smile and reminded me of how significantly I had recovered. She told me how I better do something good with my life because I was given a chance not many other people get. She asked me if I was going on to college and I nodded with excitement. I couldn't wait to tell her my major.

"What do you want to study in college?" she asked.

My face grew triumphant. I was eager for her reaction. My entire life I had been interested in the human body. While my mom was in nursing school, I would read her books and try to understand the anatomy and physiology of the organ that interested me the most.

The brain.

RYAN TROUTMAN

"I want to be a neurosurgeon!" I exclaimed. My mother and the neurosurgeon glanced at each other with looks of concern.

"Ryan, you have proved all of us wrong. You are recovering and evolving into a great young man. But, neurosurgery is very tough and takes many years of college and training," she explained. "Based off of your personality, I think you would enjoy and even excel in psychology. There is even a field called neuropsychology that I think would interest you the most. It doesn't require intense dexterity, and I think fits you very well."

Those words sort of hurt to hear. All through my childhood, I had planned to become a neurosurgeon. They make a very large salary and have an awesome title. They are people who save lives and do great things for the community. But, I wasn't capable enough for that?

Soon after that office visit, I rode with my mom to the admissions office at a local university. It was down the road from my parents which would make it easy for me attend my classes. My mom parked the car and turned to face me. She planned to give instructions prior to us getting out of her car.

"Alright, so when we get in here, I'm going to ask them about your classes and how to utilize your vocational rehabilitation," my mother declared.

Thanks to me, my family was now struggling financially due to all of the time they spent out of work to take care of me. And let's not forget the mile-high stack of medical bills. College was so exciting because I didn't have to feel guilty. I didn't have to dig mom and Tony's financial pit any deeper since vocational rehabilitation would fully take care of my tuition costs.

———

"Good morning, how can I help you?" a stout women asked from behind a gray counter. The look on her face was grim and too settled. Everything about her seemed like she might have once before had high hopes and aspirations to live a magnificent life.

One that would be full of excitement, growth, and satisfaction. But now, she was behind this counter, asking every one how she can help them. Did she lose sight of how she can help herself? Did financial stress or lifestyle choices cause her to feel subdued from living her life the way she wanted it to be lived?

That woman made me stop and think. She wasn't the first person of her kind, but for some reason she opened my eyes to how many people were just like her. At what point do we throw in the towel? What if that woman wanted to be on the other side of that counter, signing up for her first semester? Many times, I hear people tell me where they want to be or how they want to live but yet a lot of people never take the first step towards changing their life. Time goes on and every day they stand behind their "counter" wishing to be on the other side.

Because of my new outlook, I couldn't understand why people like her weren't as obsessed about life as I had become. I wanted to help her and everyone like her. I wanted to support people's lives to the point that I held their hand and walked in to a new job interview or first semester class, or sat next to them on a plane as they traveled the world for the first time. Everyone tells me I did something that they didn't think was possible when I fought through the hospitals the way I did. Now, I am reminded of that every time I come up with a crazy idea that I want to accomplish. If I've already experienced what appears to be the toughest time of my life, how hard could anything else be?

Nothing is impossible.

We walked into the advisors office. The lights were turned off and she was working vigorously on paperwork and at her nearby computer. Rays of sunlight pierced through the large window blinds behind her.

"Hello. How can I help you?" the woman's tone reminded me of the lady behind the counter in the other room.

"I'm here to sign up for my first semester of classes."

RYAN TROUTMAN

The woman let out a long, noticeable sigh and pulled out some paperwork from a cabinet. She plopped the stack of papers down in front of me and slid a pen across her desk.

"Let me know when you're finished," she huffed.

This woman wasn't being mean. I didn't have a problem with her but I could just look and see how unhappy she was. Was she just having a bad day? Or were all her days in this office bad?

"Done." I said before sliding the papers and pen back across her desk.

"He also has vocational rehabilitation paying his tuition costs. Is there any other paperwork we need to complete?" my mom asked.

"Just call your rehabilitation counselor. They'll figure it out." The advisor replied before turning to me. She had no idea what I had gone through but stared at me like I had somehow finagled a free ride through college.

If I had a choice between slamming my head into concrete at one hundred miles per hour or finding a way to pay for these courses, I'd choose the latter.

"Alright. Here's your schedule. It has class times, room numbers, and professors on it. That's it. Do you need anything else?"

Again this woman wasn't being mean to me but I could tell she wasn't happy with what she was doing. This advisor probably made twice the salary of the woman at the front desk. Compared to the front desk woman, this advisor is financially stable. She drives a nicer car. She goes on vacations and wears nicer clothes. Everything seemed better about the advisor but why was she sounding just like the woman at the front desk? She had everything she wanted but her voice sounded just as defeated.

"No that's all. Thank you for helping me."

I looked at the advisor one last time then walked out into the lobby to lock eyes with the front desk woman. Their faces looked the same. Each of them looked like life had taken them in a direction they didn't want to go. The advisor's direction just happened to lead to more money but that didn't matter.

Money can't accomplish goals for you.

The ending of that meeting resulted in me officially becoming a college student with my first semester courses already registered.

My first college course was ENC1101. When I walked into the room, I locked eyes with a ton of over-achieving high schoolers that managed to work their way into a college classroom.

This school believed in small classrooms and the one I was in looked like it had come right out of a middle school. Arts and crafts were proudly hung along the walls near the ceiling. A book shelf stood in the back of the class loaded with hundreds of worn fiction novels.

"Good morning! My name is Dr. Clay. I prefer to be called Dr. Clay because I went to college for many years to gain that title. If I wanted to be called Mrs. Clay I would've saved a lot of time and money," she said sarcastically.

The class couldn't decipher whether she was a cool professor that made the class enjoyable or if she was going to exhaust her frustration by giving us unnecessary amounts of assignments.

"Today, we are going to go around the room and introduce ourselves," she continued. I gazed around at the students and noticed that many of them appeared to be much younger than me. Each student cowered in their seat at the idea of speaking first. I, on the other hand, was eager to tell everyone who I was and a classic interesting fact. The only problem was that I was sitting in the far back corner of the classroom. The rebellious section. I always thought of this area of the classroom as a place where uninterested students concealed themselves. Years later, I'm in my first college course and I chose to sit in that infamous section. Why?

"Who would like to go first?" the professor asked. Heads twisted and gazed off into the nether as if something extremely important had just floated by. Everyone was too occupied in their personal endeavors to volunteer to go first. Moments later the professor extended a finger to a random student in the middle of the classroom. I bet this kid thought he was a chameleon and blended in with all of the surrounding desks. You would expect the professor to pick a student in the front row or start in a corner and work down the aisles. Nope, this young kid froze in horror when the pointing finger caused all eyes to turn towards him.

"You first," she commanded.

The boy gagged and cleared his throat. Nervousness crept through him. "My name is Timmy," he began.

Really... Timmy? Where was I? Preschool? I expected college to be like it is on TV. Where students are named Shawn or Brett and wore backwards hats of their favorite beer. I surely didn't expect to be sitting behind belt-buckled Timmy who may have been dressed by his mother for his big first day. But who was I to talk? My mom had dressed me, too.

"Like I said, my name is Timmy," he restated. "I took some college courses in high school so I'm off to a good start, but here I am!" he ended. The professor glared back at Timmy waiting for more.

"Is there anything interesting about you?" she asked.

Timmy spun his head around locking eyes with other students. "I guess, I could say I grew up in Wisconsin," he replied.

I instantly thought of all of the things I could say when it was my turn. *My name is Ryan and, boy, do I have a story for you!* I imagined. But was that all I wanted to be known for? It seems like up to this point everyone knew me from my story. I was always "that kid with the crazy story". But that wasn't what I wanted my life's work to focus on. I wanted college to be a fresh start. I hoped for it to act as the engine to my future success.

One by one, the students introduced themselves. "This is my second semester. I plan to become an English teacher," a girl paused. "As far as interesting facts? I'd have to say that I really enjoy riding my horse."

I heard each of these students briefly give us insight into who they were and what they liked. But what would I say? I was never good at telling short stories and without all the details it wouldn't necessarily be very interesting. *My name is Ryan. I have a traumatic brain injury*, I thought of saying. But an ambiguous statement like that wouldn't showcase how I overcame that injury or all of the trials and tribulations I endured along the way. Instead I chose to show everyone how I overcame my injury. I wanted to prove to myself, the professor, and every student why I wasn't going to let my injury stop me from succeeding in college.

"Alright, your turn," the professor locked eyes with me.

I gazed around at the rest of my classmates. Everyone seemed to know what they liked and who they were. Unfortunately, I was still trying to answer those questions about myself. I didn't want to speak up and say, "It wasn't too long ago that I learned my name was Ryan. I don't know what I like and dislike. I'll get back you once I know."

The class continued to stare me down. "Hello? Anyone in there?" The professor sarcastically questioned.

"Sorry. My name is Ryan." I began. This moment meant more to me than telling the class who I was. It was a time for me to tell myself who I was. It was the first time I consciously chose to not default to my big story. "This is my first day in college. I've lived here my entire life and still don't own a horse," the class snickered and smiled.

I simply left my introduction to my name and a joke. People would notice the challenges I overcame with time. This little exercise taught me to not use my accident as a crutch. If someone is asking about me, they want to know about me, not my injury.

After class, I waited outside like an elementary school car rider. I was waiting for my mom to come pick me up. The sedan coasted up and a pollen-coated window rolled down to reveal my mother's waving hand. "Hello, little sugar-bottomed Booman! How did my little sweet thing do on his first day?" My mom humorously asked. She knew I felt embarrassed about not being able to drive so she decided to lighten the mood with a little healthy laughter.

"It wasn't too bad. We just introduced ourselves and went over the syllabus." I replied while climbing into the passenger seat. My parents lived fairly close to the college so it wasn't long before we were parked out front of the garage door. "I'll go ahead and start cooking dinner soon," she concluded.

"Alright, mom. I love you," I said before casually making my way to my bedroom.

"Hey! How was class?" Tony asked as I walked through the living room.

"Good. I'm excited for the semester!" I exclaimed.

Was this what it was like for Timmy? Did he get a ride home from his mom and run to his room to play video games until dinner was made? Or did Timmy fit the mold for the college student I expected to encounter? The kind of students who are eager to get out of class so they can skateboard home and finish their pending game of beer pong.

One decision I had to make during the beginning of college was what kind of person I wanted to be. I could be the inspiring kid who overcame a traumatic event and lived to give back to his community. Or, I could sulk in my sorrows, give up on life, and fall victim to alcohol and drugs.

LIFE IN THE FAST LANE

I now had a car that I could drive alone and a little plastic card loaded with cash. I had no idea how to manage money or make strategic investments.

"Hey, I'm trying to get some friends together and go smoke some hookah. Want to come?" I dialed many phone numbers and pitched my idea. It wasn't long before I had twenty-two people agreeing to hangout. Only a handful knew about my riches but that didn't matter. I was beginning to feel more confident around other kids and used my story as an icebreaker. Everyone loved to hear how I flew out of a car at one hundred miles per hour and stopped breathing. People fed off the idea of me dying that night.

"Hey. I'm going over to my friend Joe's house for a bit. He's just down the road. We're just going to watch a movie and maybe grab some food." I told my parents as I paraded through the living room with my shiny key.

"Alright. Let me know when you get there," my mom replied uncomfortably.

If by saying "friend" I meant twenty-two acquaintances, then I was telling the truth. I never liked lying to them. But my social life seemed to be all I had at the time. "I will. I love you." I ended before closing the front door. I turned to see my silver chariot eager to carry me to a night of pure bliss.

RYAN TROUTMAN

When I sat down and cranked the ignition, I felt the car rumble as it chugged its first gulp of fresh gasoline. I strapped a seatbelt across my chest and rolled away from the house. My mother was standing outside and watched my car drive off into the distance.

Electricity began to course through my veins. I passed sleeping silhouettes of my neighbor's houses and shadowed trees. Wooden fences barricaded yapping dogs from chasing me down the road. The night had an eerie glow that was cast from the hovering full moon above my pacing car.

It still wasn't very long of a drive before I rounded a corner and saw a line of teenagers ready to blacken their lungs. Among the crowd were a few of my friends already in line waiting to get us a table. Brent was a friend of mine who was nearing the host stand. While I whipped my new car into the parking lot, he stared in awe at the recently polished rims and washed body. As I cruised past the line, I watched him take his boney fingers and make a whistling noise. They were all cheering me on. It felt like it was just yesterday that I didn't have any friends. Then all of the sudden I get a car and money and everyone remembered me. Everyone.

I parked the car and went to join the line. Before I could even approach any of my friends, they were all making their way to three connected tables.

"About time you made it!" Brent shouted. He brought a girl with him. She probably wouldn't last longer than a night. "Meet Sandi."

The girl delivered a subtle wave.

"Let's go ahead and order up," I commanded.

By now everyone had arrived and joined the table. It didn't take me long to realize that there were many people I had never met before. At the farthest end of the table was a tall, blonde girl who seemed lively and extremely immature. Beside her was a nerdy, skimpy guy with glasses and shaggy brown hair. He was probably the dude she was working for a night. Then there were

RYAN TROUTMAN

twins sitting across from him. They both had shoulder length brown hair and big, bulging eyes. They kept to themselves to the point that you'd think they had joined the wrong table. Close beside one of the twins was my friend Jones. He had a burly beard, enjoyed cold beers and jamming out on one of his many guitars. Oliver was sitting across from him and the remainder of the table included a bunch of new faces. Ones I had never even spoken to nor seen before. It felt like everyone I had dialed chose to send someone in their place.

"Let's get Blue Mist, Tequila Sunrise, and Code 69," a voice shouted from the end of the table. It was too dark to see exactly who made the order.

Ironically, those were three of the most expensive items on the menu. I wondered if whoever said that knew about my money. Regardless, I planned to conservatively order a water and maybe a cheap hookah flavor to share on my end of the table. After I finished making my decision, the server approached the table for drink orders.

"What can I get everyone to drink?" she asked.

We had seen this server so many times that she was now considered a friend of ours. She was a simple, smoked out white girl with jet black hair tied off into a ponytail and wore beaded bracelets. Her sleepy eyes and relaxed tone of voice exploited her potentially high mind. She scanned the table to oversee the people she was about to give drinks.

"Beer."

"Beer."

"Yeah, beer."

"Beer over here."

Everyone wanted a cold mug of cheap beer. My original plan was to order a cup of water. Not only could I save a few bucks but I wouldn't consume any alcohol and then try driving home. One by one, they ordered drinks until the choice finally arrived to me.

"And what about you?" I looked around at everyone's face. The looks on their faces told me they expected to hear the "b" word. My feet began swiftly tapping beneath the table and I suddenly became short of breath.

"Beer." I answered.

Peer pressure is a real thing. Nobody checked our IDs or cared to look at my medical records. Although it was a thrill for the other kids, it made me feel guilty. I knew I shouldn't be doing any of this. Even the lack of sleep was detrimental to my recovery.

Eventually the beers were dropped off at the table and like everyone else, I chugged down the frothy liquid. The table was awkwardly quiet and everyone seemed to tend to their own business. Finally, someone broke the silence with the worst possible open-ended question.

"So Ryan, what do you plan to do with all that money?" a voice shouted from the opposite end of the table.

Instantly, I curdled up and tried to appear like I didn't hear the question. Everyone had their eyes locked onto the side of my face while they waited for my response. The hookahs we ordered lined the three tables and sat idle between me and the impatient onlookers.

"I'm not sure. Save it, I guess," I responded.

This was a major let down to everyone at the table. They hoped to hear some marvelous plan to live an exciting, thrill-seeking life. But to hear me say I wanted to just save it made people began to ignore me.

Were these the right kind of people for me to be around? Was I living a life conducive to my health and future? I began asking way too large of philosophical questions. Regardless of how deep in thought I got, I had to snap back to reality and realize that I was losing them. I was losing another opportunity to feel accepted. To feel normal.

After the hookah coals had burned out and the beers mugs emptied, I raised a hand to signal our server who happened to be passing by. She plopped over at the side of my table with a sense that she was too busy to just stop and chat.

"Yeah? Everything cool over here?" she asked.

"Can we get our checks?" I asked with an eagerness to get home.

"Sure. I'll be right back," she fled to retrieve a handful of checks.

I scanned the table and saw the nerdy guy's lips curl into a half-cracked smile. It appeared he had something witty to say and was eager to share it with the table. Before opening his gaping mouth, he locked eyes with me in a sinister joking way.

"Hey man, you're pretty much rich. Shouldn't you cover all of the checks?" he asked.

The table erupted in an agreeable laughter. Everyone began sarcastically chanting, "Do it. Do it. Do it."

I asked myself once again *who are these people?* I wanted to call them my friends but I knew they weren't the right kind of friends I needed to have—especially not now. But to be honest, I still felt like an outsider. I still felt weird and singled out. The fact that these people graced me with their presence was something I couldn't ignore.

My hand shot into the air to flag our server down. She wandered over looking confused. She brought with her a smell of a body that hadn't seen a shower in ages. She stood by my side and rested her hand on her hip.

"Yes?"

"I'll take it all on one check."

Everyone's jaw dropped. I literally followed through with what they seemed to be just joking about. But honestly, was it a joke? Or did they know a helpless brain-injured kid with a lot of money would be easy to exploit? The server trotted off to consolidate the hefty bill. When she returned, I casually slipped my debit card into the black leather booklet and shooed her away to the cash register. The money gave me power. It gave me happiness. More importantly, I didn't feel like the injured kid nobody liked.

When the server returned, I tipped her $170 just because I could. I didn't quiet know how to perceive what had just happened. Was I using money as a scapegoat to artificial happiness? Would all of these people leave me once my bank account hit rock bottom?

I was still on my way down that slippery slope.

From that night forward my life had broken down into shambles. I let money and the popularity I felt from telling my story get me into some serious trouble. The choices I made on my adventurous days and wild nights sent me to the emergency room numerous times. It's amazing what greed, popularity, and immaturity can do to an innocent soul.

Weeks passed and I was beginning to become comfortable behind the wheel. I would drive around town alone in search of places to visit or things to do. Life was beginning to become much more exciting. But there's always someone waiting to rain on your parade, right?

His name was Alan. He was a used car salesman and one night while I was driving down the road he decided to exercise a little road rage. He was driving extremely close to my back bumper in order to get me to speed up. I had learned my lesson about fast cars and decided to continue abiding by the law and driving the speed limit. This apparently enraged him. We were on a one-lane road that merged onto a busy boulevard. The sun was beginning to set and busy drivers paced the roads in search of the quickest route home. Powerful gusts of wind whistled over my windshield.

Behind me, Alan was burning with anger. Road rage is a serious disease and this guy obviously was infected. As we approached the end of the merge lane, Alan darted into a small pocket and cut in front of me. He slammed onto his breaks and came to a complete stop. My car slammed into the back of his vehicle. The hood crunched into his trunk. The smell of heated metal and burnt rubber had become all too familiar. Fortunately, I was wearing my seatbelt so I was tightly restrained and uninjured.

It was still bright enough outside for customers at a nearby ice-cream parlor to witness the entire event. They shrieked in horror. One lady's ice-cream scoop plopped off of her cone after she jumped in startled fright. A small boy tugged his dad's pant leg and asked what had happened. He was concerned that one of us had gotten hurt.

"What the hell!" Alan shouted as he lunged out of his car and stared at the damage to his vehicle.

"But, you cut in fro—"

"I didn't do shit, little kid. You piled into the back of my car!"

"I didn't do anything! You slammed on your breaks!"

"I'm calling the cops," he threatened.

Was I going to lose my license? It seemed like I had just got it reinstated. Some random guy who must have had a bad day at work decided to take it out on a helpless kid who happened to be driving properly.

Alan was in his mid-fifties. He had a tattered face that was worn from lost sales and missed opportunities. He was dressed in a stereotypical car salesman get-up. His navy blue slacks were neatly pressed and his white shirt with the lanky shop crest embroidered on it was unbuttoned to reveal his greying chest hair. His attire shouted, "I can be a cool, fun guy but in the end I'm here to ring you out of every dollar you own."

"Get out of the damn road before you ruin someone else's car," he commanded.

I hopped into my mangled Mazda and slowly wheeled off into a nearby parking lot. Alan reached into his shirt pocket and pulled out an old-fashioned flip phone. He mashed in a few numbers and stared me down with a heated expression.

"Yes, hello? I was just hit by another vehicle. The culprit is standing in front of me now!" Alan paused for a second before continuing his rant. "No, he doesn't appear to be dangerous. Well, for now at least." He flashed a slick, devious grin.

I was close to losing it. Some guy just told the police I committed a crime and that I possibly could harm him! At this point, I matched his anger. I didn't know how to respond other than just screaming at the top of my lungs. As a precaution, I released a deep, meditating breath and dialed my mother.

"Hello?" she asked.

"Mom. I got into a car accident."

"You what?!" Her voice quickly filled with alarm.

Alan eyed me, listening in on my conversation in order to hear my side of the story. I decided to minimize my words. My mom quickly thought through ways to handle the situation.

"Are you hurt? What happened? Was anyone else involved? Where are you?" she decided to fire off every question that came to her mind.

"I'm not hurt. I was driv--" she stopped me. All my mother needed to hear was that I wasn't hurt.

"Stay right there," she demanded. I'm heading there now."

Her hurried voice shuffled out the next question by asking me where I was located. She wanted to see for herself that I wasn't hurt or that I hadn't lightly bumped my head which could lead to more serious problems. I told my mom what intersection I was at and where my car was parked.

Alan's eyebrows rose in curiosity. The annoying smile painted across his face began to tremble at the ambiguity of who I had called. His shiny leather shoes began tapping in hesitation and a glistening patch of perspiration began forming on his over-sized forehead.

I could tell he knew his wrong-doing would be exposed. Moments later flashing red and blue lights swerved into the parking lot just past the ice-cream parlor. Two cops emerged from their cars holding small spiral booklets, ready to ask questions.

"Hello, gentlemen," a tall officer said beneath his burly mustache. He had a hidden sigh in his voice that told us he'd rather be at home watching a movie or playing with his kids.

"Hello, Officer. Thank you for arriving so quickly" Alan said in his best angelic voice.

The officer gave Alan a snide look as if to say, "Cut the crap. I'm not here for your game of charades." Then, he commanded that both of us distance ourselves from the vehicles. He pointed to a crack in the pavement and advised us to stand still and only speak when spoken to.

"So how did this happen?" he began. The plump officer behind him looked just as unenthused.

"He—"

"This kid sla—"

We both shouted out in unison. A battle commenced on who would get the first word. The officers were already irritated but chaotic banter made the situation worse.

"STOP!" he shouted at us.

"One at a time you two," the officer behind him added.

Alan and I exchanged hateful looks. The eyeball combat we were engaged in deterred us from even telling our side of the story. Alan broke our eye contact and faced the officers. He took the lead and opened up with a horrid fable.

"Sir, I was driving down this road," Alan pointed behind him.

"This kid piled into the back of me. He probably was texting or messing with his music. You know how kids are these days. For all I know, he might be drunk or high." Neither officer appreciated Alan's ploy to vilify me because of my age.

"Alright, enough," the officer hushed Alan. "What's your side?" He looked into my eyes. By this time, the sun was below the horizon, and the temperature began to cool. The customers at the ice-cream parlor were dialed into the whole spectacle. They shoveled sweet sorbets into their mouthes and stood in awe at the suspenseful ending to this entire situation.

RYAN TROUTMAN

I cleared my throat and took a deep breath. "I was driving the speed limit and I noticed that this guy was driving dangerously close behind me. I didn't want to speed up and risk bumping into the car ahead of me so I continued to drive at the same speed. Once he had the chance to swerve around me, he slammed on the breaks and came to a complete stop." I said so calmly that I surprised myself.

"Bullsh—"

"QUIET!" the officer belted. "Now I'm going to ask you one time and one time only. Did you purposefully slam on your breaks?"

"No! Not at all! I'm just trying to get home to my family. This reckless kid needs to get some experience being in a car!" Alan quickly blurted. He was witty, quick, and had an agitating urgency in his responses.

"That's not true!" a voice blurted from behind the cars.

The people eating ice-cream couldn't take it any longer. The lies pouring out of Alan's mouth were nerve-racking. A herd of dessert-eaters began to migrate over to our cars. Just behind them, my mom and Tony spun into a parking spot.

"Leave that boy alone!" a woman shouted from the outside parlor's cash register.

"Yeah! You're horrible!" added a young boy sitting with his dad.

My mom and Tony strafed through the crowd and stood by my side. They stared Alan down with looks of disgust. He had no idea what I had been through. Mom and Tony couldn't believe a grown man would intentionally cause a dangerous wreck and follow it up with lying to the police who he had called to the scene.

"Are you his parents?" the mustached officer asked.

They nodded their heads sternly then returned their gaze to Alan. My mother scanned me from head to toe to make sure I had not been injured.

"Are you in pain?" she whispered.

RYAN TROUTMAN

"No. I just want to go home," I responded sadly.

"We will go soon. I promise."

The officers didn't need to hear any more. They closed their booklets and reached for a clipboard.

"Alan, we're writing you a ticket for reckless driving." the tall officer revealed.

Anger bulged from Alan's face. His eyes burned with fury and his hands gripped tightly into stone fists. His response seemed excessive.

"I need to see your insurance cards," the assisting officer asked with his hands held out.

"I don't have insurance," Alan admitted.

The ice cream crowd went wild. I wouldn't have been surprised to see soft drinks and boxes of buttery popcorn go soaring into the air. It was like they were in a 4-D theatre watching an action film about a piece-of-crap adult trying to bully an inexperienced driver. The cop shook his head at the idea of having to fill out more paperwork. The tow trucked signaled the end of our show for our parlor fans.

"We're leaving. I'll help you sort through all of this tomorrow," Tony said with a deep, stern voice. I got in the car with my parents, while Alan got in his beat up car and drove away.

The drive home was full of recapping the accident. While my parents were on my side, they still wanted to see if there was any point where I could've made a wiser decision. Their faces showed their exhaustion. A guilty feeling started to ignite within me.

My mother turned to stare me in the eyes. Lights from passing streetlights whipped across her moving lips. "The important thing is that you're not hurt. Your car will get taken care of. I love you."

Days after the accident, Alan called me and sold me on the idea of letting him use his dealership's mechanics to repair my car. I felt it would be the easiest way to get a working car. A week later, we rode to the dealership to negotiate a deal on my car's repair. The small dealership was swarming with well-dressed minions hustling cars of all shapes, sizes, and colors that lined the lot. A small, white office building seemed to be carelessly plopped down in the middle of the car lot while the magnificent main building beside it contrasted with glamorous clear windows, modern furniture, and flashy vehicles parked in an omnipotent showroom.

It wasn't long before Alan emerged from his white-walled hut with a painted fake smile and extended arm. "Good morning!" he cheered while shaking my parent's hands. He intentionally disregarded my presence. "Come in, please!" he continued his circus act.

"Start telling us what you can do for my son's car," Tony quickly shunted Alan's over-exuberance.

"Well, we're going to take his vehicle to a customization shop right down the road. They'll replace his bumper and any other mechanical or electrical damage."

What?! This guy wanted to take my car to customization and detailing shop? This was a car accident not another episode of Pimp My Ride. But, Alan's tactful skill at selling convinced us to move forward with his attempt at repair.

Many days had passed before I received a phone call. His cheerful voice sounded as if it was holding back important information. "Hey, Ryan! Everything is good to go. Come by the shop later today and pick up your car."

I obsessively nagged my parents to drive me to the lot. After numerous pleas of "Can we go? Can we go? Please! It's ready," they drove me to what looked like a chop shop just down the road from Alan's office. As we rolled up to the rows of garages, a big-boned Spanish man leaned back from the car he was repairing. A tattoo was etched just below his eye with the letters L and A. To make it even more interesting, the letters had jet black droplets hanging in dramatic suspense. Was that how many people he killed back with his gang in Los Angeles? He wore a dirty, backwards New York Yankees baseball hat and his camouflage cargo shorts were torn and stained like the one's I wore the night of my accident. Why couldn't I get my car repaired at the main showroom in the place where I could get a cup of nasty black coffee and flip through outdated car magazines scattered on a table.

"My name is Ryan. I'm here to pick up my car that Alan sent here."

The man looked me up and down with a look of preemptive dislike. He must have only heard Alan's side of the story. "Ey man, your keys are over there. Get em' and go. We got other cars on the way."

Really? This guy was going to just let me grab some key off the cork board and drive off without showing any form of identification. I guess my face looked like someone who had been wrongfully played by a used car salesman. I hurried past the oil stained concrete and empty bottles of Mountain Dew to the makeshift cork board with numerous keys hanging by thumbtacks. My key looked helpless and alone like it hadn't connected with its one true love in more than a week.

"Let's take a look at it before we leave," Tony instructed.

After circling the vehicle numerous times we came to the conclusion that the bumper had been repaired and the matching paint was applied. I grabbed my key and turned on the silver car I claimed as mine.

"You need anything else?" the Spanish guy asked with an irritated tone.

"Let's go before we have to deal with any more crap from these people," Tony openly voiced.

I drove home that day in what appeared to be a functioning car. There was a subtle clicking sound that I attributed to the old, cracked road I was driving on. Alan's resolution seemed to have worked in everyone's favor. He arranged a discounted repair and avoided legal action. I got my car back without expense, and my parents still had a son.

RYAN TROUTMAN

Not even a day later I was driving down the road and heard a metal pin clink and fly out from below my car. Suddenly that subtle clicking sound turned into a loud, blunt snap. Every time I drove over 35mph the snapping sound would drown out any music coming from the radio or any conversations I might have been having. I drove back to the dealership on my own one day only to have everyone posse up to tell me that my car was still safe to drive. Every time I would point to a damaged part of my car they would deny all responsibility. This was the end of my experience with repairing my car through Alan. He left me with a makeshift bumper, a bent rim, and significant parts underneath that were now missing their screws. Thanks, Alan.

'CAUSE THE PARTY DON'T START TILL I WALK IN

The interconnection between partying and feigning friendships became problematic. None of these people were my true friends, but my desire to feel *normal* again, to feel like my true self was far greater a concern than whether or not they are committed to me.

One night, I was at a big house party filled with rowdy college kids. Like everyone else, I shouted and laughed deep into the night. I had drank enough that the tips of my fingers began to tingle and my racing mind was calmed. These sensations were a result of the empty bottle I gripped my hand around.

"Yo! Go to the fridge and grab another. You're not going to get much more out of that one!" A guy who'd dyed parts of his hair with blue and green streaks said from a nearby table. Everyone around him glanced at my bottle and laughed at the comment. Feeling pressured and a little jaded, I began wobbling my way back into to the kitchen. The sandals I had on were tattered. Like most flip flops worn constantly over time, they became paper-thin.

For a college house, the kitchen was fairly nice. It had marble counter tops and an island equipped with drawers of new cooking utensils. Countless empty liquor bottles lined the tops of cabinets. All along the kitchen walls, half-empty and empty bottles of rum and vodka presented their own stories of past wild nights.

RYAN TROUTMAN

The stainless-steel fridge was glistening through the clouds of smoke that drifted around the kitchen and living room—and probably throughout the entire house. I maneuvered through the crowded kitchen spaces heading for a cold beer. Just as my hand went to clasp the refrigerator's door handle, I felt slick tile under my feet. Apparently, someone had spilled beer on the floor and decided not to clean it up.

My foot slid across the tile and flung from under me. Both of my feet swung through the air. My body came flailing to the ground with my head just missing the marble counter top of the nearby island.   Everyone's eyes widened in horror. This was the biggest party fail of the night.

Some people knew my story which made the situation much worse. Others never had a chance to meet me and hear my exhaustingly long story so they just thought it was a laughable tumble.

I reached back and felt the spot that took the majority of impact. It was soft, spongy, and felt just like a bad bruise. Probably because it was.

So much raced through my mind the minute my head hit the floor. I could've died instantly! After all of the hard work and recovery I had accomplished, one stupid mistake on one stupid night could've ruined it all.

I made a few too many mistakes and this hit to my head behind the pursuit of beer was no exception. I scurried to my wobbly feet and glanced around the kitchen at the bulging eyes watching me. "Are you okay?!?" people would ask from every corner. I told everyone I was fine but deep down inside I knew I wasn't.

I was rushed over to my parent's house late in the night. I crept inside and lightly knocked on their bedroom door. This wasn't the first time they had heard that something-awful-has-happened knock on their door during the early morning. "What?!" my mother shouted with a groggy voice as she woke from her slumber.

RYAN TROUTMAN

"I hit my head."

That's all I had to say before she was out of bed and rushing through the door. She asked me countless questions about how it happened and I kept telling her I just slipped in some guy's kitchen. The room was dark but her silhouette moved swiftly past the bed to care for her son.

I told my mom that I truly was okay and that I didn't need to go to the hospital. She continued to remind me that although I didn't feel much pain, I could be bleeding out of my brain and could die days later.

That freaked me out.

I was walking around and talking with no problem. I didn't feel anything wrong and the pain was beginning to die down. But, the thought that something subtly may have happened to my brain struck fear in me. From that point on I felt haunted by an uneasy feeling.

Fortunately, the pain and injury was not as bad as it could've been. I had bruised my head and got beat up a little bit, but I wasn't bleeding. I went to sleep that night wondering if the hospital machines could've missed something or if the radiologist wasn't fully aware of what had happened. You want to talk about an uneasy feeling? Go to sleep one night and truly have no idea if you're going to wake up the next morning. All because you made some stupid mistake—*again.*

For months after that fall, there were even mornings when I would wake up and jump out of bed only to come swirling down in a hazy tumble. The moment I stood on my feet, everything began to spin and I would have an uncomfortable lightheaded feeling. My lack of sleep was beginning to have an effect on me. One that was much more serious than someone who didn't have an atrophied brain.

The point of telling you this side story is quite substantial.

From that point forward, I knew things needed to change. Partying was fun but it wasn't my life's work. It wasn't going to be the one thing I could tell my grandchildren later in life. I wanted to be something, and I wanted that something to be big.

The following week, I made it to class on time. In fact, I showed up early. My professor stared at me with a confused look. She didn't know whether to be appalled that I was making a late effort at coming to class or to jump with joy.

"Nice of you to join us," she would mock. One day, she instructed me to stay in the class while the other students left. The stern look on her face told me she didn't have nice things to say. All of my fellow classmates had left the room and it was just her and I standing beside her desk. The lights were turned off allowing a faint beam of sunlight to shine through a small window above the classroom door. She cleared her throat and stared at me with piercing eyes.

"Ryan, we need to talk," she started. "You have to get a grasp on your coursework. I usually tell my students college is optional and that they have to make the choice to succeed. But, I see your potential." Her voice became mellowed and sincere.

"I know you don't want to keep acting the way you are. But I can't do anything else other than push you to at least complete the work for my class," she said.

It was almost like she wanted it more than I did.

"I know, Dr. Clay. Sometimes, I don't wake up to my alarm or there have even been times that it doesn't work," I lied.

"I don't care! You can't live your life not waking up to alarms and missing every opportunity," the volume of her voice soared. "Every other student in this class seems to wake up to their alarm just fine. I won't accept that as an excuse." Her lips crinkled, and her eyes narrowed.

"I don't know what to do. My injury has made college too tough to handle. My disabilities have made the work harder for me than the other students in this class. I can't really explain why or how but it has been a burden since the first day of class." I lied once again. I was hiding behind my injury and letting it protect me from the bad choices I made.

RYAN TROUTMAN

My atrophied brain was my Get-Out-of-Jail-Free card that I always conveniently carried with me. If I ever got into a dicey situation or did something wrong, I could just whip that card out and everything would be okay. People would understand and apologize for not first learning about the challenges I faced. But, Dr. Clay wasn't following suit. She saw right through my facetious words.

"Ryan. Stop. Just stop. I've taught for a long time. Many different types of students have sat in these chairs and each of them have had their own unique stories. Some couldn't afford college. Others just didn't care. There have been students who thought college was only created to join a fraternity or sorority. I've dealt with people like you, too. You limit yourself behind your injury. You're the only person telling yourself you can't do something. Nobody can help you unless you first accept their help." She had to stop herself before continuing on with a lengthier speech.

"But.. but you don't understand," I gave her my best plea. "I have trouble with comprehension, and my processing speed is delayed. The doctors told me life will be hard and that I will face challenges. They tried giving me accommodations for school because they knew I would need them. I never used the help and, now, I wish I would have. My math skills aren't what they used to be."

I stopped and watched her face before continuing, "You just don't understand. I have a traumatic brain injury, and I can prove it. It is the reason all of this is happening. It is why I can't succeed!" I was pleading my case to this professor. Like everyone else, she didn't truly understand why I did the things I did. She didn't know what is like to go through each day with a mental delay.

"Listen to me. I believe you. I have no doubt that your car accident was horrible. You have experienced some very tragic things. But let me ask you a question?" her eyebrows rose.

I swiftly nodded my head.

RYAN TROUTMAN

"You may have trouble with math. Sometimes, it may be hard to think through complex material. You claim to have a mental fog that apparently can only be cleared by the accommodations you didn't accept. You're telling me all of these things that are wrong with your brain," she paused, still had yet to ask her question.

"But does challenging schoolwork prevent you from hearing a loud buzzing alarm? Do your headaches make it impossible to get here on time? Does having a brain injury make you want to drink the nights away instead of choosing to better yourself?" We stared each other down in silence. She called me out on everything.

Those words hit me hard.

I didn't know how to respond. She exposed all of my bluffs. I felt stripped of the card. She left me defenseless. She didn't want to hear my answers to those questions but wanted me to internalize them. To really ask myself those questions and find an honest answer.

That was the moment I realized I can't hide behind my brain forever. I couldn't continue deceiving people or making them feel bad when I call them out for not knowing about my disabilities. I especially could no longer fool myself. Dr. Clay's words stuck with me and I laid in bed that night asking myself those questions over and over.

The answer to every question was "no." The assignments I had in class were never the reason I decided to go to a house party until 5 a.m. The occasional headaches I had weren't even that disturbing. In no way did they prevent me from getting to places on time. The sleepless nights I had parading around town was the reason I was never punctual. My lack of care was the only thing I was trying to give accommodations to. My professor couldn't have said it better when she bolted out with, "Just stop."

I was beginning to become tired of it just as she was. I still went to an occasional party and would rage through the night with a bunch of disorderly people. The only difference is that I would be in bed by 11 p.m not 11 a.m. I wanted to change for the better.

My brain injury became my ability rather than a disability. It empowered me to seek more and challenge myself everyday. I stopped using it was a ploy to make life easy. I viewed my injury as the greatest thing to ever happen to me.

PLAY HARD, BUT WORK HARDER

I stared out at the sea of students. Each of them had a look that said, "no matter how much you come to class on time, you've already failed." I began working much harder at my coursework. I began showing effort in every aspect of my life. Sure, I had quite a bit happen to me and there was a lot of ground to cover. But I wasn't going to throw it all away by getting wasted and not being able to function as a decent person.

Honestly, college was tough. Without my individual education plan my courses became hard to manage. While trying to find new friends, hoping a girl would look past my imperfections, and rediscovering myself, I still had to keep working hard on my classwork in order to graduate.

I can't stress how bad I wanted to change the trajectory of my life. There were many times I daydreamed about the grand life I could live now that I was given a second chance.

My unrelenting drive to change has sent my life spiraling in an upward trend.

As time went on, I began noticing positive and negative consequences from my lifestyle choices. Some nights, I was bundled up in a computer chair playing an addicting video game. Other nights I was at a raging house party being the person I didn't want to be.

RYAN TROUTMAN

This constant struggle followed me all through my time in college. I made Ds and Fs because I would never show up and there were even times I just truly couldn't do the classwork.

I constantly had to report my grades to the vocational rehabilitation counselor who was funding my college. This lady left a bad taste in my mouth. I remember this one time when she called my phone and asked to speak. She always needed to "update my file."

"Hello, Ryan. I just have a couple of questions to ask in order for me to update your profile," she robotically murmured.

"Alright, I am ready," I sluggishly responded.

"After you graduate, what do you plan to do with your degree? What career are you interested in?"

I majored in psychology so I thought of all of the options available to me. There was always the option of continuing on to graduate school to become a psychologist or maybe a professor who does research on the side.

"I want to become a behavior analyst when I graduate," I said with a hint of excitement.

She chuckled in the most insulting way. Then, sighed and scoffed, saying, "Let's pick something more realistic."

That's all she said. There was no explanation behind why she didn't think that was a good idea. She didn't even follow her statement by telling me about other great career options. No, she just told me that she was going to write down a career that best fits my abilities. The career she wrote down was one that did not require a college education.

Here was some random lady, from a government program that is paying for me to get a quality education. An education that I can later take and do something great with. But she thought she was qualified enough to tell me that my aspirations and goals weren't realistic?

Although I was never able to get her reasoning, it only led me to think that someone who does not have a traumatic brain injury is telling me I can't be like them. I wasn't capable enough. That I'm not like everyone else.

Well, that might have been true because my goal was to be better.

I dealt with this lady all throughout my entire college career. Each semester we would go through the same issue. She would try to tell me that my courses weren't applicable to what I planned to do later in life. She would always taunt me by trying to hint that my classes wouldn't be paid for. There were even times she would hang the thought of unpaid tuition over my head as a way to get me to answer personal questions about myself.

"How much money do you make an hour at your current job?" She would ask.

This always made me worry because I didn't know if I was making too much for them to pay for my college. Let's get something straight. I was not making enough money to take care of myself let alone pay for a bachelor's degree. I would always ask her why she needed to know and her response was "because I just do."

Although my part-time minimum wage jobs weren't preventing me from getting the financial support of this office, I still felt nervous. I always tensely walked between my classes not knowing if I would be attending much longer.

This was the start of my big upward momentum, but it was people like her who were dragging me down. She wasn't the only one. No, almost every boss I had—except Tony—was just like her.

Regardless of the frustration she caused, I was beginning to get a grip on my college courses. In addition to dealing with my vocational rehabilitation counselor every three months, I was doing everything I could to keep my grades up. The only thing I seemed to have trouble with was finding a job and keeping it longer than one semester.

RYAN TROUTMAN

I jokingly tell people they can think of pretty much any restaurant and I've probably worked there at some point. I've been a pizza delivery guy, sandwich maker, front desk guy at a gymnastics gym, restaurant host, barista at Tony's coffee shop, sign holder, pizza guy who just took orders, and the list just went on. I've been a door-to-door salesman and tried to sell outrageously overpriced junk. I've tried driving around town and selling water filtration systems and thousand dollar cooking knives. But I didn't stop there. I've been an insurance agent, a fry cook, a bus boy, lawnmower guy, and so, so much more.

My experience at many of these places was horrible. I couldn't make it longer than a week as a pizza delivery driver because I had trouble with directions even after I went out and purchased a fancy GPS. Then, I was only a host at a restaurant for only a couple of months because I had trouble staying organized and remembering what tables needed to be sat and in what order. As an insurance agent, I sat in a training room with a bunch of middle-aged men who sometimes had two or three children. My youthful face stood out like a sore thumb and it quickly had me searching once again. I got fired as a bus boy because I did not want to climb a giant rolling ladder in order to get some products down from a shelf. I couldn't stop thinking about the Navy man from therapy that fell off of a ladder. Of course they couldn't fire me because of that so their reasoning was that they "had to downsize and no longer needed me."

I remember working for the water filtration company and how miserable that went. Their training involved reading a 28-page packet over and over all day long, repeatedly studying the words on the paper. They did not give us the autonomy to try our own sales tactics. Their instructions had a word-for-word script that started off with "Hello (customer name)." After ruthlessly studying, we all had the entire script memorized from beginning to end. We all made calls to prospects who were interested in having us visit their home so we could robotically recite the script that sells. I made endless amounts of these calls and finally got one family to agree to a demonstration.

I drove far out of my city to this family's rickety house. They lived on the side of a road out in the middle of nowhere. Just me, the customers, and gallons of dirty water that surely needed to be cleaned, filtrated, and everything else I was ready to boast about as soon as we got to talking. When I knocked on the door, the smell of alcohol nearly knocked me over and the woman in front of me had no idea who I was or why I was standing at the door of this horrid home.

But, the day finally came when the career gods graced me. I was unemployed at the time and driving around to find something that I would be able to do. I pulled up to a GameStop and asked for an application. A tall, slinky man with a tattered beard told me that the whole process was done online. He then proceeded to lean in and whisper the words I didn't want to hear.

"But to be honest, man, we're not hiring right now."

I slumped out of that store and was heading back to my car when I glanced over at a corner store. It was a coffee shop with an eloquent sign gleaming just above the front door. That sign was about as bright as the lightbulb that went off in my head.

My family owned a coffee shop that I worked at for quite some time. I knew how to pull shots, brew coffee, and clean up the shop towards the end of my shift. This was definitely a place I would shine and I hoped they were hiring. Everyone loves coffee, right? Surely they could use the extra help, I told myself. In all honesty, I was fired from Tony's coffee shop three separate times for slouching, but this time I swore I'd be different.

Walking into this place was a refreshing break from the typical Starbucks. A delightful scent floated through the small shop. It was a combination of freshly brewed coffee and new furniture. The orange walls were stained. Small tables were covered with magazines and were softly positioned next to every chair. Book clubs, Bible study groups, starving artists, and busy students would all call this place their home.

RYAN TROUTMAN

"Hello! How can we help you today?" a stout man asked me as I strode through the front door.

I was the only one in the cafe, so I braced myself to receive undivided attention. "Welcome. How can we help you today?" he asked again.

I was broken from my gazing trance and looked back at the counter. Honestly, I didn't know whether to ask for a coffee or an application. Both sounded appetizing.

"H..hello. I wanted to know if I could grab an application. My parents owned a coffee shop and I'd worked there for a while. I feel I'd be a great addition to your team," I muffled back at him.

The man let out a deep sigh. His eyebrows softened and he stared back at me with a face filled with bad news.

"Sorry bud, unfortunately we're not hiring."

"I am available for any position. It doesn't necessarily have to be a barista," I jolted back.

It seemed that I had already exhausted all of my other options. Well, at least all of the ones that were "realistic."

This man and I ended up talking for hours. He seemed like a genuinely nice person who wanted to help me but financially was not prepared to hire an additional employee. We spoke about my degree and the courses I was taking. Through the banter, we still weren't connecting. I would awkwardly sit in one of the cafe chairs waiting for the next question or chance to break the silence. Finally, he asked me what that dark spot on my nose was.

The icebreaker.

That was my cue to tell him my life's story as vividly as could. The conversation went on much longer and I wanted to do everything I could do help this guy grow his business. I wasn't worried about getting hired or making money. It just was a way for me to thank him for really caring about my interests. It was my way of congratulating him on being such a kind-hearted person.

RYAN TROUTMAN

For many days, I would drive back to his shop and help out in any way I could. I would stand on the side of the road and hold a sign while waving at oncoming cars or clean off tables after customers finished their coffees.

One day, I was walking inside after a hot day outside near the road. I set the sign down and picked out my day's pay: a fresh cup of coffee and a sandwich. This was the least he could do since I was volunteering my time and effort. While the sandwich was delicious and the coffee was superb, I still needed a job.

"Do you think maybe now I could get an application? I hope I've proven my work ethic and eagerness to be apart of your business," I said confidently.

The first time I asked the man for an application, his face sunk. He declined my request initially but when I asked this time, his eyes widened. I watched as his eyebrows rose into what looked like the famous McDonalds golden arch. It appears he had an idea. One that would be the next step in my life's upward trend.

"I still an unable to hire you," he started.

My face drooped once again. I had given all the effort I could to get a job here and now I braced myself to get back on the road in search of another business.

"But," he paused.

My eyebrows shot up just as high as his after hearing that hopeful word.

"Do you know what you look like?" he leaned in with inquisitive eyes.

I shook my head frantically. I didn't have a clue what I looked like. Maybe a scared rag doll that was thrown around on the road a couple of times. I probably looked desperate.

"You look like a guy who would work here," he said while handing me a business card. "That is my son's business card. I'll give him a call and see if he is able to meet you."

I was standing still with a professional posture, but in my head, I was jumping up and down doing the backflips I was never able to realistically do.

Later that night, I met up with his son at the same coffee shop I couldn't get a job at. The coffee shop that was right beside the GameStop where I couldn't even apply for a job which was right across from the sports bar I got fired at for not climbing a rolling ladder.

I was in college and doing well, and had just landed an interview that I would have never dreamed of getting. It was for a sales job but didn't come with a script or tyrant bosses who wanted their bonuses. This was a job that would later help me find myself. It helped me find the new me.

Life was beginning to brighten up for me. The dark days of lying in a hospital bed and not knowing if I would even be alive much longer were over. The days I would cry myself to sleep at the ambiguity around my future and all that I had lost in the present were gone.

That night I reflected on all that had gone well for me and saw that it as a result of my hard work. I put in the time and effort to recover myself both physically and mentally. I tried doing things for myself and no longer allowed nor demanded people to hold my hand through life. From making peanut butter and jelly sandwiches all the way to driving around town looking for a job. I was beginning to look in the mirror and no longer see a damaged blur. The person looking back at me was finally transforming and re-forming. He was becoming me at my best.

All of this hard work surely deserved a reward. The reward I chose happened to come from a consistent patron at my family's coffee shop. She came to the shop every morning. Both of her arms were covered with tattoos all the way to her inked up neck. She had massive gauges in her ears that looked like they came from an exotic bazaar. Her nose piercing sat just above her lip ring while her eyebrow piercing towered over her left eye. I didn't take this woman for a business consultant or a medical professional but she would soon lead me to my reward. I was helping Tony out at the shop and took a moment to spark a conversation while ringing her out for her coffee.

"Nice tattoos. Where did you get them done?" I slyly said.

She chuckled and smiled.

"I'm a tattoo artist at the parlor down the road," she replied. She would pass the coffee shop on the way to work.

My eyes lit up. This would be the woman to give me my next artistic marking. People say that once you start getting tattoos, you just can't stop. I was afflicted by that craving.

"Awesome! I've been thinking about getting another tattoo," I puffed out my chest and slid up my left pant leg proudly rotating my leg.

She forced a smile and commented on how well I took care of it. She could see that I treated that thing like it was a newborn child.

"Well, I am setting up a table at a tattoo convention soon and still need a person to work on. If you let me do your tattoo at the convention, I'll give you a discount," she positioned almost a little too quickly.

My mind spiraled to what I could get. I wanted the discount more than I wanted the tattoo.

"Let me think about it. I'll stop by the shop and let you know what I want," I said with an empty tone in my voice.

Later on that evening, I drove to the tattoo parlor. A group of bikers sat outside donning their bandanas and gripping bottled beers. They wore sunglasses even after the sun went down. They glared at me through my front windshield.

"Hey, boy. Can we help you?" a biker grunted.

I stared back and felt my heart began to beat swiftly.

"Yeah, I'm here to talk about my next tattoo," I said while slowly directing my attention forward. I stuck out my octopus leg to show that I was just like them. A badass.

"They're inside. Go in and someone will find you." The man said, before allowing me to enter.

RYAN TROUTMAN

When I walked inside, I noticed that the walls were covered with framed photos of all of the shop's artists with famous musicians, actors, and comedians. It kind of made me feel like I was going to get V.I.P. service.

"There you are," a woman's voice echoed from a distant hallway as she began making her way down the hall toward me. "Let's get down to business," she commanded. "What did you decide on?"

"I want a pirate ship," I noted.

Did I really want a pirate ship? I didn't know. But, I was standing in front of her and she was demanding an answer.

She quickly sketched a mock image of the tattoo. It was an outline of a classic battered pirate ship. Its sails were ripped and torn and the wood was cracking along the side of the ship. The ocean water violently whipped around the vessel.

I agreed that this should be the second picture that would remain forever blotted under my skin. It will also be my well-earned reward.

"Alright, sit down. I'll get the outline done tonight and we can do color at the convention this weekend," she directed. I stared back with a spaced out look. Whatever she said sounded good to me. I was just ready to feel that familiar needle pry beneath my skin.

"Ready when you are," I gave her the green light.

She grabbed her tattoo gun and began going through the proper cleansing procedure. It was nice to know that she cared about safety and hygiene.

BUZZZZZZZZZZ

The tattoo gun kicked on and quickly emitted a painful sounding noise. Like nails on a chalkboard. She dug the outline of a ship into my right leg. Like my first tattoo, it also had no purpose. A ship that set a course to absolutely nowhere.

"How does it feel?" she asked.

Just before I moaned out in cries, I looked down at the octopus on my left leg. I've already experienced this. I couldn't show any signs of weakness.

"Feels like they always do," I said, followed by a cool-guy sigh of relief.

I went home that night with the outline of another tattoo that had no meaning. One was an lonely octopus and the other just a stranded ship with no captain in sight.

The following weekend, I went to the tattoo convention to get the coloring and shading done. I brought my friend along for the experience. He was the guy who would back me on all the stories I would have to tell my friends. He was short, like me, and had shaggy curly hair. Occasionally, he would invite me to one of his church's college nights and somehow I always ended up attending.

He drove us downtown to the tattoo convention on the very road where my major car accident took place.

"You excited?" he asked without breaking his attention.

"Yep," I slyly replied.

"What colors are you going to get?" he turned and glanced at the side of my face. I watched the road closely. I surely was not about to turn and stare him back in the eyes. I have had enough trouble already even when my eyes are on the road.

"Don't know," I honestly replied.

Just like my octopus, I didn't know what colors I wanted. To tell you the truth, I didn't even know if I wanted an octopus or pirate ship. They were two choices I made in a swift manner—two irreversible choices.

We got to the tattoo convention and walked through the front doors. A burly-bearded man checked tickets at the door. He reminded me of The Empire's bouncer.

"Next!" he shouted.

My friend and I approached the man and squirmed out our tickets from the tattoo shop.

"In there, on the right," he directed us.

RYAN TROUTMAN

As we began to stroll through the convention hall, we saw things we had never seen before. It was like a contained freak show. People had piercings in places I never knew possible and tattoos of the most vulgar images. And then there was me. Just a guy wanting a modest pirate ship tat.

"Hey! Over here!" my artist shouted. She wore a black coverall that looked like it had been drug from the Renaissance. Her pale face and narrow eyes turned to me. "Let's get started. These people are waiting," she commanded.

There was a small group of bystanders lingering around the booth, eager to see me get inked up. Just before plopping down into the chair, I noticed a small trashcan full of beer cans under the fold-out table.

I stopped for a moment and connected all of the dots. This was her shop's booth, she was the only person in attendance from her shop, and I highly doubt anyone politely asked if they could dispose of their cans. It suddenly occurred to me that this woman could've crushed a six pack just before attempting to steady her hand on my right leg.

"Take a seat," Kate impatiently whispered.

Her makeshift audience was ready for the show to begin. The buzzing needle on the tattoo gun began to whistle once again. An older man was fascinated by the display. He looked so perplexed at the sight of me getting a tattoo. He may have wondered how an intoxicated artist was doing such a good job.

The look on my friend's face let me know that he was ready to leave. It wasn't very interesting to watch but the end result came out just the way I wanted.

The ship had torn and ragged sails and the blood red ocean it floated on almost popped off my leg with bright color.

"Thank you!" I said.

I pulled out my wallet and paid for my second tattoo.

Now I had two large tattoos on my legs and had not given any meaning to either. I had an octopus with a skull for a head and a ship that looked like it was about to sink. Unless I was a captain who once had to wrestle a giant sea creature, there wasn't much meaning to be given. Regardless, this was another reward. It was a youthful treat for all of the hard work I had done towards being a better person.

I was moving fast and couldn't stop now. Full-time school while working forty hours a week was challenging at times but it kept me on my toes.

While attending my classes and clocking in at work, I also had to complete projects for my courses that required me to spend a day at a clinic. The class, "Abnormal Psychology," gave me the opportunity to learn about all of the mental illness and injuries that can occur to the human brain. Ironically, we spent a whole chapter on traumatic brain injuries. I was a pro on this subject. It was as if the material we discussed was already driven into my head.

One day in class, my professor spoke about our next project.

"Alright everyone, settle down. We are going to outline a project in class today. It will require you to visit a local hospital or clinic, and shadow the staff around the work they do," he directed.

Everyone in my class that day grew excited at the idea of an actual clinical setting. This would give us all the opportunity to see if psychology truly was what we'd imagined and if it was what we wanted to do.I glanced around at my fellow students and saw bewildered looks on their faces. They had no idea what to expect.

The professor began listing off places that normally accept students for this project but I zoned out after going deep into thought.

I knew exactly where I wanted to go.

THE DAY CENTER OF OUR LIVES

I contacted the rehabilitation hospital I was in for eight weeks and tried to set up a time to visit. This clinic had not accepted university students in the past, but I thought they may make an exception for me. I called the main office and spoke to a woman who you could tell was anxiously waiting for her quitting time.

"Thank you for calling, how can I help you?" she asked.

"My name is Ryan. I am a previous patient of the hospital and wanted to know if I could set up a time to come and shadow my neuropsychologist," the sound of hope echoed in my voice.

"Honestly, there wouldn't be anything you could do here. A rehabilitation center just opened down the road as an extension of the hospital. I think you would find better luck there," she responded.

Back when I was a patient my occupational therapist always dreamt about opening a day center. She wanted a place where people with brain injuries could feel apart of something. A place where they could practice their daily living skills without feeling incapable or belittled.

It surprised me to know that the center I was about to call was the one she had planned to open many years ago. I got the phone number from the woman and mashed it down on my phone's keypad.

"Hello?" she asked.

RYAN TROUTMAN

I must've called her personal cellphone because that typically isn't the way to professionally answer the phone.

"My name is Ryan. I was once a patient at the rehabilitation hos…" I tried to finish my opening line.

"RYAN! It's so nice to hear from you! You really sound great! How can I help you?" she asked while trying to subdue her excitement.

To tell you the truth, I didn't want to ask her to help me any more than she had. This woman helped me become functional again. She knocked the sense back into me and gave me back my autonomy. This therapist worked a miracle on me and I will forever feel in debt.

"Hi! I am currently at the university. I'm studying psychology with a course that requires me to visit a clinic. I wanted to know if I would be allowed to come spend the day with you," I hesitated.

I didn't hear her say anything. The only thing coming through the phone was the sound of shuffling papers and the occasional "hmm..". I waited anxiously for her answer. Visiting that day center would do so much for me than just completing an assignment. It would give me the opportunity to see where I once was. I would get a chance to see some of the obstacles I had to overcome. To top it all off, I could give the satisfaction to those therapists and show them what their hard work and skill did for my life.

"Ryan, I would love it if you could visit next Tuesday. Does that work for you?" the therapist was ready to pencil me in.

"That is perfect! I don't have school that day and I would love to spend the day with you!" I exclaimed.

Days went on and my excitement grew. I was eager to get the good feeling of helping others who are fighting through some things that I was lucky enough to overcome. At the core of it all, I just wanted to give back the same thing that was given to me. Love.

RYAN TROUTMAN

I readied myself for an eye-opening day back in the rehabilitation center.

When the day finally came, I drove to the one-story brick building stashed away from the road and hidden by deciduous trees. It was like a secret clubhouse and I wouldn't have been surprised to see Brain Injuries Only sign etched in a stone post at the entrance.

My eyes began to truly open the moment I walked through the automatic doors. It was so nice to know that the therapist who helped me recover my daily living skills had opened a center specific to the overwhelming needs of people with traumatic brain injuries. I looked around the building with a little sense of pride knowing that this center was helping people like me feel empowered and a part of a community.

"H...hello. How can we help you?" asked a young lady who was seated behind a desk. It was apparent this girl had cognitive issues. I began stating who I was and why I was there. The girl stared blankly back at me, quickly nodding her head up and down.

"Follow..me. I will take you to her," she sprang from her chair and led me through the corridors into the day center.

Aside from the familiar walls and broad doors, the center looked like it was designed for kindergarteners. It had board games, puzzles, and coloring books scattered across tables. There was a dry-erase board next to the table that listed everyone's name and what their job for the day was. Some were assigned to clean while others helped cook lunch. It smelled like an arts class only the paint and model clay had been cleaned up and put away. The girl led me through a few rooms and I still had not seen anyone. "We are almost there," she said.

She flung one last door open before I was standing in front of a crowd of people. Each person in the room stopped and quietly stared back at me. They had no idea who I was or why I was there. But more importantly, they didn't know that I was just like them.

RYAN TROUTMAN

I began making my way through the crowd to shake hands and introduce myself. Some people did not want to be touched while others were overly affectionate.

"Hello. My name is Ryan. It's nice to meet you," I said repeatedly. I was finishing up on introducing myself when I shook hands with a very tall man who towered over me.

"He..he...hello," he said deliberately.

My jaw dropped. A new perspective ran through me. I was almost breathless. As he shook my hand, my mind flooded with memories of all of the recovery I had done and all of the miracles I received. This man was in my group therapy back at the outpatient rehabilitation clinic in 2007—three years before. He and I were injured around the same time and took this same recovery journey through the hospital together. There was only one difference between us now. I was at this day center because I needed to complete an assignment for my college course. He was here because his brain injury was still preventing him from being able to rightly function in society.

I stood there, wondering, why me?

Shaking this man's hand really hit me hard. I was given a chance that he was not. It made me think back to the front desk lady and advisor. The advisor seemed much better off than the front desk lady. But did that make them any different?

They both seemed miserable with their lives.

The man I was standing in front of still had many cognitive problems. He still was acting like a toddler just like the days we spent in therapy. I, on the other hand, was succeeding in school and performing well at my new job. I was beginning to gain control over my behavior and live a better life. But does that make us different?

We both still have brain injuries.

The thoughts I had while staring at the tall man brought me down to earth. It reminded me that I wasn't too different than they were. I realized I had worked through many of the obstacles they are currently facing and that they are just as deserving of a second chance as I was.

I began looking around the room and daydreaming about the tragic stories each of these people must have went through. The tall man who was in group therapy still hadn't fully recovered. His wife left him and took the kids. His job fired him and he may not be able to function in a work setting. His friends may have forgotten him and moved on to hanging out with more "capable" people. Some of the people in the room suffered strokes, car accidents, or diseases that worsened. They were at a different stage in their recovery. Their injuries were endless but it was certain that each of these unique people were fighting through their own battles and coming out on top.

This crowd of people intrigued me in such a powerful way. It was like I was staring into a window of my past. I saw myself in each of these people.

The tall man and a few others who I had just met moved to the side to make way for a woman who was rushing toward me with arms wide open and a huge smile. It was my occupational therapist and she was absolutely delighted to see me.

"Ryan! You look great! I am so happy you're here with us today!" she said, grabbing hold of me and hugging tightly. I was a result of her hard work. This woman looked at me and was filled with confidence. I knew this moment gave her the assurance that she could work the same kind of miracle on the people surrounding us in that moment.

She turned to the group and gave them a lengthy introduction of me followed by instructions for the next group activity. She and I began working through various activities with the group. I went around the room and partnered with people on completing their tasks. Each person I interacted with had a drastically different personality. Some would not talk or even look at me while others could hardly complete their work from being so social and talkative. Regardless of what they shared with me, I was able to observe the obstacles each of them faced. Obstacles that I had faced—and some I was still facing.

One guy had a pile of puzzle pieces on the table in front of him. They were the overly large puzzle pieces that made it easy to complete. He had trouble beginning with the first piece and called me over to help. I laid the puzzle pieces out neatly in a way that showed a pattern in how they connect.

I could have easily completed this puzzle. But it reminded me of the organizational and spacial challenges that I still faced.

A young girl began shouting for my help. She was working inside of a coloring book and wanted my recommendation on what colors she should use. I set the man up for success by helping to begin his puzzle before making my way over to the girl.

"What should I pick next?" she spoke at a loud volume.

"You can choose whatever color you would like!" I replied with an excited tone.

The colored pencils meant so much more to me than just a way to complete the picture. They were an arsenal of opportunities available to this young girl. Opportunities and choices that were not limited by her brain injury. I spent time with her, telling her that she could choose whatever color she wanted and that she didn't even have to stay inside the lines. I gave her a wide smile and explained that if she chose a color that didn't look good, all she had to do was grab a different pencil and color over it. She could even turn the page and begin working on a totally different picture. I wanted to show this girl that she could do whatever she wanted and that the only thing she couldn't do was give up.

Working with each of them gave me such a good feeling. It was great to reunite with a community I had become so familiar with—a community that I will forever be a member of.

Later that day, the occupational therapist signed off on my paper to signify that I actually showed up somewhere. Honestly,

RYAN TROUTMAN

she didn't have to sign it. My excitement alone was proof that I spent the day at a center.

I returned to school a few days later and listened as we all presented our clinic visits to the class. One by one, students would walk up to the front of the classroom with their shoulders shrugged like they had nothing to say. Some people walked up and began their presentation with an infamous "uhh...."

I glanced over at my professor who looked drained of his energy. The lackadaisical speeches did nothing more than show him that the students weren't fully prepared. Only a couple of students' presentations would wake the class from their deep slumber by sharing some interesting material.

Towards the end of the class, the professor said we only had time for a couple of more presentations. He gazed around the classroom and cleared his throat. "Any volunteers? If there aren't any, I'll start picking," he recited the famous line every teacher says.

My hand shot high into the sky. I was eager to tell everyone about my experience. I wanted to create awareness of the injury I had become so knowledgeable on. As I walked up to the front of the class, I locked eyes with various students. The teacher's pets glanced up from their front row thrones with a challenging, competitive look. They were confident that I wasn't going to wow the professor like they had.

"Hello. My name is Ryan, and I did my assignment on a local rehabilitation day center." I opened up like I was reading from a teleprompter. "This visit was truly an eye-opening experience. I was able to spend time with patients who each have a traumatic brain injury. After these patients completed their rehabilitation at the hospital, they've used this day center as a way to continue improving their cognitive, occupational, and physical skills."

I was losing them. Smartphone lights flickered on and people began snickering at memes they saw on social media. An occasional sick person would make an unnecessary cough that said they were more bored than they were ill. There was even a guy way in the back who put on his overly large headphones and began bobbing his head to music at a low enough volume so that the professor wouldn't turn around.

"I have a traumatic brain injury," I blurted. This surely made some heads perk up. "In 2007, I was in a car accident that put me in a coma. I had to relearn nearly everything about myself and my life. Fortunately, I've recovered enough that I'm able to stand at the front of my college classroom and tell you about my experience at this day center." Smart phone lights began to go black, and the kid in the back even managed to slide one of the speakers away from an ear.

"Those people at the center meant a lot to me. They were part of an assignment but they are also a part of my life. These were people I connected with on an entirely different level. For once, I was able to be on the other side of a very bad situation. I was able to see the challenges I overcame. I was filled with hope that these people were as blessed as I was during recovery." My voice became shaky, and I began talking fast. It was almost proof that I wasn't fully recovered when occasionally I would slur my words or mumble them all together.

Regardless of my articulation, everyone could see how proud I was to complete this assignment. My professor reveled at the fact that he gave me this opportunity. Then, my exciting presentation was thwarted when the clock made its final tick which signified the end of the class.

"Alright everyone, great work today. I will see you all next week," the professor dismissed the students and gathered his belongings from his desk. I was approached by some students after class who wanted details. Like nearly everyone before them, they asked me what it was like to be in a coma or if I saw a light. Sadly, no question pertained to my day center visit or to the class in general.

So, I decided to satisfy these students and their need for gory details. "I flew out of a car and hit the ground head first. My body slid down the road and ripped off the skin on the right side of my body. When I finally woke up, I didn't know my name or what had happened to me." I began telling my story. One that I've told to nearly every person I've met.

The point of telling them the story was not to glorify my accident or injury. I wasn't proud that I didn't wear a seatbelt and that I just so happened to come out alive with a cool story. I wanted to tell my story from beginning to end. I wanted people to realize that it wasn't the gruesome details of the accident that were the moments I wanted to remember. Instead, I was eager to tell the story of how I recovered and how I challenged myself to become someone I had nearly forgotten. The students and I sat on a bench outside the classroom and I was able to fully go through all the ups and downs of my time through the hospital. It makes me feel good when I speak to people about my injury because occasionally I see someone's eyes truly open up. I notice the times when people think back on the choices they've made or considered the future they have ahead of them. My goal was to inspire as many people as I could to break the barriers, take hold of their life regardless of bad decisions they have made, and accomplish any goals they've ever had.

RYAN TROUTMAN

THOUGHTS FOR YOU

I was overwhelmed with a sense of purpose, a sense of fulfillment, and even a sense of confusion when I walked away from the day center. My mind returned to the two patients working the puzzle and selecting pencil colors. I saw my life as the puzzle and this second chance as the colors of change.

Have you ever had a time where you weren't able to complete your life's puzzle? Or maybe sometimes you've felt like you haven't connected the first two pieces. Has there been a time where you have been faced with a tough decision but felt bound by having to stay inside the lines?

We all complete our picture with a different color.

Some of us look around to see what colors others have chosen. Some of us will only use one color for the entire picture. Sometimes we make small marks on multiple pages; sometimes we deliberately run off the edges of the book. And, sometimes, we just close the book and put it back on the shelf.

How have you colored your life?

Every color we've ever chosen has a reason behind it. We thought it would make our picture look good. Or sometimes it just felt like the right color to use. There have been times where we made a mark on our picture and instantly regretted the color we chose. At times some of us have considered ripping our picture out of the book and throwing it away. Regardless of our de-

RYAN TROUTMAN

cisions, we are all given a picture. A picture that without color, is nothing more than an outline.

I felt like I truly made an impact on the lives of others that day. It may be an impact they won't remember. They may not have even asked me what my name was. But that didn't matter. I was happy knowing that I did something good for a group of people while they were enduring the most challenging time in their lives.

That visit to the day center has motivated me to continue volunteering my time in my community. I became addicted to helping others. It gave me a high to see people set goals or take a big U-turn with the direction their life was heading.

Every semester, I would meet new people who eventually would ask me what the dark mark on my nose was. Or occasionally people would talk to me for an hour with uncomfortably tense shoulders and tapping feet. They finally would shout out, "Ok! I can't take it anymore. You have something on your nose."

The Icebreaker.

These people became my friends. Some of them would invite me to the movies while others wanted to go out for a drink. Regardless of their agendas, I remained focused on completing what I had set out to do: *graduate*.

RYAN TROUTMAN

The Show Must Go On

My family was extremely proud to know that I was nearing graduation. It was a day nobody thought they would ever see. I woke up that morning and stayed in bed long enough to reflect on the challenges I had overcome. I even thought about the possible dangers I could experience in my future if I didn't stay steady.

I've made a lot of bad decisions on both my life and health. Like many people, I went to parties and drank my way through college. I would stay awake through the night long enough to see many sunrises. Sometimes a lack of motivation prevented me from acting on opportunities that could have changed my life in amazing ways. I've been depressed and saw no prosperous future ahead of me. I've felt isolated, stranded, and different. The things that have occurred to me have given me great stories to tell of how I victoriously fought my way through the hardest time of my life. But this story has been filled with struggles—many that I still face today.

Before I graduated college, I got one more tattoo. A lot of my friends had corny phrases dug into their collar bones, and it inspired me to want the same. Except I didn't want to have a cheesy sentence etched onto my body like "Friends are Forever" or "Stay True To Yourself." I didn't want to get something that I would regret years down the road. I didn't want to go to the beach in my mid-forties and take off a shirt so everyone can see "Strength ~ Respect ~ Loyalty" because it's something that

RYAN TROUTMAN

would make no sense. I wanted something that had meaning. Unlike my previous two tattoos, I was determined to find the right words to have permanently printed on my chest.

For weeks, I searched the Internet and scrolled through photos of other people's chests. I saw all of the cliche ones and would occasionally come across someone with a massive Chinese symbol that stood for "honor" or "water".

Until one day I was driving down the road and it hit me. Not another car or a fire hydrant. No. This time, the words I wanted tattooed on my chest hit me like a whirlwind of an epiphany. I quickly pulled over into the nearest parking lot and called my friend who happened to be at his tattoo shop.

"I got it! I know what I want!" I shouted into the microphone.

He patiently waited for me to continue with my excitement. I'm not one to tell short stories. Ironically, dragging out stories or seeming to find no ending when talking is a symptom I discovered for traumatic brain injuries. Let me be the first to tell you that it was nothing more than a symptom of me being my normal self. My entire life I've always had long, engaging stories to tell. On my call to him, I began elaborating on all of the reasons I felt the words were right for me. There were times I would have to pause and take a breath due to me talking so fast. Finally, after I had exhausted every description possible, I waited for him to speak. I expected a long response on when he was available or what I needed to do prior to arriving.

"That is absolutely perfect" were the only words that came through the phone's speaker. I never like to postpone things that I am excited to do so I turned my car around and drove to the other side of town. I've said it before and I'll say it again. No time is better than the present.

I drove to his tattoo shop and felt the needle dig into me once again. This time I hardly felt any pain due to the build up of scar tissue near my collar bone. He even had to stand up from his stool and lean in at times to really get the ink settled into my skin.

RYAN TROUTMAN

"Alright man, you're all done," he said proudly then signaled for me to rise from the chair. "Go take a look in the mirror and tell me what you think." I rose from the black leather chair and hurried to see my shirtless chest in the closest mirror. It was perfect. This tattoo was everything I hoped it to be.

Written in beautiful cursive letters were the words *Second Chance*. They were the two words I had heard over and over from practically everyone who has known me since my accident. They would always say "you've been given a second chance and you better do something with it" or "you're lucky to have been given a second chance at life" Those two words really stuck with me and now they will forever.

Every single morning for the rest of my entire life. I will stand in front of a mirror and be reminded of my second chance. I will become aware of my purpose and the goals I have set for myself. I will dismiss any idea of making bad choices because that isn't what you do with a second chance at life.

I now had three tattoos but only one of them told a story with meaning. Until one day I stared down at my legs and began to creatively formulate meaning to my skeleton octopus and mangled pirate ship. By the end of the night, I had one combined meaning for all three of my tattoos. A meaning that was almost as long as the story it related to.

The first tattoo I got was the octopus. It had a skull for a head and waves crashing around it. I looked down at the tentacles and counted eight. It somehow made me think of the phrase "cats have nine lives." Now am I saying I'm a cat? No, if I was I probably would've flown out and landed on my feet and not my head. Then I looked at the skull. It reminded me of a skull and crossbones which usually stood for death. All throughout 2007 and into 2008, I lost a lot. My high school sweetheart dumped me, friends ditched me, my personality changed, and the foods I ate didn't even taste the same.

Everything I had learned to love had become medically restricted and the adventurous plans I had for my future were quickly forgotten. My boisterous personality was now shuttered by the thought of always being disabled or only getting to live a short and limited life.   One bad decision caused me to lose everything. I lost a life.

Skulls represent death and cats have nine lives. One of my lives died. Bringing me down to eight. An octopus has eight tentacles.

The waves crashing onto the octopus made me think about my life. Just like a wave, my life was growing bigger and bigger until one day it came crashing down. While in one of my psychology courses, I learned that colors have a relationship with moods.

When my family got the knock on the door and heard I was in a trauma center they were instantly struck with fear. Soon, all of my family and close friends had driven to the hospital only to hear a doctor say that I probably wouldn't be alive for much longer. My family was crushed. They all got to hear that their son, brother, friend, nephew, or grandson was about to die in the room down the hall from them.

The color of the waves are blue and blue represents sadness.

The octopus had red spots on it that covered the tentacles. A few weeks into the in-patient rehabilitation hospital my mother asked me if I knew what had happened to me. I gave some wildly incorrect answers and finally she quieted me long enough to tell the story in full detail. I hated myself for not wearing a seatbelt. I hated my friend for driving so fast. I honestly hated everything about the world and everyone in it. Why did it have to happen to me? I was extremely frustrated and angry at the thought of my dim future.

The color of the spots are red which represents anger.

The main part of the tattoo was the octopus which I decided represented me. Today I am living a new life as an entirely different person and I am loving every second of it. I've been through hell and back and have learned to see the brighter side of life. More importantly, I've gotten better each and every day.

The octopus is green which represents new life and growth.

The second tattoo I got was the pirate ship. Have you ever heard the old myth of Kraken? It's a massive octopus who would terrorize ships passing through the ocean. It would bash the sails and break the ship down until it sunk to its misery deep beneath the ocean's surface. Remember when I said the octopus represented me? Well, the ship represents me as well. What does that mean? It means that all throughout this story, my greatest enemy has been myself and fortunately, I won.

That is the reason why I've been given a Second Chance.

My friends and family laugh when someone looks at one of my tattoos and says "second chance on what?" or "cool octopus! Does it symbolize anything?" I always grab the nearest chair and slide it underneath them before I begin with "February 18, 2007 was the day I died..."

That tattoo means so much to me. It's a daily reminder of what I've done and what I still have left to do.

It feels great knowing that I've accomplished a lot. From graduating college to finding a career, I managed to recover from my disabilities and improve myself into the greatest person I've *ever* been. I've helped other people in times of need, tried being the best brother, son, boyfriend, and friend a guy could be, and constantly had a hunger to better my life.

On the day I walked across the stage and earned my bachelors degree, I kept asking myself if I was really the one who made it this far. That one question continued to circle around in my mind. Luckily, I pocketed it for a later time and focused on my special day and enjoying it with my family.

The graduation ceremony was unforgettable. The university's stadium was filled with family members and friends who anxiously waited to hear their graduate's name called. Every graduate frantically peered around looking for their loved one. My cap and gown muddled me into the sea of other students wearing the same. These caps and gowns shuddered our uniqueness. We all looked the same but each of us had different walks of life. At some point, each of these students had a life changing experience. One that drove them to the success of graduating college. Nobody sitting next to me or staring down from the stadium seats knew what I had been through. They didn't know that shortly before beginning my Senior year in high school I didn't know my name.

The students around me each had a story. Everyone does. Have you ever had a unique experience that you felt was left unheard? Has it changed you in ways that you feel have gone unnoticed? We all live in different ways. Our choices are what make all of the chapters of our lives different and exciting. Be proud of what you've written so far in your life's story. Be open to others about the choices you've made and the stories you have in your life. Because one day you might tell your story to a person who is moved by the life you've lived. It's these moments where we can change the lives of others.

Students in front of me began lining up to head towards the stage. This was the moment we were all waiting for. For some of us, this was the final chapter. For others it was just the beginning. One by one we would hear names announced and watch a student stride across the stage to grab their degree. Some studied biology, engineering, computer science, music, and mathematics while others majored in psychology, philosophy, and education.

It's makes me wonder how each of these majors were chosen as they could be an indication to each person's story. When people ask me why I chose psychology, I launch into the massive story I'm telling you now. I wanted to ask the girl beside me why she chose education or the guy in front why he kept changing his major.

We have no idea what kinds of lives other people have lived. Each of these graduates may have overcome an extremely hard time in their life to get to this stage. Now, they could go

RYAN TROUTMAN

on to becoming the next teacher who helps to educate children. Some could even be inventors and design the next globally admired product. There may even be people who later become surgeons like the one who saved my life.

My name was finally called. I slowly strode across the stage and tried to take everything in. When I grabbed ahold of my degree, I was instantly filled with a feeling of achievement. Grabbing that degree signified grabbing hold of my life. Here in my hands was a piece of paper that told me I was ready to take on the next exciting chapter of experiences, choices, stories, and successes. It felt great to see my family and my girlfriend cheering me on from up above.

Each of them have played a special role in getting me to where I am today. They all helped steer me away from danger and inspired me to get my life going in the right direction. My family would help me through the hard times I experienced in college. They would always keep me on track towards succeeding and inspired me to do my best. I met my girlfriend during my last semester in college. I admired the focus she had in nursing school and it pushed me to complete my final courses the best I could. She even supported me when I told her I was finally going to buckle down and write this book.

Each of these people have made a positive impact in my life and I proudly watched as they cheered me on from the stands. With all this love, support, happiness, and success you'd never guess anything was wrong with me, right? But the happy ending to this story is still one filled with obstacles.

My brain is damaged, bruised, scared, atrophied, and worn. As a result, my days are met with a range of challenges from driving directions and being forgetful of simple things I need to complete to fighting my words so that my speech makes sense and being able to read words without jumping around the page. A lot of times I have trouble understanding complex stories. Drama movies with intricate plots leave me lost and confused. So you can imagine how difficult it has been to recall the details of my life in order to write this book.

I still get headaches and live in a sometimes extremely uncomfortable body. My bones are misaligned, popping, cracking, and locking as I move throughout the day. Instead of being satisfied by shopping for clothes or buying nice things, I get excited about my next visit to the chiropractor and even about trying a new herbal tea or supplement known to improve one's health.

People always tell me that if I didn't tell them my story, they would have never known anything was wrong with me. They say I'm the most recovered person they've ever seen. I'm always reminded that I have "an angel" or that "the man upstairs is looking out" for me. Yes, it is exciting to know that I've been blessed enough to even come out of any of this alive, not to mention as recovered as I have.

Millions of people go through just one of the experiences I have and die instantly like Jordan or they are forever disabled and challenged like the man in my group therapy. Millions of people didn't have such a great ending to their story like mine. A lot of them didn't even get a chance to finish writing it. My story has had countless tribulations and achievements but there is one drastically important thing about my story that I haven't told you.

It's that it isn't over.

I am trying to be the greatest person I possibly can be. That is the purpose behind challenging myself with volunteer work, a college education, a career, and writing this book.

No one knows what day they'll write their last word. None of us even know what our next chapter will look like. Regardless of how much I've recovered or how awesome of a story I can tell you, I still have a brain injury.

I still have to live each day with the weary feeling that my brain could one day give out on me. The choices I make today carry with them a feeling of guilt. Every time I take a sip of alcohol I'm reminded of the damage I'm doing to my brain regardless of how much moderation I enforce. My wild experiences parasailing or the stupid times I've skateboarded at fast speeds without a helmet. All of the times I've driven a car and nearly killed myself. Every time I've ended up almost getting into a fist fight with belligerently drunk people who could knock me out cold or even kill me with one hit to the head. I went to rock concerts and head banged to the music which made me lightheaded as I stumbled to the ground. I got into smoking hookah and prided myself in how big of a puff I could take or all of the cool tricks I could do with the smoke. I get people worried when I tell them I want to skydive or wakeboard. All of these activities have given people brain injuries and a lot of them didn't make it. So why should I continue to roll the dice?

I'm not invincible. No matter how much I've been through, I wonder if one day it will all catch up to me. All the force I had taken from car accidents could one day reveal its true damages. My brain could one day fall victim to a mental illness or become completely impaired from the choices I've made in my past.

To be honest, I don't know what my future looks like. But one thing every person takes with them into the future is their past. I will always have a brain injury.

But, we're always told to not live in the past and that is a standard I set for myself each day. We all make stupid decisions and everyone experiences hardships throughout their life. But it's how we deal with them going forward that truly shows our strength. If I let my brain injury or the unsafe choices I've made prevent me from progressing through life I wouldn't have to wait for something to happen to my health because I would've already been defeated.

What's done is done and what's going to happen will happen. All we can do is be the best we can possibly be in the present and feel confident in knowing it will give us a bright future. Everyone is on this earth for a different number of years.

RYAN TROUTMAN

There is no way to change how many you have but you surely can change how they are lived.

I will continue living my life in the best way I can but will forever feel indebted to the people who truly sacrificed to make it possible. I didn't do this all by myself. But, at the same time, it wasn't all just handed to me. I had the love and support of all my family and many of my friends.

My mom constantly watched over me when I was injured. She cared for me in ways I couldn't even begin to explain to you. If it wasn't for her constant love and support, I surely would be dead. She saved my life. I love her with every ounce of me and will never be able to truly tell her how amazing of a person I think she is. Tony helped me in school with challenging math and drove me to success all throughout school. He showed me what it meant to have good work ethic and to never slack off on anything I do. He helped me realize the kind of man I want to grow up and be. Tony inspired me to never give up on my goals.

I had an amazing little sister who loved me enough to endure my sudden tantrums and shouting. She knew that wasn't the person I truly was and that I loved her just as much as she loved me. I am happy to be alive and watch her grow into the amazing person that she is.

My little brother had just been born but was someone I could mentor. His importance in my life drove me to be the best person I possibly could be in hopes that he would someday do the same. I am honored to be someone he can look up to. He will forever be one of my best friends.

My mom's best friend Janet rose to the occasion and supported my family through some of the toughest moments of their lives. She juggled being a mother to her own kids while being a best friend to my mother and doing anything she could to make things better.

Nurses, doctors, and surgeons worked ruthlessly through the day and night to make sure someone they didn't even know was taken care of in the best way possible.

RYAN TROUTMAN

Therapists helped me restore every ability I lost from my injury. I will forever be grateful for the amazing work that they've done. Their love and care was unparalleled and helped me to receive the highest quality care possible.

The high school teachers who once despised my childish behaviors gave their loving support and organized the students to put together that touching banner.

My grandparents, aunts, uncles, cousins, friends, coworkers, and so many more people all are the reason I am writing this story. They all supported me in any way they could. Their love was unconditional. They never gave up on me. Ever. They are the reason I'm alive.

Now I have to go on knowing that I have a purpose. I wake up each morning eager to make it better than the last. I'm set to defy every odd standing against me. People have always told me the things I can't do. Well, let me tell you something I CAN do. I can come back from the most traumatic event of my life and live to tell the story. I can work each day to make the lives of those around me better. Each and every day I can better myself and learn from my mistakes. I can, and will, live the best life I have ever had the chance at living.

My name is Ryan, and this my Second Chance.

RYAN TROUTMAN